Compassionate Ministry

Compassionate Ministry

Theological Foundations

Bryan P. Stone

ORBIS BOOKS

Maryknoll, New York 10545

The Catholic Foreign Mission Society of America (Maryknoll) recruits and trains people for overseas missionary service. Through Orbis Books, Maryknoll aims to foster the international dialogue that is essential to mission. The books published, however, reflect the opinions of their authors and are not meant to represent the official position of the society.

Published by Orbis Books, Maryknoll, NY 10545-0308
Manufactured in the United States of America

ORBIS / ISBN 1-57075-069-6

For my brothers and sisters
in Polytechnic Heights, Fort Worth, Texas
who will always be known to me as
"Liberation Community"

Contents

Introduction: Jonah and the Worm—
A Call to Compassion   ix

1   Getting Theology and Ministry on Speaking Terms   1

2   Created in the Image of God:
Freedom, Community, and Creativity   18

3   The God of Compassion   44

4   Jesus: The Compassion of God   68

5   The Church as a Liberation Community   97

6   Compassionate Evangelism   143

Conclusion: The Hope of Compassion   157

Bibliography   161

Index   165

Introduction

Jonah and the Worm

A Call to Compassion

Most of us are familiar with the story of Jonah and the whale. We grew up hearing the story as children, and early on we were fascinated by the tale of a man who was called by God to go to Ninevah but who disobeyed that call and eventually found himself in the belly of a whale. The story of Jonah and the *worm*, however, never seems to get quite the same press. Worms are not as glamorous as whales, and many of us have never even heard the story at all.

The details leading up to the Jonah-worm encounter are relatively simple. Jonah was summoned by God to leave the comfort and security of his homeland to serve as a prophetic presence in the city of Ninevah, the capital of the "evil empire" of Assyria. Assyria was the current superpower in a long list of superpowers that occupied and dominated neighboring nations. One of those nations was Jonah's native Israel. The very idea of Jonah crossing over from his clean and holy culture to the politically and racially different (read "inferior") culture of Ninevah was as disgusting and reprehensible to Jonah as it could possibly be. Jonah chartered a boat heading the opposite direction.

What happened next is familiar to most of us. A fierce storm came up at sea while Jonah was asleep down below in the boat. After praying to their own gods with no results, the sailors woke Jonah up and asked him to pray to his god. Still no results. On the assumption that the god of someone on board must be angry, the wind-blown and rain-drenched mob resorted to a more primitive form of the state lottery and drew straws to determine the guilty party. Jonah got the shortest straw, entitling him to an unsolicited deep-sea diving expedition. God now appointed a whale, so the story goes, to swallow Jonah alive.

Contrary to popular opinion, the whale was actually God's instrument of salvation, not punishment, in the story. Jonah sang out in praise to God while in the belly of the whale:

Water encompassed me to the point of death. The great deep engulfed me,
Weeds were wrapped around my head. . . . But Thou hast brought up my
life from the pit, O Lord my God. (2:5–6)

We don't know how long Jonah could have lasted in the whale. We do know that
the whale grew weary of Jonah after just three days and regurgitated him onto
dry land. Jonah got up, brushed himself off, and began vowing never to eat at
Long John Silver's again. It was at this point that God called Jonah a second time
to go to Ninevah. This time Jonah obeyed. He proceeded directly to Ninevah
and began to walk the length and breadth of the city, preaching to its residents,
denouncing their wickedness, and announcing God's future wrath and punishment if they should fail to repent and change their ways. A remarkable thing
happened! The people of Ninevah began to repent! From the poorest peasant to
the king himself, the whole city began to heed Jonah's message! It is even
recorded that the Ninevites put sackcloth and ashes (symbols of repentance) on
their animals—a pretty stout revival even by today's standards!

Jonah, however, was far from pleased with the results of his ministry among
the Ninevites and went off to the suburbs to pout. He had secretly hoped that
Ninevah would disregard his message and that God would go ahead and zap a
few of those godless foreigners! In fact, Jonah admitted that this was why he
didn't want to go to Ninevah in the first place. He knew that God was a
"gracious and compassionate God" who was "slow to anger and abundant in
loving-kindness." Jonah was a persuasive evangelist with effective preaching and
revival skills, but he felt nothing for the people themselves. Jonah practiced what
we might call *oppressive evangelism.*

But there is more to the story. As Jonah sat on the ground and began to pout,
God appointed a plant to grow up over his head to shield him from the
scorching sun. Jonah, fickle as ever, was now happy once again. He began to
settle in under his beloved plant and enjoy the shade. During the night,
however, God appointed a worm to devour the plant with which Jonah had
become so enamored. Jonah, upon waking up, became angry at the worm and
even more angry at God. He began to beg for death, to which God responded
with the following interesting words:

You had compassion on the plant for which you did not work, and which
you did not cause to grow, which came up overnight and perished overnight. And should I not have compassion on Ninevah, the great city in
which there are more than 120,000 persons who do not know the difference between their right and left hand?

Jonah, it seems, had a bad case of misplaced compassion. Like many of us, he
had placed trivial things above human beings. Jonah was a superb evangelist,
but not a very compassionate one!

I will not pretend that the four short chapters of Jonah provide a thorough guide to the nature of compassion or to the practice of *compassionate ministry*. But I do think we would do well to follow up on what is communicated so imaginatively in the story of Jonah—namely, that God is fundamentally compassionate and that there is a distinct and significant link between God's compassion, on the one hand, and the kind of ministry to which God calls us as human beings, on the other. Compassionate ministry is not just one type of ministry alongside others. It is the first and last word in any ministry that understands itself as an authentic response to a compassionate God.

Like Jonah, we are all called by a compassionate God to a ministry of compassion in our world. Like Jonah, many of us find ourselves, as well as the churches and denominations in which we serve, in the belly of the whale. We, too, have been called by God to minister to the "great cities" where, like the Ninevites, people "do not know the difference between their right and left hand" (a phrase that signifies confusion and disorientation if ever there was one). Instead, we have turned and run in the opposite direction, and we now find ourselves surrounded by the blubber of suburban comfort, security, and prosperity. It's no wonder that Christian ministry in North America is too often reduced to church-building programs, teen choir trips to Six Flags, or mid-week Bible studies that consist of little more than the pilfering of a few meager scraps thrown from the table of pop psychology. It's no wonder that our worship and evangelism have become insulated and isolated from situations of massive poverty, hunger, and oppression around us. Like Jonah, we are being called by God a second time to be compassionate to Ninevah. Like Jonah, many of us and many of our churches are heeding the call. But simply responding to Ninevah with an arsenal of programs, plans, and technology is not enough. We must respond with the compassion of a compassionate God. Our ministry and our lives must be thoroughly shaped by this compassion.

So what is compassionate ministry? Is it just another passing fad in the church? Is it simply opening up a food pantry or clothes closet? Is it the calling of a minority or a chosen few who don't mind working with the elderly, the sick, or the poor—those few who are just simply wired that way? What do the words "compassionate ministry" mean? And if there is such a thing as compassionate ministry, does that imply that there is such a thing as *non*compassionate ministry? This book tries to probe some of these questions.

A Theology of Compassionate Ministry

The word "compassion" originally comes from the two Latin roots, *cum* (with) and *pati* (to suffer)—thus, "to suffer with." The idea is that one individual enters into the hurt and suffering of another with true feeling and solidarity. To be compassionate to others, therefore, is to be there with them, to hurt with them, and to feel with them. Compassion is much more than a general benevolence or pleasant disposition. To be compassionate, as Salvadoran priest Jon Sobrino says, is to "internalize" the suffering of others (88).

Today, of course, the word "compassion" often means little more than feeling sorry for someone. Indeed, the King James Version of the Bible, reflecting word usages over three centuries ago, regularly uses the word "pity" instead of compassion. But pity, as we use the word today, is hardly the response of the God of the Bible to the large-scale injustice, poverty, and suffering in our world.

A Christian is one who is convinced that if we genuinely want to understand and practice compassion, the place to begin is with Jesus of Nazareth. There not only do we find the definitive model of a compassionate human being, we also experience, in a decisive way, the reality that God is compassionate—that God suffers with us and has internalized our suffering. But beyond the identification with our suffering that takes place in the person of Jesus, we also discover a restoring and humanizing love that springs forth from that identification. In other words, God through Jesus enters into intimate community with us and at the same time struggles with us for our liberation. And, thus, out of the compassion of God are born these twin movements, *liberation* and *community*, which, I will argue, form the central framework for an authentic compassionate ministry in our world today.

The pages that follow were born out of the conviction that the notion of a compassionate ministry requires more careful consideration than we in the church have tended to give it. In fact, nothing less than a fully reflective theology of compassionate ministry can serve as a warrant against compassion becoming simply a passing fad or fashionable trend in the church. Then, too, such a theology could guard against the equally disastrous trend of viewing compassionate ministry as the calling of a minority within the church. There certainly are commonly practiced forms of ministry (if, indeed, they can be called "ministry") which are not only *non*compassionate, but are, at worst, down-right oppressive and, at best, charming distractions from authentic Christian ministry. The work of a theology of compassionate ministry is, negatively, to criticize those forms and, positively, to contribute toward a more adequate vision of what ministry ought to look like in our world. In other words, a theology of compassionate ministry is committed to making explicit what is implicit in Jonah's story—that the character of God as compassionate has decisive implications for how we understand, imagine, and go about the practice of ministry today.

The aims of such a theology will require us to take up three tasks simultaneously. The first task is to be explicit about what we believe. This book attempts to take a serious look at some of our most fundamental claims as Christians. Being explicit about what we believe, of course, requires more than merely repeating worn-out dogmas. It requires a self-critical attitude that is willing to expose our beliefs to theoretical and practical acids. Are our beliefs coherent and credible? Are our beliefs relevant and liberating? Are our beliefs consistent with the apostolic witness to Christ discovered in the New Testament?

The second task of a theology of ministry is to be explicit about what we take to be the most important challenges and opportunities of contemporary human existence. In other words, we must be clear about the context in which and for which ministry is to be carried out in the world today. I make no attempt to hide the fact that I write from a North American perspective with all of its advantages and limitations. I have a great interest, therefore, in the North American context for doing ministry. But I also understand that just as the church of Jesus Christ is a *catholic*, or universal, church, so a truly adequate theology of compassionate ministry must never fail to situate itself within the global context of human living and suffering today. Whether rich or poor, young or old, sick or healthy, we all experience suffering at different levels in our lives, and an authentic ministry of compassion attempts to bring liberation and community to every instance of bondage and alienation. In the absence of a consciously global perspective, we fail to recognize just how massive is the suffering brought on by poverty in our world. There is a vast difference between suffering that is related to issues of fulfillment in our lives and suffering that is related to issues of pure survival. In other words, without a deliberately global perspective, our theology—and, by extension, our ministry—will fail to be *real*. We will deceive ourselves as to our own involvement in systems and institutions that cause the kind of brutal suffering associated with a poverty affecting the vast majority of human beings living on our planet. To take life for granted, to enjoy comfort, prosperity, and dignity, is to be an exception, an anomaly, in our world. A theology that forgets that fact will mask that fact and will inevitably end up perpetuating that fact.

Thirdly, we must find a way to interface our beliefs with our context. We must ask whether—and, if so, how—our beliefs are decisive for human existence today, given its challenges and opportunities. We must ask whether—and, if so, how—our beliefs can best be expressed and implemented through the practice of Christian ministry. Until and unless Christians begin the critical task of structuring their faith in terms of a concrete practice of ministry on a daily basis, we can only expect the world's problems to grow ever more intractable, while Christianity sinks deeper and deeper into irrelevance.

All three of these tasks must be done at the same time. I see no profit in segregating theology from the practice of ministry. We must instead commit ourselves to an unremitting dialogue between what we believe and what we do, between our theology and our ministry, between faith and life. Furthermore, you the reader are invited to approach this book not merely to find out what the author thinks, but to take the steps toward the construction of your own theology of ministry. If this book can help, that is because it urges you, first, to ask about the meaning and truth of your most fundamental beliefs. It asks you to be explicit about what you believe and to open those beliefs to scrutiny. In other words, this book asks you to do theology. But, second, this book implores you to take up the more practical task of interpreting your world, to imagine more adequately the form that Christian witness should take when expressed in terms of ministry today. In other words, this book asks you to do practical theology.

It may be that this book will be helpful to those who are already engaged in ministry. I add one word of warning, however. What is offered here is not a how-to manual for the practice of compassionate ministry, but a reflection on the *why* and the *what* of that practice—its motivations, context, and aims. It is never too late for such reflection in ministry. Indeed, the gap between faith and practice may well be as characteristic of lifelong ministry practitioners as of anyone else. Nonetheless, this book is for any Christian who wants to think more carefully about what it means to put her or his faith into practice in the world today. Accordingly, I have tried to keep my reflections as free as possible from technical theological jargon and ecclesiastical inside secrets, thereby making it possible for those who are less theologically trained to be able to read and to use it.

Chapter 1 attempts to describe the kind of dialogue or *circle* that must occur between theory and practice (or theology and ministry) today. Not only must we move deliberately and imaginatively from theory to practice, but we must also move from practice to theory in a way that does not simply serve to rationalize or justify our present practice or ministerial options. Also, the kind of prior commitment we bring to the theology-ministry circle is critically important. I defend the notion that a commitment to those who suffer in our world has an incredible way of opening us up, not only to the truth about our context, but also to the truth of the gospel and its relevance for our context.

In Chapters 2 through 5, I explore four fundamental Christian beliefs and their relationship to the practice of compassionate ministry today. In Chapter 2, I begin with what Christians believe about human beings—our creation in the image of God as free, creative, and communal creatures; our subsequent corruption of that image; and how ministry might be envisioned as the restoration of that image. Compassionate ministry, as I understand it, is essentially humanizing ministry, and so this chapter lays the basic groundwork for the rest of the book. In Chapter 3, I discuss the decisive relevance of what we believe about a compassionate God for the practice of ministry. Since the relationship between theory and practice is two-way, however, I also attempt to show how our practice shapes our knowledge of God. Nowhere is this more true than throughout the biblical witness, where to "know God" is not neces-sarily the same as to "know about God," the former being an intensely practical activity that takes up the enterprises of compassion and justice in the world.

In Chapter 4, I explore the significance of Jesus of Nazareth for Christian ministry. This chapter has two parts: The first part is a reflection on what Jesus himself preached about the inbreaking of the Kingdom of God and what a conversion to that Kingdom means for human liberation and the restoration of human community (the sources for which are found primarily in the N.T. gospels of Matthew, Mark, and Luke). The second part represents a shift from Jesus' proclamation of the Kingdom to Paul's proclamation of Jesus and of what it means to live "in Christ." Though the logic of the gospels is quite different from the logic of Paul's epistles, in both sets of New Testament writ-ings we are introduced to a Jesus who is the very "compassion of God," and we are pointed to a new way of living marked by a fundamentally new freedom, new community, and new creativity—a life that is humanized and restored in the image of God.

Chapter 5 takes up the question of what we believe about the church. I survey various models of the church and the way they both reflect and shape a particular understanding and practice of ministry. I then propose that we understand the church as a *liberation community*, and I go on to suggest what a ministry of liberation and a ministry of community might look like in actual practice. Chapter 6 focuses on the ministry of *evangelism* in the church. I call into question what I take to be a popular consensus regarding evangelism, and I suggest an alternate model of evangelism as *compassionate evangelism*, a thor-oughly "worldly" endeavor to which all Christians are called.

I developed many of the ideas in this book in the context of an economically depressed urban neighborhood. Although that was my context, I am hopeful that many of the theological motivations for compassionate ministry expressed here will have application in any context where the church takes seriously its responsibility to meet people in need with the love of a compassionate God. I cannot hide, however, that the needs of the urban poor, and the day-to-day involvement in working with the urban poor to meet those needs, provided the soil for much of what lies in these pages. My hope is that just as the themes of this book have served as an impetus for my own involvement in compassionate ministry, so also they can provide direction and motivation for others who are doing or who wish to do compassionate ministry.

The first drafts of this book were deployed in urban ministry classes I taught at Bresee Institute in Los Angeles. As with every good teaching experience I have had, the teacher became the learner. The students themselves ended up shaping not only the form but the content of what I have ended up saying— and this not only in a conscious way, but in many ways of which I am probably unconscious. Therefore, I wish to express my gratitude to Alice, Cynthia, Deth, Doug, Jill, Joanna, Krista, Pam, Todd, and Vicki who wrestled with many of these issues, grumbled about some of them, and offered other valuable feedback and suggestions along the way. I am a better person for having spent time with them. The book is undoubtedly better also.

In the inner-city neighborhood of Polytechnic Heights in Fort Worth, Texas, I was privileged to live, work, and worship with a small community of Christians who were the inspiration for this book. This group of African-American, Hispanic, and Anglo believers demonstrated to me the power of the gospel in crossing cultural and racial lines to create genuine Christian community, while preserving diversity and creativity in the service of liberation. My heart is filled with gratitude for having been able to worship in and dialogue with this community of faith and, thereby, to develop my own vision for what the church should be in our world. To those brothers and sisters who, whatever else happens, will always be known to me as "Liberation Community," this book is dedicated.

Getting Theology and Ministry
on Speaking Terms

"Action-Reflection-Action" is a phrase often used these days to summarize the never-ending process appropriate for doing theology in our world—a world where we can no longer take for granted the influence of our daily commitments, activities, and social context on the way we understand and express our faith. It has become increasingly impossible (if it ever was possible) to acquire a database of eternal, fixed truths and then to apply them to life and ministry in a simple, straightforward way. As Robert McAfee Brown says, "There is no true theology without engagement; theology must both *issue from* engagement and *lead to* renewed engagement" (1978: 71). Action causes us to rethink theory, and renewed theory leads us to revitalized action.

But how do we get this circle between action and reflection moving? How do we get theology and ministry on speaking terms and how do we keep them on speaking terms? How do we go about prompting theology and ministry to inform one another and revitalize one another consciously and deliberately? And how do we keep this happening in the lives of most of us, for whom a huge gap exists between the world of the theology classroom, on the one hand, and the actual practice of ministry, on the other?

Imagination: Moving from Theology to Ministry

If we can visualize the relationship between theory (theology) and practice (ministry) as a circle, perhaps we can think of imagination as the conduit, or path, that leads us from theory to practice. Imagination is often treated as little more than a synonym for "daydreaming"

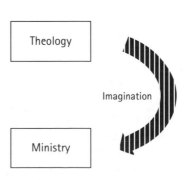

Theology

Imagination

Ministry

or "fantasy," but that is not its only or even its best meaning. Imagination is the ability to see something without eyes. It is the capacity for painting a picture on the canvas of the mind. We use the paints of our previous experiences, but we employ the brushes of novelty and creativity.

One defect of much of what passes for contemporary education is that imagination is neglected, if not censured outright. We pour dates, names, facts, figures, and events into each others' heads, but rarely do we educate the imagination. In general, we fail to recognize how much of our thinking is cultivated through images rather than statistics, through metaphors rather than propositions. Imagination is the key to invention and novelty, the pathway to creativity and hope. We should not be surprised then, given our predominant model of education, that human activity is generally conservative—reflecting and preserving what is rather than projecting and adventuring what might be. Sadly, Christian ministry is no exception.

One might argue, of course, that the movement from theory to practice (and, thus, the capacity for imagination) is not the same in all fields. Students of chemistry, for example, must first acquire an intellectual grasp of fixed chemical properties, formulas, and procedures. They can then move from this textbook understanding of chemistry to the actual practice of chemistry. This is the static model of theory and practice: straightforward, linear, and direct. Learn it. Apply it.

When it comes to the relationship between theology and ministry, however, the movement from theory to practice requires far more than sheer memorization of scripture or a textbook understanding of fixed theological creeds, formulas, or doctrines. The static model will not do. If ministry is to be liberating and creative, the movement from theology to ministry requires the ability, on the basis of our theology, to imagine what Christian ministry should look like. Indeed, we should probably question whether the static model is appropriate even for the physical sciences. Many chemists, for example, would argue that good chemistry requires just as much imagination as any other field of inquiry. In fact, what does the classical scientific method begin with? A hypothesis! A possibility! It was a physicist named Albert Einstein, after all, who once said, "Imagination is more important than knowledge."

Ministry is not the mere implementation of theology in some immediate, rigid, or simple way. When it comes to the authentic practice of Christian faith, there is no direct route from intellect to activity. Rather, our theology must be allowed to shape our imagination of what ministry is and of who we are as ministers. In this model, ministry becomes the immersion and engagement of our theologically informed imagination in the concrete struggles and needs of the world.

When you think about it, imagination is uniquely suited for this middle role between theory and practice. Even though imagination is not a purely theoretical exercise employing strict reason and logic, it is certainly a mental activity. Imagination is the attainment of a goal, but never in fact. It is a halfway house between theory and action, and we delude ourselves if we blur the line between envisioning something, on the one hand, and actually bringing that something into existence concretely, on the other. But even though imagination is not yet practice, it is certainly not *im*practical. Imagination anticipates practice and guides it; it is the first and most important tool our minds use in the attainment of goals. Many star basketball players, for example, claim that before big games they find themselves imagining shooting baskets—interestingly enough, usually in slow motion. They imagine the ball leaving their hands, sailing through the air, and swishing through the hoop. The same is true for many great football receivers and quarterbacks. They prepare for games by imagining a spiraling football released, floating through the air, and caught precisely in the intended hands—here again, usually in slow motion. Perhaps Christians should also become more intentional about imagining ministry before and as we go about doing it. Hopefully, we will not always see the church moving in slow motion!

In using imagination to mediate theology to ministry, however, there are at least two possible distortions of imagination. On the one hand, imagination can easily become mere fantasy if it fails to take into account the reality into which we are called to minister—the world of suffering and misery, the world of joy and opportunity. On the other hand, imagination loses its creative edge if it is swallowed up by reality and becomes simply a mirror of reality as it is, society as it is, suffering as it is, people as they are. Imagination is partly a hunger for what should be, partly a hope for what might be, and partly a vision of what can be. Only as we begin to educate and cultivate the imagination by giving conscious, sustained, and deliberate attention to what Christian ministry and ministers can look like, will our practice of ministry be transformed into something purposeful and effective—something that is guided and intentional rather than haphazard, stale, and pointless.

Spirituality: Moving from Ministry to Theology

If imagination can play an indispensable role in the route from theology to ministry, then perhaps *spirituality* can serve a similar role in the reverse route from ministry to theology. To understand spirituality in this role, as mediating what we do to what we believe, some explanation and clarification is re-

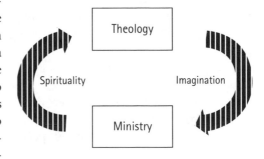

quired. There are, after all, a variety of ways that practice can be related to theory. Spirituality is one such way. We will look briefly at two other candidates and then return to the path of spirituality.

The first possibility is, of course, that practice will be related to theory in such a way as to make no difference at all. In other words, practice never makes it back around the circle to theory. Theory and practice are then segregated and allowed to proceed down their own separate tracks. This is especially tragic in the case of the relationship between theology and ministry. On the one hand, we end up with theologians who become recluses in the ivory tower and who are of little or no earthly good. They may know the four standard theories of Christ's presence in the Eucharist and a whole bagful of theories of the atonement, but their vast amounts of knowledge make only minimal connection with the world of utility rates, land development, corporate mergers, and unemployment. On the other hand, we end up with ministers who have left the thinking to someone else and who are content merely to marry and bury, report statistics, attend meetings, and implement programs to their hearts' content.

Both of the above are caricatures, of course. Few, if any, ministers (either lay or professional) would be content to completely yield to someone else the task of reflecting on their beliefs. So also—even if there truly are theologians who have little or no relevance to the decisive crises of our time, let alone the daily routines of our lives—no theologian is completely devoid of some practical context that informs and makes a difference to his or her beliefs. Where we stand, our allegiances, our social locations, and those on whose behalf we have already made some kind of ministry or life option, all form a framework—a context—that pervades virtually every theological choice we make and, in turn, informs our theological imagination as a whole.

I have already suggested that imagination plays an important role in the movement from theology to ministry. John Patton, in *From Ministry to Theology*, makes the point, however, that our experience itself enriches the imagination and provides the soil from which it recognizes possibility and potential. Patton argues that "Christian ministry involves not only understanding what we do in the light of our faith, but also understanding our faith in the light of what we do" (12). In other words, rather than our thinking being solely determinative of how we experience life, our thinking is also reflective of how we experience life. Really, what we have here is a relationship between thought and experience that is a two-way street. Just as theory informs practice, so also practice informs and shapes theory insofar as it contributes to an overall context out of which we think and believe. There are no believers whose beliefs are shaped in a vacuum.

As urban ministers, my coworkers and I would sometimes invite or allow suburban youth groups to invade our neighborhood for paint projects, cleanups, and other such activities. On one particular occasion, I remember guiding a tour of white, middle-class, suburban teenagers through a piece of property intended for renovation into a homeless shelter. As I explained the proposed placement of bunk beds in the large sleeping quarters, one of the teens nodded affirmingly and said, "Oh, yes, like at summer camp!" A month later, I gave the same tour to a group of the teenagers who lived in our own impoverished neighborhood, again explaining the proposed setup including the placement of bunk beds. On this occasion, one of the teens asked, almost in horror, "You mean like in jail?"

Whether we are interpreting life, interpreting scripture, or simply looking at old buildings, where we stand makes all the difference in the world. Where we stand makes a difference in what we see. Where we stand makes a difference in the way we think. Where we stand makes a difference in what we hope for. All the more so with our theology and practice of ministry. If the primary focus of our ministry is funding and building a cathedral, watch how our theology reflects that endeavor! If our ministry is centered around entertaining comfortable, well-fed teenagers for the summer, watch how our "theology of youth ministry" reflects that practice!

It is often difficult for us to recognize just how true this phenomenon is. We are rarely self-critical of the way our practice contributes to a wider context that shapes our thinking. Such shaping is unavoidable and need not be an obstacle to a lively and creative theology. But when we fail to be self-critical about the way our context and practice shape our beliefs, it is all too easy for our beliefs to become strictly determined by our context and practice. In that case, theology is reduced to ideology, a mere rationalization of what we already do and where we already stand.

In other words (to return to our original question of just how practice makes a difference to theory), if the first possibility is that practice will fail to make any difference to theory, the second possibility is that practice may simply determine theory, in which case theory becomes ideology. With regard to this second possibility, there are certainly those, especially some Marxists, who have emphasized the role that our practical infrastructure (especially our economic and political arrangements) plays in determining our theoretical superstructure (our philosophical and theological beliefs and opinions). So, for example, Marx himself believed that religion was little more than a theoretical byproduct of bad economics. If we could just correct the economic alienation between classes, religion would simply disappear.[1] While many would agree that Marx over-

---

1. Marx is rather inconsistent on this point. He anticipates a transformation of philosophy and the arts in the wake of an economic transformation. But he sees no such transformation in store for religion—or, by extension, theology. Religion, as the "sigh of the oppressed" will simply disappear when oppression disappears.

stated his case, the influence of economic and political arrangements on the way we think and believe is indisputable. Perhaps practice can never totally determine theory, but the sobering fact remains that, for many of us engaged in ministry, our theological beliefs are but a pale reflection of the sociological conditions and practical tasks imposed upon us. Ministry, rather than feeding and nourishing theology, too often preys upon and displaces theology.

The process whereby theory increasingly justifies or simply mirrors our experience occurs little by little and is barely noticeable. But watch how our theological optimism with regard to grace is gradually chipped away by the five o'clock news. Having been assaulted daily with reports of slayings and brutalities, many Christians have given up altogether on the notion that people (or at least some people) can ever be changed. Or, as another example, watch how the duty of fundraising that often accompanies the task of ministry tends almost imperceptibly to shade certain of our theological convictions toward those held by the group or persons from whom we are raising money. Practice certainly does shape theory. Our choices of ministry (where, with whom, and for whom) have a way of transforming and conditioning our theology by locating us with a unique set of resources, limitations, and commitments, all of which form a context in and through which our theology is born and reborn, shaped and reshaped. But if ministry really does transform and shape theology, and if we wish for this to happen in something other than a deterministic or ideological way, is there a third possibility—perhaps a liberating possibility—for the movement from activity to thought?

I think that there is and I suggest that spirituality, properly understood, can become just that route. But if ever there was a difficult word to get a handle on, that word is "spirituality." For many of us it refers primarily to prayer, meditation, private piety, and worship, understood as nonphysical and nonworldly pursuits. But this identification of spirituality with such a narrow slice of human activity only shows how *un*spiritual our spirituality tends to be.

One of the primary difficulties at this point is that the words "spirit" and "spiritual" have taken on an almost entirely other-worldly meaning—one that is perpetuated and reinforced by an enormous dualism that permeates our thinking and living. This dualism is characterized by a tendency to split up life into two distinct and opposed realms: the physical and the spiritual, the political and the religious, the public and the private, the body and the soul, the church and the world, loving God and loving our neighbor, the list could go on. Spirituality, when understood from within this dualism, is typically a form of activity marked by withdrawal from the world and from our daily struggles and projects. But this misunderstanding is as unbiblical as it is destructive of the relationship between ministry and theology.

Spirituality is the process of discovering meaning in and making meaning out of the whole of our lives. In this understanding, spirituality has both an objective dimension (we discover the meaning that is already present in our lives, whether we have ever recognized it before or not) and a subjective dimension (we actually give meaning to the various dimensions of our lives, to the extent that we integrate them into the whole that grounds and gives meaning to our lives). Authentic, or holistic, spirituality, then, is both active and passive, public and private, individual and corporate, religious and political. Authentic spirituality is both the experience of grace and the activity of being gracious to others. It is the ongoing journey of integrating the entire texture of our everyday and ordinary living into what we take to be the whole in which we find ourselves.[2]

If this description of authentic spirituality is valid, we must be extremely cautious about identifying spirituality with flight or withdrawal from the world. Authentic spirituality is instead a particular way of being fully engaged in the world of everyday activity rather than simply rushing through it. The Bible provides numerous examples of this down-to-earth spirituality. Moses communing with God on Mount Sinai, for example, is no more or less engaged in spirituality than when he is standing before the Pharaoh or treading across the desert of Saudi Arabia. So also, Jesus, on the Mount of Transfiguration, is no more engaged in spirituality in those glorious few hours than he is when involved in meeting the very physical and earthy needs of hurting individuals moments later at the base of the mountain. Spirituality is not moments apart from the crowd or segmented retreats from the world. It is the way we experience and interpret both our activity and our inactivity, both our worship and our politics. Indeed, it is precisely a holistic spirituality that can help us to overcome the dualisms in our life and to see that our politics may very well be an expression of worship to God.

Spirituality, then, is not worship, prayer, or meditation as distinct from ministry, politics, or work. It is the way we wrestle with our buying and selling, working and playing, loving and fighting, voting and praying, ministering and being ministered to, integrating them all into a single response to who God is. Our prayers are no more or less a response to who God is than is our public policy. Spirituality is a matter of who I am, but never apart from what I do. It is being and doing in unison. And so, while "who I am" is never fully disclosed by "what I do," "what I do" is always incorporated into and is never separate from "who I am."

If we return to the question of the relationship between ministry and theology, just how does spirituality provide a distinct and liberating channel

---

2. For the Christian, of course, this whole includes not only self and world, but the God discovered in Jesus of Nazareth. On the level of a strictly formal definition of spirituality, however, some such whole operates in all of our lives, regardless of whether we understand it to include God or not. Thus, there is certainly such a thing as a Buddhist spirituality, a Hindu spirituality, or even a Marxist spirituality.

for taking activity (ministry) and mediating it to our thinking (theology) without strictly determining our thinking? And are there any specific examples of how a Christian spirituality might actually go about doing this?

To begin with, spirituality mediates the practice of ministry to theology by unveiling the depth, meaning, and purpose of what we do. In other words, authentic spirituality places our activity in front of our minds, but in a way that is hardly a mirror of that activity. Indeed, a creative and holistic spirituality often confronts and challenges our practice, laying bare its inconsistencies and disjointedness. So, for example, when the prophet Isaiah simulates a dialogue between God and Israel about the spiritual discipline of fasting, the discipline itself does not cease to be a spiritual activity, but it suddenly begins to look very different. Now fasting becomes rooted in the concrete struggles and suffering that human beings face in our world. Fasting becomes much more holistic and authentic:

> "Why have we fasted and Thou dost not see?
> Why have we humbled ourselves and Thou dost not notice?"
>
> Behold, on the day of your fast you find your desire, and
>   drive hard all your workers. . . .
> Is it a fast like this which I choose, a day for [people] to
>   humble [themselves]?
> Is it for bowing one's head like a reed,
> And for spreading out sackcloth and ashes as a bed?
> Will you call this a fast, even an acceptable day to the Lord?
> Is this not the fast which I choose,
> To loosen the bonds of wickedness,
> To undo the bands of the yoke,
> And to let the oppressed go free,
> And break every yoke?
> Is it not to divide your bread with the hungry,
> And bring the homeless poor into the house;
> When you see the naked, to cover him;
> And not to hide yourself from your own flesh? (Isaiah 58:3–7)

What a picture of fasting! When set in the context of a holistic spirituality, fasting is no longer a form of retreat or withdrawal from human activity. It is a means of exposing our practice for what it is and then renewing it as a response to God.

Another example of how an authentic spirituality is capable of channeling ministry to theology in a liberating way can be found in the way the so-called

Negro spirituals have functioned in the life and history of African-Americans from the time of slavery until today. James Cone, in his book, *The Spirituals and the Blues*, argues that the spirituals, born out of slavery and oppression, expressed the "somebodiness" of a people who were and continue to be systematically stripped of personhood. The spirituals were an intense and profound form of resistance to exploitation in situations where little else was a possibility. And this resistance, as Cone says, "was the ability to create beauty and worth out of the ugliness of slave existence" (1972: 29). Thus, while the spirituals affirm the dignity of the black person in the context of white racism and slavery, they also express protest and hope in the midst of injustice and suffering. Consider, for example:

> O Freedom! O Freedom!
> O Freedom over me!
> An' befo' I'd be a slave,
> I'll be buried in my grave,
> An' go home to my Lord an' be free.

The spirituals have a functional character for an oppressed black people. They express in an imaginative way, the way things should be. They reinforce conviction and determination, as in the words of the spiritual, "Ain't gonna let nobody turn me around." But the black spirituals also interpret the experience of suffering from within a deep-seated hope and confidence in the God of Moses and Jesus, the God of liberation from slavery. In other words, the spirituals are a form of finding meaning in and giving meaning to the daily existence of those who sing them. Consider the following song:

> When Israel was in Egypt's land,
> Let my people go;
> Oppressed so hard they could not stand,
> Let my people go;
> Go down, Moses, 'way down in Egypt's land;
> Tell ole Pharaoh
> Let my people go.

When black slaves prior to the Civil War or blacks today who live in a racist society sing "let my people go," they are not just setting a Bible story to music. They are moving from experience to theology. They are providing an interpretation of their misery—indeed, a subversive and even revolutionary interpretation—and setting it within the framework, or whole, that gives meaning and hope to that misery. They are engaged in the practice of spirituality. And this spiritual exercising need not happen only within an explicitly religious environment. Cone points out that just as the spirituals function in the religious community as an expression of hope in the midst of suffering, so also the blues function as a kind of "secular spiritual" that gives meaning in a situation of oppression and offers an indirect but radical form of "social protest." (133ff.)

A holistic spirituality unites our practice and context with our minds and beliefs. It is the movement toward purity of heart because, while it finds its point of origin in the doing of many things, it is nonetheless aimed at, as Søren Kierkegaard said, willing "one thing." In willing this one thing, however, no dimension of life becomes slighted or understood as inferior to another. The one thing at which a holistic spirituality is aimed is not one particular dimension or activity in life that is higher or more important than other dimensions or activities. The one thing is the depth and purpose of all our other things. The one thing is that which gives meaning to the totality of our life, activity, and ministry—namely, its being lived as a response to God.

Commitment Is the First Step

Imagination and spirituality, then, may combine to form something of a circle between theory and practice, between reflection and action, between theology and ministry. What this book asks the reader to do is to consider jumping into that circle with a specific kind of commitment—a commitment to those who suffer, a commit-

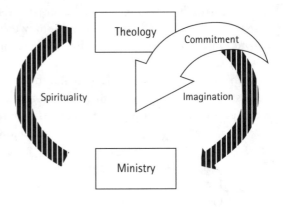

ment to those who lack dignity and are treated inhumanly, a commitment to those who are locked out in our society, a commitment to the victimized.

This request is not the typical one made by theologians to their audiences in the tradition of academic theology over the past two hundred years. Modern theology has, both for good and for ill, been the product of the Enlightenment, the heir of the scientific method, the glory of impartial reason and unbiased investigation. "Just the facts, please!" To ask people deliberately to be biased up front runs against the grain.

In the last few decades, however, theologies emerging from the so-called Third World have been challenging academic theology on this point and insisting on the priority of commitment in how we come to understand the

Christian witness and in how we try to express its significance for contemporary human beings. In one sense, these theologians are simply bringing to light what already takes place! We are all influenced by our context and commitments in how we read scripture, understand the Christian faith, and practice ministry. Third-world theologians are simply asking us to become more honest and critical about how that happens. They are suspicious when the wealthy and comfortable of the world read the Bible and conclude that the root human problem is spiritual poverty and that the solution to this predicament is a private and individualistic salvation from sin effected by a colorless (read "white") Christ who hovers above and beyond the differences of race, gender, and class that divide our world.

These theologies from impoverished regions of the planet understand first-hand that the status quo is not worth maintaining and that a private and individualistic reading of the Bible only serves to reinforce the status quo, whether consciously or unconsciously. They point out that the poor read the Bible and discover the promise of transformation and the hope of a radically different social order. The poor read the Bible and discover a Christ who takes sides with the forgotten, the despised, and the victimized—who in racist white America is black, who along the American-Mexican border is an exploited *maquiladora* worker, and who in the Appalachian mountains is "poor white trash." In other words, these third-world theologies argue not only that commitment plays a role in the shaping of our understanding of the gospel, but that a particular commitment—namely, a commitment to the poor and suffering of the world—plays a central role in a true understanding of the gospel.

So, for example, Juan Luis Segundo, a Jesuit priest from Uruguay, claims that, whereas others derive their response to human problems from theology,

> Jesus derives theology from the openness of the human heart to [humanity's] most urgent problems. Indeed Jesus seems to go so far as to suggest that one cannot recognize Christ, and therefore come to know God, unless he or she is willing to start with a personal commitment to the oppressed. (1976: 81)

This is a radical claim. But Segundo sees the basis for it in a recurring contrast in the gospels between the attitudes toward Jesus of those who were wealthy and powerful, on the one hand, and those who lived daily with poverty and oppression (the *amaretz* of Israel—"the people of the land," the "common folk"), on the other hand. The wealthy and the powerful are typically presented as those who were orthodox but whose minds and hearts were closed to Jesus. The poor and outcast, on the other hand, though uninformed theologically, are typically presented as the ones who recognized God in the life and teachings of

Jesus. Is this contrast merely a coincidence? As Segundo asks, "Is it possible to know and recognize the liberation message of the Gospel at all without a prior commitment to liberation?" (81)

Gustavo Gutiérrez is a Peruvian priest and theologian who would answer Segundo's question with a resounding "No!" When it comes to grasping the truth and meaning of the content of Christian faith, where one stands makes all the difference in the world. About the gospel of Jesus, Gutiérrez says,

> But this is made real and meaningful only by living and announcing the Gospel from within a commitment to liberation, only in concrete, effective solidarity with people and exploited social classes. Only by participating in their struggles can we understand the implications of the Gospel message and make it have an impact on history. (1973: 269)

If what Segundo and Gutiérrez are arguing is true, then a sensitivity to the deep struggles and suffering of the poor, the elderly, the orphaned, the diseased, and the marginalized in our world—our receptivity to their cries, our capacity for seeing through their eyes—opens up to us, in an unparalleled way, the true nature of the predicament of human beings today, as well as the significance of the gospel of Christ for bringing hope and healing to that predicament. The point here is not that the gospel was proclaimed by Jesus in a kind of code that only those who suffer and are marginalized can understand. The point is, rather, that a prior and lived commitment to those who suffer and are marginalized can go a long way toward liberating us from the individualistic and *conserv*ative biases that cause us to turn the gospel into something it isn't—a vague summons to abstract, private, and other-worldly piety, along with a general civility toward our neighbor.

The implication for Christian ministers ought to be clear. I may have better grammar, math, and spelling skills than the dirty, smelly, and neglected inner-city child who constantly disrupts my sermon by swallowing pennies and making the other children laugh. I may even know more theology. But that child is my window to viewing the God of compassion, in a way that I may never be for him. I become the needy one.

This book, then, is devoted to considering the implications of jumping into the "Action-Reflection-Action" circle with a prior commitment to those who suffer and experience pain, exclusion, oppression, and poverty on a daily basis. Given the fact that this circle moves back and forth between theory and practice, between theology and ministry, we should not be surprised that this commitment will yield at least two consequences: a theoretical consequence and a practical consequence.

A Theoretical Consequence: "The View from Below"

The life and experience of those who suffer affords us a unique and genuinely privileged perspective on what God is up to in the world and what, therefore, we ought to be up to. If God is to be found in our world today, it is, as always, with those who suffer and are trampled upon—not because God prefers some people to others, but because wherever God's children are being excluded from human community, God is at work bringing liberation and healing. Given the overwhelming reality that a grinding and structural poverty is now the status quo for a majority of human beings living on our planet, we may, without risk of overstating the case, refer broadly to those who suffer as "the poor." But poverty is not the only cause of suffering. There are those who suffer from illness and disease; those who suffer rejection and loneliness because of their age; those who suffer as victims of violence—whether in the form of sexual violence, emotional violence, or even economic violence. It is in their lives and experience and through their eyes that the truth can most clearly be discovered about ourselves, the world, and what God is doing through Jesus.

This is so, in the first place, because theological claims have a way of being bound up with and lending support to oppressive structures in society. Viewing our beliefs from below can help us cut through this ideological use of the Christian faith to support and rationalize the interests of the powerful and wealthy and show how practically incredible such claims are. The view from below can accomplish this (1) by providing an alternate interpretation of the Christian witness in scripture that, in many ways, is closer to the meaning expressed by the original witnesses; and (2) by providing an alternate interpretation of human existence that, in many ways, is closer to the way things really are.

Being poor and powerless, or standing with those who are, often has a way of bringing us closer to the truth of a situation than is available to those who see the world from the vantage point of the comfort and power they wish to retain. That does not mean that the poor or oppressed always see or express reality with absolute clarity and accuracy. As Segundo warns, the poor are not only the object of structures of oppression, they also internalize those structures, depriving themselves, to a great extent, of the ability to consciously reflect on or analyze those structures (1990: 360). What often occurs, claims Segundo, is a warping of their own theology into a kind of spiritualized resignation to their plight and a preoccupation with other-worldly ambitions. One thing is certain, however; the poor are those for whom the announcement of the inbreaking of God's kingdom is a piece of good news. And if anything is clear from Jesus' life and ministry, it is that the coming of the kingdom of God is not automatically good news for everyone! The presence of the kingdom spells an end to those who profit from the misery of others. As Jesus says, "Blessed are you who are poor, for yours is the kingdom of God. Blessed are you who hunger now, for you shall be satisfied. . . . But woe to you who are rich, for you are receiving your comfort in full. Woe to you who are well-fed now, for you shall be hungry" (Luke 6:20–25).

At the very beginning of our reflection on compassionate ministry, then, we are called to recognize that the placement of ourselves alongside the poor and the suffering is not simply for their benefit or for their liberation. On the contrary, the context of human poverty, suffering, and oppression provides an indispensable position for sensing the heartbeat of God and for discovering the decisive significance and relevance of Jesus Christ for all of us. Far from being merely one particular perspective among a plurality of equally valid perspectives, the view from below is an essential starting point that opens up who God is for the world and sets the agenda for the structure and mission of the church in the world as a liberation community. Christologically, this means that the emphasis of the apostles on Jesus' birth in a manger, his life of homelessness, poverty, and suffering, and his death on a cross are not merely coincidental to Jesus' significance as revealer and savior. The two are somehow bound up together and even imply one another.

But why is it that the life and experience of those who suffer is so transparent to who God is? Is there something meritorious, for example, about experiencing violence, exclusion, or material poverty? On the contrary, violence, exclusion, and material poverty are detestable states of affairs which God simply cannot put up with. And because God cannot put up with the destruction of human life through poverty and oppression, God sides with those who are trampled on and who suffer. It is neither accidental nor arbitrary that God should reveal himself to be a compassionate God by historically choosing sides for the oppressed and against the oppressor. As long as there is injustice in our world, as long as there are deeply imbedded structures of domination and subjugation in our society, as long as there is the grinding poverty of the many, side by side with the comfort and profit of the few, and as long as God is God, then the life and experience of the poor and the suffering will continue to provide a unique window for discovering who God is. And the God we find when we look through that window is a God of compassion—a God who enters into the situation of those who suffer, and in suffering with them, redeems us all.

Of course, it might be objected that employing the life and experience of the poor as a unique and privileged theological window carries very little weight since we already have the Bible. It is our window. The problem, however, is that not all of us come away from the Bible with the same conclusions. Even those who attempt to take every word of the Bible literally still end up approaching the text like the rest of us, with a multitude of presuppositions, biases, and concerns. And these biases and presuppositions each in their own way yield a different perspective on who the Bible says God is and who, therefore, the Bible says we are called to be.

It would appear, then, that we face an incredibly difficult predicament. We want to know who God is, but we can never attain a neutral perspective above the particularity and bias of our individual social locations and struggles—not even through scripture. In fact, it is precisely in our reading of scripture that these biases come through most noticeably! The distinctively biblical response to this predicament, however, is far from a cynical relativism ("we can never know who God really is") or even a consistent pluralism ("all perspectives on who God is are equally valid"). Rather, the God of the Bible is the one who today, just as yesterday, can be found in extraordinary ways, binding up the brokenhearted and healing the wounded. It is in these situations of brokenness and marginalization that the Christ in whom we have discovered God's character most clearly is to be found again and again—in the soup kitchens, tenement slums, sweatshops, barrios, and prisons. It is through the eyes of the victim that the message of the Bible unfolds before us as the two-edged sword that it is. All perspectives prejudice our knowledge; but the perspective of the dispossessed of the earth prejudices our knowledge in the right direction!

A Practical Consequence: Preferential Option for the Poor

There is a second consequence that follows from entering the "Action-Reflection-Action" circle with a commitment to those who suffer and are victimized. That consequence is a practical consequence—a ministerial preference that both precedes and follows from the view from below. Here again we find ourselves back in the circle between theory and practice. On the one hand, making a practical life commitment on behalf of those who suffer opens up to us a theoretical view from below. On the other hand, viewing life from below compels us to make a practical commitment on behalf of those who suffer. It is this practical life option, or ministerial preference, to which all Christians are called by Jesus' own life and witness.

Of course, the notion of a ministerial preference for the poor and the suffering is certainly not new to Christians. Throughout Christian history, this preferential option has occasioned a number of reform and revival movements in the church. One thinks, for example, of the various mendicant movements of the twelfth and thirteenth centuries associated with Francis of Assisi, or the various Wesleyan and Holiness denominations that appeared six centuries later with explicit (and what to some would even seem downright myopic) callings to the poor—for example, Methodism, the Salvation Army, or the Church of the Nazarene.[3] These movements all have in common a ministerial preference not unlike the kind of preferential option for the poor recently advocated by various forms of liberation theology.[4]

The significance of a ministerial preference for the poor and marginalized lies in its conviction that all Christians, both individually and communally, have a responsibility to enter into solidarity with the suffering and oppression of exploited and victimized people so far as possible. It is our responsibility thereby to adjust our wants in accordance with their needs, and to work together to place the full resources of the church and society at the disposal of relief, empowerment, justice, and community. It is essential to recognize that this preferential option for the poor is not an exclusive option for the poor, as if no other persons on the planet were the objects of ministerial concern. On the contrary, the very logic of a ministerial commitment to all humanity is precisely the foundation of making a preferential option on behalf of those who are being excluded from full participation in the human community.

A number of implications for the practice of ministry follow from the exercise of a ministerial preference for the poor and suffering. Some of the most conspicuous are, for example, how the church allocates its resources, makes decisions, trains laity and clergy, or measures success in ministry. In essence, a ministerial preference for those who suffer implies a particular model of being the church. The church that takes up a ministerial preference for the poor and suffering is a church that is thoroughly engaged in daily political, social, and economic reality rather than merely the practice of individualistic piety. The church that takes up a ministerial preference for the poor and suffering is a church that is determined to bring about the liberation of the oppressed rather than the mere maintenance of ecclesiastical machinery. The church that takes up a ministerial preference for the poor and suffering is a church that is devoted in its genuine search for dialogue and community, especially with those who are

---

3. So, for example, the founder of the Church of the Nazarene, Phineas F. Bresee, can say, "We can get along without rich people, but we cannot get along without preaching the gospel to the poor."

4. It is important to recognize the fact that the movement known as liberation theology has been not only a theological renewal movement, but first and foremost a renewal movement in the practice of ministry across the continent of Latin America and elsewhere. It was the CELAM (Conference of Latin American Bishops) conferences of Medellín (1968) and Puebla (1975) that responded to some of the key insights of Vatican II (especially its "Constitution on the World," *Gaudium et Spes*) by calling all Christians to make a "preferential option for the poor." Since then, however, the notion of a preferential option has ceased to be the sole possession of Roman Catholics or even a handful of Latin American bishops, but a widely adhered to, even if somewhat controversial, principle for numerous Christians in many world areas.

traditionally excluded and voiceless not only in the life of the church, but also in the reflection on our faith that we call theology. I call that model of being the church and of engaging in ministry a liberation community.

A prior commitment to those who suffer deeply in our world, then, yields both theoretical and practical consequences for the development of a theology of ministry. The pages that follow attempt to detail just some of those consequences in a systematic way. All of this, of course, is not to say that a theology of ministry can ever take the place of ministry itself. Instead, the work of a theology of ministry—and, therefore, of this book—is to reflect critically on ministry and on the meaning and truth of the Christian witness that is presupposed by and incarnated in ministry. The theology of ministry should never, however, become a substitute for ministry, as though when we had finished talking about what ministry is or ought to be, we had actually done it.

2

Created in the Image of God

Freedom, Community, and Creativity

In the previous chapter, I tried to show that a commitment to those at the bottom in our world's scale of values provides a unique and even privileged perspective from which to develop a theology of ministry. This commitment is grounded, first, in the overall impression we gain from the Christian witness— that looking through the eyes of the poor opens up new and liberating paths for understanding who God is and what God is calling us to do and to be. As Paul says, "God has chosen the foolish things of the world to shame the wise, and God has chosen the weak things of the world to shame the things which are strong" (1 Cor. 1:27). It is grounded, secondly, in an age-old suspicion that contemporary sociologists of knowledge increasingly show to be well-founded; namely, that where we stand—including our political, social, and economic interests—biases and shapes our thinking at every turn. For those who have relatively easy access to resources, position, power, wealth, and opportunity, theology tends to be shaped in a way that is protective of the status quo, even to the exclusion of those who lack such resources and opportunity. For those who have little or no stake in the system, theology is understandably biased more toward inclusion, liberation, and change. In today's world, as in the world of the first apostles, it is those who find themselves or place themselves with the poor and the powerless who are most likely to comprehend the gospel and to recognize Jesus as the compassion of God.

We may say then, that the view from below is a critical safeguard in doing theology. It is not, however, a guarantee of theology's validity. Simply because persons are poor or suffering, or are engaged in ministry with the poor and suffering, in no way certifies that their theology will be relevant, liberating, faithful to scripture, or even make sense. Nonetheless, a living and dynamic commitment to the poor is an indispensable tool in unmasking where oppression breeds oppression in theology—especially in our attempt to discover the truth about God and ourselves. And, after all, the truth about God and ourselves is at the heart of a theology of ministry.

But with which question do we begin—the question of who God is or the question of who we are? As a matter of sheer method we have to make some kind of decision about where to begin our theological journey. It might seem proper to begin with God. After all, God is the creator of everything and should obviously be accorded preeminence. The problem, however, is that we are not here primarily concerned with contemplating God's nature in itself or in the abstract (as important as that question might be in a purely philosophical context). Rather, in a theology of ministry, we are interested in the existential meaning of who God is. In other words, we are interested in the question, "Who is God for us?" Thus, the question of who we are and the question of who God is are not finally two independent and unrelated questions, but rather two complementary and interrelated aspects of one question (Ogden, 1982: 29–30).

It is precisely this kind of mutuality and interdependence, between the question of who God is and the question of who we are, that is so beautifully expressed in the creation narratives of Genesis. The conceptual vehicle used to integrate these two questions is the notion of the *imago dei*, the image of God, in which we have all been created. This chapter will explore just what it means to be created in that image and what difference that makes for how we understand ministry and go about engaging in the practice of ministry. In so doing, hopefully we will move down the path toward answering both of these fundamental questions—about God and about ourselves—and do so simultaneously.

There can hardly be a more fundamental and astounding statement in the entire biblical witness than that which is found in Genesis 1:27: "God created humanity in His own image. . . ." What at first sight looks like a statement about us is also a statement about God, and what looks from a different angle like a statement about God is also a statement about us. The idea of our creation in the image of God is a theological tool that allows us to talk out of both sides of our mouths at the same time (a favorite indoor sport of theologians!). It allows us to talk about the structure and purpose of our existence as human beings and at the same time to talk about the One who grounds that existence, gives it meaning, and authorizes a particular way of living and ministering as the authentic possibility of our existence, as opposed to other ways of living and ministering.

Throughout the Genesis creation stories, we discover the profound truth that the character of God is a character which human beings also share, even if in a radically limited and derivative sense. But this story is more than just a statement of how we reflect God's nature in our very being; it is also a statement of what we do with that reflection. We must not forget, after all, that the creation story also includes the story of the fall. If we share the character of God, we also distort and corrupt that character.

In a real sense, the story of Adam and Eve is the story of us all. It is a statement of the way it is with all of us and the way it goes with all of us (cf. Tillich, 1951: I:252ff). The real danger of a literalistic interpretation of the Genesis creation accounts and the figures of Adam and Eve is not that we may end up treating as historical fact what many biblical scholars take to be ancient Hebrew mythology. It is instead that a preoccupation with a literal Adam and Eve or a literal six-day creation causes us to view creation as an event once upon a time, as something which happened in the past, the results of which we must now cope with. The real value of the creation story is not that it provides us with scientific detail about the creation of our universe or that it supplies us with historical data about two primitive ancestors, but rather that it communicates to us just who we are as human beings in relationship to God. In other words, it affirms to us that we are indeed created in the image of God. This fundamental claim is of enormous theological consequence and is so serious and important as to have direct implications for virtually everything else we believe, say, and do—not the least of which is the form of ministry to which we understand ourselves to be called today as Christians: namely, compassionate ministry.

We lose or distort what it means to be created in the image of God, however, when we consider it from an allegedly neutral perspective above and beyond the predicament of real people who hurt and suffer. But when considered from the standpoint of those who live on the margins of society and through the lens of their daily predicament, answers to the question of just what it means to be created in God's image become not only more clear, but more relevant, and even revolutionary.

Welfare Mothers from Hell!

It would be easy, at this point, to launch into an abstract philosophical analysis of what a human being is, or, perhaps even more tempting, to draw together the diverse biblical data on the subject and then lay it out before the reader. We could then try to synthesize this data, apply our conclusions to contemporary human existence, and be done with the matter. But is it possible instead to begin with the life and experience of the poor and suffering themselves? Can we allow their struggle and the data of their predicament to provide the starting point for our approach to the biblical notion that we are created in the image of God?

A friend of mine and fellow minister, Mark East, was once training a college intern in urban ministry at the inner-city church where we both served. After the intern's first full morning of counseling and assisting the steady flow of people who had come through our doors seeking emergency assistance, she was visibly upset and almost to the point of tears. She had been lied to by some, cried to by others, and even yelled at by one young single mother who decided to vent her frustration on the young intern. Mark came up to the intern, hugged her, and asked, "What's the matter, did you get attacked by the 'welfare mothers from hell' today?" Laughter replaced anxiety, but not the painful awareness that within a couple of miles radius were thousands of impoverished single mothers trying to raise their families and make ends meet, but who were daily defeated in their attempts to do so. If many of these mothers acted like demons, that was only because their life was, in many ways, a daily, living hell.

Some of the stories of such women—numbers of them quite courageous, most of them not very demonlike at all, and many of them devout Christians —tell the story of the human predicament, with both its challenges and opportunities, perhaps better than any textbook on the subject ever could. I would like briefly to relate the stories of three such women, whose lives are representative of the blend of tragedy and unyielding strength, despair and hope, that characterizes so many human beings today. Hopefully, their predicament can serve as a starting point for our theological reflection on the meaning of contemporary human existence.

Debra is a single African-American woman who lives in a severely distressed and blighted inner-city neighborhood. Her last job was as a maid in a local motel, but when her boss found out she couldn't read or write, she was let go. It seems he felt there might be instances when her illiteracy could prove to be a liability for the motel. Debra owns no car, and she couldn't read the road signs to get a driver's license, even if she did. Finding work is extremely difficult, but she keeps on trying. Debra rents her own house but rarely lives alone, mostly for financial reasons. She has had several different men who have lived with her over the last few years. If and when they work, she can count on a few extra dollars to pay the bills. She's used to taking money from men for sexual favors; as early as age eight, her mother used to invite men over to receive oral sex from Debra. Her mother would get $5 each time. Debra got used to that kind of life and it's helped to keep the electricity and water running on several occasions. Still, she hopes that someday she may get a good job and settle down with that one right man.

Maria is a single Latina woman with twelve children. She lives in the same neighborhood as Debra. Maria moved to the neighborhood from a nearby city in the middle of the night, after loading up her children, a few important papers, and just the clothes on their backs. Her husband had beat her and threatened her dozens of times, but this time he had pulled a gun on her and her children. She felt she could take no more. Over the few years since then,

Maria has tried to create a life of her own. She has had three or four live-in males, none of whom have held steady jobs. Maria loves companionship, however, and the task of raising twelve children gets a bit overwhelming sometimes. Maria went through a federal job-training program and even worked at a community center for a year or so as a counselor. She was eventually terminated because many of the clients knew her personally and complained that if she couldn't keep her lights on, she could hardly presume to counsel them about their money management. Maria loves to help people, but presently she's unemployed. She barely makes ends meet, and even that is thanks to a federal housing-assistance program, food stamps, and a monthly welfare check. Her older children have come to resent her much of the time because they have always had to work just as soon as they became old enough. Maria takes their paychecks and only rarely gives them a few dollars to spend on themselves.

Finally, there's Pam. A single, African-American mother in her late forties, Pam became the victim of a crippling disease that took its toll on the limbs of her body. She eventually lost her job and her house. Pam eventually discovered that one of her legs had become so badly infected that she needed to have it amputated, and so she went to the county hospital to have it removed. The doctors removed the wrong leg. Horrified and embarrassed, Pam told no one until it was too late. She passed away due to heart failure from toxins that had entered into her bloodstream from a leg that should have been amputated early on but that was mistakenly left to destroy the whole body. Pam is not untypical of the kind of careless and mass health care that is provided to poor people who, without insurance or personal funds, are herded through county indigent hospitals and treated more like statistics than genuine human beings. Pam was a woman of faith and strength to the very last.

Each of these three brief stories may sound like extreme situations. But even if they are extreme, they are not rare. Hundreds of thousands of people in America's inner cities, with hundreds of millions more globally, live life on the margins and are just like Debra, Maria, Pam, and their neighbors: struggling to survive, searching for answers to life's dilemmas, and hoping—always hoping— for a way out. Debra, Maria, and Pam are average citizens with families, friends, churches, and even roofs over their heads. But they are the poor, even though they would probably not use that four-letter word to describe themselves.

The situations of Debra, Maria, and Pam may seem far removed from the comfort and privilege of those of us who write and are likely to read books like this one. However, there is something about their lives and experiences that, when used as a window for reading the Genesis stories of creation and fall, are nothing short of revelatory, not only of the situation of the poor in general, but of all human beings. Their predicaments, as diverse as they undoubtedly are, elucidate three crises faced by contemporary human beings—especially, the poor: a crisis of freedom, a crisis of community, and a crisis of creativity.

Each of these crises, in its own way, reflects what it means to say that we are all created in the image of God and that this image has likewise been impaired in each of us, threatening our authentic humanity. But just as these three crises illustrate the predicament of human existence in something of a negative way, so also they can serve to point us positively toward the practice of Christian ministry today if we want that ministry to be effective and liberating. Through the lens of the experience of the poor, then, perhaps we can comprehend (1) the structure of the image of God in each of us, (2) the way that structure has been defaced in each of us, especially in and through the humiliating and oppressive condition of being poor, and (3) the direction and shape that the church and its ministry must take today if it desires to participate in God's liberating and sanctifying activity of restoring the divine image in each of us.

Created for Freedom

What becomes so painfully obvious at first in reflecting on the experience of the three women mentioned above is the crisis of freedom in each of their lives. When we hear their stories, it doesn't take long for the suspicion to surface that, when it comes to freedom, something is not quite right here! No one, we suspect, should be locked in to a cycle of despair and destruction from generation to generation the way the poor are. No one, we presume, should have so few options from which to choose in life, so few paths to follow in leading life.

As in the case of Maria, no one should be forced to choose between what amounts to three options: (1) work for minimum wage while leaving children unattended at home, (2) stay home with the children but stay dependent on welfare, or (3) allow your children and family to go hungry and homeless. As in the case of Debra, no one should be forced to choose between only two options: (1) electricity and running water or (2) prostitution. As in the case of Pam, no one should be faced with no option other than to be treated like little more than cattle at the county indigent hospital where an individual is forced to sacrifice not only her dignity, but, finally, her very life.

When we view the Genesis creation accounts through the window of the life and experience of those such as Debra, Maria, or Pam, our suspicion that something is dreadfully wrong is confirmed by our reading that we have all been created in the image of God and that at least one piece of what that means is that we have been created in freedom. God placed Adam and Eve in the garden, so the story goes, to exercise their freedom in making their world whatever they wanted. The original couple was created with the capacity not merely to live their lives, but to lead them. Their freedom had its limits, of course, but the possibilities for self-fulfillment and living in harmony with each other and with nature were virtually unlimited. The message that comes through loud and clear in this story is that what it means to be created in the image of God is that a fundamental freedom is intended for every human existence. In fact, after reading Genesis, it is hard to avoid recognizing that this freedom is precisely what constitutes us as humans—it is what makes us uniquely human. Image-of-God freedom is a freedom to choose our future, a freedom to have a say in where we are headed. And if freedom is what constitutes us as humans, then to be robbed of that freedom, or to be seriously and unduly restricted in the use of that freedom, is, to that extent, to be dehumanized, to be stripped of at least one fundamental dimension that makes our lives human in the first place.

The crisis of freedom experienced by so many of the poor is, of course, both personal and social. The poor, like anybody else, do make bad decisions, often early in life, that serve to enslave them and shut them off to opportunity and liberation for years to come. But to focus guilt solely on the bad personal decisions made by poor people themselves is little more than victim blaming. For example, the fact that teenagers from poor families consistently tend to drop out of school at an early age can hardly be attributed simply to a mass bad personal choice by all the teenagers involved. Economic factors, racism, teenage pregnancy, rampant crime, and drug-infested neighborhoods, and abuse or neglect by overworked and underpaid parents all provide a kind of prison cell in which hundreds of thousands of inner-city children grow up, become teenagers, and move on into adulthood today. If the story of Adam and Eve means that we are all created in the image of God as free beings, then we can only conclude that for a significant segment of humanity today that image is being destroyed, squashed, stolen, and defaced.

But if the poor are those who, at virtually every turn in life, are enslaved either to someone or something (whether the federal government, the landlord, drugs, alcohol, poverty, prostitution, or finance companies), what about others in the human community who are quite comfortable and whose quality of life is characterized by virtually unlimited freedom—freedom to do what they want, go where they want, buy what they want, be what they want? For this segment of the population, if a leg gets infected, the finest medical specialists will be called in, the patient will be admitted and treated comfortably at a nice hospital, provided superb follow-up care, and, best of all, it's all paid for by the individual's health insurance policy provided by his or her employer. Surely there is no crisis of freedom here? Surely the image of God is firmly intact here?

On the contrary, the crisis of freedom which the life and the experience of the poor make so vivid is a crisis in which we all participate. In fact, the view from below forces us to take a hard look at how the relatively unrestricted use of freedom by some is related to—and in many ways the cause of—the restriction of the legitimate use of freedom by others. It is not necessarily the absence of freedom nor is it necessarily limitations on freedom that corrupt the image of God. Our fundamental image of freedom is also defaced insofar as it is cut off from the other two dimensions of that image yet to be discussed—creativity and community.

Freedom without Creativity

In the first place, the kind of freedom which the biblical witness affirms to be image-of-God freedom is more creative and dynamic than the empty and hollow freedom offered by a consumer-oriented society that reduces the definition of freedom to little more than a choice between rival soft drinks or competing blue jeans. The kind of freedom that characterizes life among the relatively comfortable and affluent of our world is not necessarily authentic image-of-God freedom, but is too often little more than the freedom to consume, the freedom to buy, the freedom to possess, and the freedom to accumulate. Far from bringing novelty and vigor into one's life, this sterile substitute for freedom deadens the senses, traps the individual in a never-ending spiral of wants and have-to-haves that continually drain a family's (or nation's) resources and transform time for creativity, loving, and playing into a rat-race (or arms-race). After living in both the inner city and the suburbs, I'm not sure who has less freedom: the average poor family with relatively few choices in life, or the average wealthy family enslaved to the endless cycle of consumption, acquisition, and gratification of material desires. Both families live in a kind of ghetto. Of course, in many ways this kind of comparison is deceiving. The crisis of freedom is not at all the same for both families. The solution is not the same either. It is in the gospel's call to a conversion to the poor that the wealthy find true freedom from selfishness and stockpiling. There is no parallel conversion to the rich to which the gospel calls the poor, however, that would bring liberation to their lives. The crisis of freedom is a crisis that characterizes us all. It does not, however, characterize us all in the same way. The choice between food or electricity is not the same as the choice between Sony or Sanyo. In other words, the relationship between the slavery of the poor and the slavery of the rich is real, but not symmetrical.

Creative freedom has to do with the quality of the choices we have and not simply the quantity. Simply because I have a choice among more than 300 types of drinks when entering a neighborhood convenience store, that does not make it the freedom store (despite the recent use of just this advertising slogan by one convenience store chain). Freedom is creative when I have a stake in my freedom, when I am a participant in my choices. Creative freedom is more than the mere exercise of options. It is the expression of who I am, complete with all my gifts and defects. That is why, for example, low-income homeownership programs or cooperative tenant associations in areas of urban decay will always foster a higher degree of creative freedom than their large, top-down management counterparts, even though the actual cost of housing might be equally affordable to a poor family. Unless the exercise of freedom is a genuine extension of our own unique creativity and imagination, we are not really talking about image-of-God freedom.

Freedom without Community

The second way that all of us participate in a crisis of freedom, whether rich or poor, corresponds to the dimension of community, or relatedness, inherent in the image of God. Just as with Adam and Eve, our freedom is thoroughly social. The exercise of our freedom is never empty of a context and almost always has consequences for the freedom of others. In reading the story of Adam, Eve, and the apple, we stumble across the all-too-familiar truth that we human beings like to implicate each other in our sinning. The sin of one of us almost always has repercussions on our neighbor. As soon as one individual sins, the neighbor is immediately brought in on it. Not only are we created together, we like to sin together!

We can see how this truth functions in our own social context as we increasingly realize that the unrighteous cycle of poverty enslaving the majority of our world is not without its rootedness in the prosperity and comfort of a small minority of the world. So, for example, the fact that the 6 percent of the human population on our planet that lives in the so-called First World consumes 40 percent of the world's resources is not unconnected to the destitution that characterizes so much of the rest of the world.

We could even draw a parallel to the story of Adam and Eve that more closely mirrors our own situation. In our day, the original sin does not always take place in the privacy of the relationship between two individuals nor does it involve simply one apple. The comfortable and prosperous of our world have plenty of apples—in fact, an overabundance of apples. But this affluent minority did not simply show up magically on the scene with these apples. We have taken them from neighboring trees (while claiming to have earned them), paid slave wages for the harvesting, and, in the process, polluted the gardens that nourished the trees. In many parts of the world, we have even stolen the land out from under those who owned it, and bulldozed the apple orchards to make room for airports, condos, and shopping malls. In the real world, the alleged freedom of one person or group often results in, or comes at the expense of, the slavery of other persons or groups. As Martin Luther King, Jr., put it,

We must all learn to live together as brothers. Or we will all perish together as fools. We are tied together in the single garment of destiny, caught in an inescapable network of mutuality. And whatever affects one directly affects all individually. For some strange reason I can never be what I ought to be until you are what you ought to be. And you can never be what you ought to be until I am what I ought to be. This is the way God's universe is made; this is the way it is structured. (1986b: 269)

Image of-God freedom, however much it may characterize us all, eludes us all.

In a sense, all of creation, and not just humanity, bears the stamp of God upon it and, therefore, has a certain degree of freedom.[1] The more we know about the most basic stuff of our universe, the more we know that it is not as entirely predictable and determined as we had previously imagined. And while the society of particles that makes up a rock or tree is in no sense as free as we are, there is something about all the universe that reflects God's image—an image of freedom. Human beings, nonetheless, are unique in their capacity to make choices, to create their own future, and to do this in the context of loving, deliberate community. Humans have an almost unlimited ability to create an atmosphere of freedom for others, however rare that might actually occur in our own world.

Sadly, of course, the freedom that the Genesis account affirms to be a God-given aspect of our makeup is too often robbed or misused. But this robbery or misuse of freedom is not a part of what it means to be human. It is actually a distortion of our humanity and is a condition that is, in an original sense, alien to us. If it is true that we are all sinful, that is not because we are only human, but precisely the opposite—we have failed to be truly human and are to that extent even inhuman to one another. We have ceased to live in accordance with the image in which we are all created. To be authentically human is to live in God's image, the image of freedom.

Created Together

The second tragic characteristic of the life and experience of the poor and the suffering that reaches out and grabs us in the stories of Debra, Maria, and

---

1. While this book is not the place to develop it, one could certainly talk about a metaphysics of freedom, creativity, and community where the three elements that I here speak of as the image of God are the primary metaphysical traits of all reality simply as such. The most promising resources for such a metaphysics are to be found, I believe, in a neoclassical, or process, metaphysics such as that developed by Charles Hartshorne and others. For Hartshorne, "creative synthesis" is the central metaphysical category that points to the fact that for any entity whatsoever, its becoming is an instance of relationship (with itself, others, the past, and God), freedom, and creative self-determination.

Pam has to do with the quality of their relationships—their capacity for and manner of actually being social. Whether we consider family relationships, sexual relationships, marital relationships, parental relationships, or any other of the common relationships that take place in our society, workplace, family, church, or neighborhood, these relationships are often characterized by patterns of abuse, exploitation, violation, self-centeredness, domination-subordination, and worthlessness.

Poverty especially has a way of forcing people to live in situations of inferiority and bondage in relation to those upon whom they must remain dependent and enslaved. Life becomes not so much the experience of freedom, equality, and genuine community as the experience of being held hostage to the whims and wants of the landlord, the employer, the boyfriend, the caseworker, or the bill collector. For Maria, the relationship of parent to child becomes one of utility and manipulation rather than provision, support, and encouragement, while the relationship of child to parent becomes one of resentment, defiance, and disrespect, rather than admiration, honor, and esteem. For Debra, the relationship of male to female becomes one of domination, exploitation, and violence, while the relationship of female to male becomes one of self-negation, prostitution, and manipulation. For Pam, the relationship of individual to society becomes one of enslaved dependency and distrust, while the relationship of society to individual becomes one of neglect and irritation.

Here again, when we read the creation story of Genesis while standing with the poor, we discover that their condition reveals a fundamental disfigurement of the second dimension of the image of God: our creation as social beings, beings in community. Whether we begin with the creation story in Genesis 1 or the creation story in Genesis 2, the truth that we are created social is striking. As the writer of Genesis 1 states, ". . . in the image of God He created them; male and female He created them" (1:27). Or, to take the second creation story, God creates the first human being and then says, "It is not good for the man to be alone" (2:18). Either way, community is deeply rooted in our nature as human beings, and it is in this most important respect that we are created in the image of the one true God who is also social.

Relatedness, or community, is one of the most obvious and irrefutable characteristics that we can attach to what it means to be human, though it has traditionally been a real problem when applied to God. Everything we do is colored by influences from others and, to that degree, we are dependent on others—we include them into our own becoming. Indeed, more and more, we find that who we are involves a constellation of relationships not only with God and our fellow human beings, but with social institutions, political and economic structures, and our natural environment itself. Even my own relationship to myself, at a number of different levels, becomes a major factor in who I am. What I eat and the quantity thereof influences who I am. My location in society, my past, my genetic material, my friends, and my family all influence who I am. As we are finding out in ways that are often alarming and disturbing, our relationship to our environment, our planet, and to other living creatures has direct consequences for our own development as human persons. We are complex beings, to say the least, and that complexity is largely the consequence of the social nature of the image of God impressed on each one of us.

It is no wonder, then, that to deprive our neighbor of proper community or to misuse our own capacity for relationship is absolutely abhorrent and foreign to the biblical notion of what it means to be a human being. Here again, though the poor are not the only ones who reflect this distortion, their situation certainly magnifies it. The crisis of community is one in which we all participate.

The crisis of community can take many different forms. In some cases, individuals choose to forfeit relationships either with God or with others, thereby shutting themselves off from community and choosing instead to be selfish and turned in on themselves. In other cases, however, one could almost say that community is stolen, as in the case with victims of rape and sexual abuse, the elderly, AIDS patients, or members of racial minority groups. The value of the person too often becomes little more than his or her utility as a means to some other satisfaction. But while community can certainly be forfeited or stolen, it can also be disfigured or misused. As in the case of freedom, the problem is not that the image of God is missing, but that it is corrupted. And the corruption of community lies in the fact that it is separated from each of the other two dimensions of the image of God: freedom and creativity.

Relationship without Freedom

Relationships without freedom are characterized by domination and subordination, master and slave. Here the problem is not so much that human beings are unrelated to one another; rather, we are improperly related to one another. This pattern of domination and subordination is deeply etched into our society and world. At every turn, we find ourselves in situations where we either suppress the liberty of our neighbor or allow our neighbor to suppress our liberty. In either case, what is missing from the relationship is a genuine, reciprocal freedom.

It is precisely this lack of freedom in our relationships that turns cooperation into competition, service to neighbor into subjugation to neighbor, and compassionate leadership of others into domination of others. Rather than turning to others, we turn on others. There is, of course, a place for leadership in the Kingdom of God. Martin Luther King, Jr., in his sermon, "The Drum

Major Instinct," cites Mark's account of James and John, the sons of Zebedee, asking to be placed first in the kingdom by being seated at Jesus' left and right hand. Rather than chastise the two disciples for their request (the other ten disciples were "filled with indignation"), Jesus takes their request, turns it upside down, and fills it with a new Kingdom-meaning:

> One would have thought that Jesus would have said, "You are out of your place. You are selfish. Why would you raise such a question?"
>
> But that isn't what Jesus did. He did something altogether different. He said in substance, "Oh, I see, you want to be first. You want to be great. You want to be important. You want to be significant. Well you ought to be. If you're going to be my disciple, you must be." But he reordered priorities. And he said, "Yes, don't give up this instinct. It's a good instinct if you use it right. It's a good instinct if you don't distort it and pervert it. Don't give it up. Keep feeling the need for being important. Keep feeling the need for being first. But I want you to be first in love. I want you to be first in moral excellence. I want you to be first in generosity. . . .
>
> And so Jesus gave us a new norm of greatness. If you want to be important—wonderful. If you want to be recognized—wonderful. If you want to be great—wonderful. But recognize that [the one] who is greatest among you shall be your servant. That's your new definition of greatness. And this morning, the thing that I like about it . . . by giving that definition of greatness, it means that everybody can be great. Because everybody can serve. (1986a: 265)

Note that the ability to serve pointed to by King and discovered in the words of Jesus is far from the kind of slavery and oppression that characterizes the human predicament. What distinguishes Christian servanthood from slavery is precisely the element of freedom in the relationship. Christian servanthood respects the integrity and freedom of the individual. It is I who choose to serve. I am not made to serve. How often, both inside and outside the church, have we justified subjugation in the name of servanthood, and domination in the name of leadership? Relationships without freedom will always be an affront to the image of God in which we are all created.

In the cases of Maria, Debra, and Pam, we discover that this affront is three-fold. These women are ethnic minorities, they are women, and they are poor. They experience what some refer to as triple jeopardy! In the first place, poverty already brings with it a destructive dependency that eats away at virtually all primary relationships. As in the case with Maria, the mother of twelve children, every move must be reported to the caseworker. If she wants luxuries like a roof that doesn't leak or a toilet that flushes, she must wait weeks for the landlord who, four states away, promises to "get to it right away." She is reliant on her own children for income, and this puts her in a seriously strained position with them. Debra, on the other hand, unable to read, is dependent on others even to take medicine or to fill out an employment application. She obviously cannot get a driver's license and so is always dependent on others even to go get groceries. Finally, in the case of Pam, as in the case of so many of the poor, serious medical problems spell absolute dependency not only on an impersonal medical system, but also on family members who have too many problems of their own to be of any real help.

But poverty is just the beginning of the attack on the image of God as revealed in the situation of these three women. Each of them is also an ethnic or racial minority, and this fact precedes them whenever they walk into a bank for a loan, an employment office for a job, or even a church for worship. Poverty and race go hand in hand in our North American context, and we can no longer hide from that fact in the United States where, for example, poverty is overwhelmingly black. However you cut the statistics, blacks are still two to four times as likely to live in poverty as whites. Two hundred years of slavery, a hundred more of segregation, and decade after decade of ghettoization have so ravaged African-Americans in our society, so robbed the element of freedom from their relationships, that it is no wonder the economic effects have been crippling. Racism in America is still one of the primary assaults on the image of God manifesting itself in a variety of ways. Jacquelyn Grant writes:

Politically, racism disenfranchises; socially it ostracizes; culturally, it degrades and robs the people of those characteristics that make them a people; religiously, it brainwashes and indoctrinates so that the oppressed peoples believe not only that it is impossible for God to look like them or for them to image God, but also that God ordains racist oppression. (49)

But Maria, Debra, and Pam are not only poor and members of minorities, they are women, and if any group of people throughout the history of the planet has been dominated and forced into situations of destructive dependency, it is women. Here again it is precisely the quality of relationships without freedom that is the link between poverty, race, and gender in our society. In the United States, during the Reagan administration of the 1980s, for example, while poverty in families headed by men declined by 50 percent, poverty in families headed by women increased by 54 percent (Grant: 53). To be a female in our society still defines for many the kind of work and the structure of relationships that are possible both inside and outside the home. The female is still perceived as the weaker sex and as needing to be led and protected by (we mean subordinated to) the male. Then, too, the treatment of women in terms of their sexual utility is another clear example of the blatant corruption of the image of God, one that victimizes character and compromises integrity.

Christians, far from serving as a force for change at this point, have legitimated and bolstered these attitudes with mindless and literalistic appeals to scripture. Some even find scriptural support for the domination of male over female in the curse God pronounces after the fall in Genesis 3:16, "your desire shall be for your husband, and he shall rule over you." Unless I am mistaken, however, the very significance of Christ for us is to be found in his offer of redemption from the curse of sin and restoration to our true humanity, a humanity created in the image of God, a humanity of partnership, equality, and freedom. It is not the curse of sin but the redemption found in Christ that must define our relationships with each other.

Relationship without Creativity

Someone once asked me what the difference was between the rich and the poor, arguing that the difference was purely subjective and relative. I asked him how fast he could produce his birth certificate, copies of his children's birth certificates, a most recent copy of his pay stub (unless he was presently on welfare and then I'd want a copy of his most recent welfare check stub), and his most recent utility bills. He didn't know how long it would take. But the poor carry these with them at all times. Their identity, their proof of existence, their humanity, is lodged in these documents. They know that the housing caseworker will want to see them. They know that the social agency will require them before any food can be distributed. They know that the Food Stamp office will need to review them. The poor are those who have lost their faces and have become, instead, a traveling pile of paperwork.

This condition has similarities to what Juan Luis Segundo refers to as a "mass" existence (1976: 208ff). And it is precisely this existence, characterized by relationships without individuality or uniqueness, that we can describe as relationship without creativity. While, for the poor, this quality of facelessness and anonymity is pervasive, it characterizes existence for most of us. Sometimes I feel as though I am no longer a person, but a legion of PIN numbers. (If you don't know what a PIN number is, you are fortunate enough not to carry too many credit cards, bank cards, or long distance calling cards.)

Here again, the problem is not that we are unrelated to one another; rather, the problem is that our relationships tend to be purely external—who we really are is not allowed to enter into or shape those relationships. Rather than being genuine partners in the creation of each other, we are reduced to faceless numbers, mere cogs in the machine.

Of course, it is true that the very foundations of any society, especially its political and economic systems, depend on most of us acting precisely as a mass—predictable and uniform. Society would unravel, and there could be no law or order if there were not a good number of external relationships in all of our lives. Neither can anyone love all their neighbors with full intimacy and openness. We are all bound to keep a good number—in fact, the majority—of our relationships at arms-length. There is a point at which too many intimate relationships begin to harm the quality of all of our relationships. Despite these obvious limitations on creative relationship, however, too few human beings experience genuine community in their lives. Alienation, shallowness, and anonymity rob and distort the image of God in each of us and hinder relationships characterized by novelty, creativity, empathy, and compassion.

If we think about relationships without creativity, two words come to mind, each of which is the opposite of creative—barren and destructive. The first of these, barrenness, refers to the absence of creativity while the second, destruction, refers to the reversal or demolition of creativity. Both are apropos of the human predicament as we know it, and both are enemies of community. To begin with, barrenness is simply another way of describing the mass relationships and alienation from one another that contemporary human beings experience. But at several critical points in our world, barrenness becomes destruction, emptiness turns into injury, and shallowness is transformed into oppression. Whether we think, for example, of riots, rape, family violence, and police brutality, on the one hand, or the more silent but insidious devastation that comes with racism, poverty, sexism, and treatment of the elderly, on the other hand, the barrenness of our relationships converts itself into one of the most stubborn and implacably destructive forces in the world.

In the last several decades especially we have seen the rise of this deadly interplay between barrenness and destructiveness in the institutional violence of many transnational corporations. Mark Lewis Taylor has traced the relationship between the abject poverty of nations such as Guatemala (where over two-thirds of the population live in extreme poverty, unable to secure even a minimum diet) and the virtually unrestricted investment and business practices of first-world corporations in those same countries. Not only is labor exploited by many of these corporations in the form of slave wages, but "almost any effort at bettering the laborers' situations can result in repression and death" (107). Thus, individuals linked to labor-organizing efforts in these countries are daily assassinated or tortured by death squads, the known leaders of which hob-nob regularly with business executives and government officials. The suffering of the poor, as Taylor notes, is augmented by ethnic discrimination whereby land is expropriated and whole communities are evicted and relocated into slum living conditions. So also, the triple jeopardy that characterizes the existence of poor minority women in North America is even more intensified in third-world countries where, for example, in 1989, 95 percent of workers in textile maquiladoras (cheap labor assembly plants) were female and earned approximately 5 percent of what the comparable textile worker in the United States earned (110).

The injustice and destruction caused by transnational corporations, however, could never occur with its characteristic ferocity and intensity apart from a dialectic of distancing and destruction. In other words, as Taylor points out, it is precisely a corporation's remoteness or distance from the poor, minorities, or women that allows and even encourages it to engage in practices that oppress and destroy. So also for us, it is always easier to abuse people that we either don't see or refuse to see.

In a North American context, we can detect this same dialectic between treating others as invisible and the consequent abuse and destruction generated by this practice. One thinks, for example, of the link between imagining the poor, in the words of Ronald Reagan, as "a faceless mass waiting for a handout" and the destructive social and urban policies of the 1980s that accompanied severe rises in poverty, urban decay, and increased violent racism. In other situations, on a more interpersonal level, the same dynamic is at work. Time and again, the landlord is alienated from the renter, and this empty and purely external relationship smooths the path for harassment and abuse on the part of the landlord, on the one hand, or disregard for property on the part of the renter, on the other. Lack of genuine community with our neighbor habitually begets oppressive and violent behavior toward that neighbor. One need only think for a moment of the relationship between labor and management, citizen and politician, wife and husband, pastor and congregation, caseworker and client, or professor and student. The infertility of our relationships with others generates disastrous and destructive consequences on an almost daily basis.

Created Creative

We have seen the essential role played by creativity in relationship to the experience (and corruption) of image-of-God freedom and image-of-God community. We must now ask about creativity itself as a third crisis that manifests itself so excruciatingly in the life and experience of persons like Debra, Maria, or Pam. Creativity is the element of novelty in each of our lives whereby we receive from our past and from those influences around us, and then freely determine a future for ourselves and for our world. Thus, creativity is a function of both community and freedom. Indeed, it is the lively interplay between the two.

If we look at Genesis, we find that Adam and Eve were instructed to "be fruitful and multiply" and were given a world to cultivate into whatever they wished. In so doing, God created us to create. There is something about our very nature that drives us to bring novelty and productivity out of our world.

This creativity is more than just an ability to form what already exists into something else. We really create! And our creations are more than just the aggregates of other creations. The fact that we are able to bring something new into being is central to what it means to say that we are created in the image of God.

Over and over, in countless ways, the image of God as creative is expressed in every dimension of our lives—in our art, science, education, sexuality, politics, religion, play, and work. Creativity runs through our entire being and, though too often we find our creativity stifled and our responses to life rather unproductive, barren, and even born out of despair, it is impossible to deny who we fundamentally are: cocreators with God. Here again, however, when we consider our creation in the image of God from the vantage point of the disinherited of society, we are quickly confronted with a glaring assault on creativity. But, just as with freedom and community, the crisis of creativity, though aggravated in the life and experience of the poor, is a crisis we all share. How this is true can perhaps be better understood by considering just two of the many dimensions of life where image-of-God creativity is disfigured: (1) work and (2) sexuality.

Work

In and of itself, work is a tremendous channel for creative self-expression. Contrary to popular opinion, work is not a by-product of the fall or something dreadful injected into human life because of sinfulness. It is a primary vehicle for the expression and cultivation of the image of God. If we look once again to the story of Adam and Eve, we discover that God put human beings in the garden to work it and to preserve it (Gen. 2:15). To be sure, work does become something cursed for human beings, but in an original sense, work is fundamental to our creation in God's image. It is something positive and one of the primary avenues through which we express our basic humanity. But if this is true, then there is a considerably large segment of humanity—the unemployed—who, for a variety of reasons, are not able to express the image of God as creative through work. It is for that reason that large-scale unemployment in our society is not merely a misfortune or an economic problem. It is a sin. It is an assault against the image of God in those human beings who are able to work but who cannot find work.

But unemployment is not the only distortion of the image of God when it comes to work. Underemployment is also a crushing attack on the image of God. For those in our society who are unskilled, uneducated, or discriminated against (whether because of race, gender, age, or appearance), the only work available is typically mindless, sometimes degrading, often monotonous, and usually void of imagination and stimulation (not to mention a decent wage). Even here, there are those rare individuals who succeed in being innovative, fresh, and inventive in the face of what would otherwise be tedium and empty routine. In general, however, the poor are usually consigned to jobs that no one else wants (fast-food service or janitorial work) and which promise very little by way of long-term satisfaction. In essence, work, for most of the poor, lacks the space for creativity—for novelty and imagination. If one of the primary paths for expressing the image of God is creative work, then single parents who are caught in the trap between child care and employment (like Maria) or those who are unskilled and illiterate (like Debra) are those for whom the image of God is being repressed and falsified on an almost daily basis.

If we are honest, of course, work is not an assault on the image of God for the poor only, though their predicament certainly magnifies that assault. It would hardly be an exaggeration to claim that most human beings find it difficult to discover meaning, novelty, and fulfillment in their work. Here the problem is as much our attitude toward work, both as individuals and as a society, as it is the economic and political structures that guide and order our work. Neither socialism nor capitalism, for example, have really delivered on their promises in our world when it comes to bringing fulfillment through work. Socialist experiments in our time have tended toward depersonalizing human labor, treating workers as mere cogs in a social machine. Capitalist societies, on the other hand, true to their ideology that value is an exchange value determined by a free market, have birthed multitudes of human beings who find themselves doing work that is miserable and even self-destructive, selling themselves to the highest bidder.

The image of God in us as creative resists these forms of assembly-line or prostituted existence. In the first place, it drives us to seek out personal satisfaction in meaningful, fulfilling jobs. In the second place, it presses us, in the words of E. F. Schumacher, "to reject meaningless, boring, stultifying, or nerve-wracking work in which a [person] is made the servant of a machine or system" (119). There are, of course, millions of human beings who find it necessary to work at jobs that are degrading and meaningless for the sake of mere survival. It is the height of presumption to instruct them in some cavalier way to reject such work, even if they could. The rejection I have in mind is not merely a renunciation of demeaning work on the part of the worker, to the extent that this is possible; it is also a renunciation of demeaning work on the part of employers, managers, corporate boards, shareholders, policy makers, and even society itself through its political and economic arrangements. Thus, in the third place, the image of God as creative compels us to structure our businesses and economic arrangements in ways that are more likely to take advantage of the creative impulses with which we are all created.

The creative image of God in each of us also propels us to reconsider and reorder the relationship of play to work. On the face of it, the dimension of play in our lives seems to be the complete opposite of work, and yet the two are intimately related. Without the time and space for some degree of leisure and play, it is doubtful whether human life is truly satisfying. Work that is creative and fulfilling is usually understood to be precisely that because of the time and resources it makes available for leisure—for family, friends, and recreation. Then, too, for the extremely fortunate, work is play, or at least the line dividing the two is exceptionally fuzzy. But what about poor families where both parents or the single parent must work two or more jobs and where the children must typically begin working at an early age to help support the family, often dropping out of school early to do so? For the poor, this overloaded existence—what, in another context, we would style a workaholic existence—is not for the sake of being able to afford a nicer car, house, boat, vacation in Tahoe, or even a college education. The poor work day and night in order merely to survive.

In Eden, work and play converge. Perhaps this was even true to a certain extent during the long course of human history up to the industrial age, where long work days and dehumanizing working conditions began to stand in stark contrast to the day off, vacations, and holidays. Increasingly, however, we know clearly where work ends and play begins. We segment our lives not only in terms of play times, but play places (Hall: 52–53). But both work and play suffer in this form of cultural apartheid. On the one hand, play becomes increasingly passive and barren (watching television, visiting amusement parks, playing video games, etc.). On the other hand, work becomes pure drudgery and a necessary evil. At least part of what it means to live creatively in the image of God, however, is to overcome the opposition between work and play in our lives. That can only happen as we allow our faith to transform our work into the adventure of cocreation with God that it was meant to be.

Sexuality

If the image of God is obscured in our work, so it is in our sexuality. In fact, there may even be a close relationship between our sexual arrangements and our working conditions, as Dorothee Soelle points out:

We work for exchange value, even though money cannot satisfy real needs, and so the craving for money becomes endless. Analogously, the search for sexual objects is limitless, because the utilitarian or exchange value of bodies does not satisfy actual needs for sex and love.... The aim of sexuality is deflected from the concrete and unique person to her physical attributes or her aesthetic packaging. The person is turned into an object, a sexual commodity to be possessed or purchased like any other commodity. (1984: 117)

While this description can characterize numerous sexual relationships, Soelle specifically calls attention to two examples of this distortion of human sexuality. The first she refers to as "anonymous sex," where virtually any other person is used to satisfy one's physical passions. This is very similar to the massification of relationships mentioned earlier. It represents relationship without creativity. The individual person in his or her totality is not present. Sexuality is reduced to a biological function. The second pattern Soelle calls "sport sex," by which she means that whole process whereby we are trained from an early age how to tease, market, attract, turn on, and conquer others. Here too we find an assault on human creativity insofar as sexuality is utilitarian and exploitative. In each of these, our consumeristic mindset results in the fact that, as Soelle says, "sensation is separated from feeling and expectation, sexuality from human commitment, and loving from knowing" (117).

If what Soelle says is true, however, the loss of family values and the rise of promiscuous sexuality bemoaned today is hardly the result of life in a secular society that only a return to conservative morality can reform. Ironically, conservative Christianity in North America today is generally as tied to a capitalistic economy that treats human labor as a commodity to be bought and sold as it is resolute in its fight against the sexual implications of that very system. Even the widespread practice of abortion on demand—the holy horror of conservative religion—is little more than the application of market-determined value to the sphere of human procreation. As long as human life in our society is reduced to production, consumption, and acquisition, and as long as value is determined by exchange value, we can only expect human sexuality to reflect the corruption of our image-of-God creativity.

The situation of Maria and Debra is typical of the assault on creative sexuality in the life and experience of the poor. In both instances, sexuality is made to serve economic security. In the case of Debra, the sex-for-money trade is conspicuous and explicit. Money is paid; sexual favors are granted. In the case of Maria, the situation is more complex, but the need for financial safety is still the governing reality to which sexual arrangements are subordinated. Finally we must admit that prostitution is a way of life for many of the poor in our society, and that, really, the professional prostitute is only an exaggerated instance of a destructive process that characterizes the context of poverty in general. Here again, it is typically women who are the victims of this destructive process, but it is a process that plunders human creativity in the sexual expression of both men and women.

The poor are not the only ones for whom image-of-God creativity is under attack in and through our sexual arrangements. In fact, the enslavement of human sexuality to various factors such as economic pressure, job advancement, social acceptance, chauvinism, and physical violence is so obviously representative of our society as a whole as to require little elaboration. Image-of-God sexuality, however, is sexuality that is born in and aims at authentic freedom and authentic community. It is free insofar as one engages in sexual relationship without coercion and without manipulation. It is communal insofar as it is placed in a context of reciprocity, care, nurture, and commitment.

Dimensions of human life other than work and sexuality could be mentioned—politics, art, even religion. What we see in the two dimensions highlighted above, however, is the extraordinary capacity for creativity that comes with our creation in God's image as well as the tragic assault on that very image. This is especially evident in the situation of the poor, but it is a crisis in which we all share. Here again, the real culprit is not primarily the absence or restriction of creativity, but rather its separation from the other two dimensions of the image of God—freedom and community.

Creativity without Freedom

In the first place, the kind of creativity which the biblical witness affirms to be image-of-God creativity can never be entirely compulsory or completely thrust upon us from the outside. We are either free participants in the ongoing process of creation, or we are really not creators at all. As we have seen in the case of work as an expression of creativity, when labor is forced upon us as something alien to us—a kind of Monday through Friday, nine-to-five parallel universe through which we drudge until we can make it to the weekend—we are essentially slaves, whether we are rich or poor. What we create is not our own, for it is not an act of freedom.

Far from bringing novelty and joy into our lives, creative expression through work, play, art, and love is cheapened and deadened when freedom is absent. Free creativity, then, is never to be confused with mere productivity. Here again, the image of God has to do more with the quality of our creativity rather than its quantity. Simply because the children of Israel turned out more bricks for the Pharaoh this year as compared to last year does not mean the children of Israel have become more creative. Image-of-God creativity is fundamentally a free creativity.

One of the obstacles to affirming the importance of our own participation in creation is that too many of us still suffer from a negative understanding of creation. This misunderstanding stems from a clear preference by many Christians for the spiritual and immaterial over the physical and material in life. The spill-over effects of this preference are most noticeable in a predominantly negative attitude toward, for example, the environment, human sexuality, or the future prospects of human existence on our planet. Over and over, Christians define their hope in terms of getting to "Beulah Land," rather than a love for, loyalty to, and participation in creation. We have a difficult time, it seems, in agreeing with God's own praise of creation: "And God saw all that He had made, and behold, it was very good" (Gen. 1:31). Perhaps that is because the ability to praise creation stems from our participation in it. Insofar as we fail to participate in creation, it is quite difficult to praise creation. In fact, for many Christians, as Dorothee Soelle once observed, it is easier to believe in the certainty of life after death than to believe in and participate in life before death.

The liberation of theology includes the liberation of the doctrine of creation as not so much a study in ancient history as an exercise in self-understanding and mission. If we really want to understand what it means to be created in God's image, we must freely participate in creation ourselves, and that includes unmasking and struggling against the attempts all around us, both consciously and unconsciously, to undo creation, whether through destruction of the natural environment, proliferation of nuclear weapons, rapid and mindless depletion of natural resources, or dehumanizing poverty. Creation, then, is not so much a doctrine to be learned as it is a choice we must make—something we are either for or against. Perhaps the most fundamental decision we must make in life is not whether we believe in creation or evolution, but whether we will choose to participate in creation or become accomplices in its undoing.

Creativity without Community

The second way that we all participate in a crisis of creativity corresponds to the dimension of community, or relatedness, inherent in the image of God. Creativity that is purely individualistic or selfish is not image-of-God creativity. While the dimension of freedom insures that I am an active participant in the ongoing process of creation, the dimension of community insures that what I create is not at the same time destructive of others or inattentive to the suffering of others. So, for example, it is difficult to claim that every technological discovery of modern human existence is a leap forward in terms of image-of-God creativity. In fact, as we are increasingly aware in our world, we humans do much better in the how-to department than in the what-for department. Image-of-God creativity is never identical with mere expertise or technique, but always includes a fundamental responsibility to others, our world, and God.

It is especially at this point that the crisis of creativity for the poor intersects with the crisis of creativity for the affluent. Less and less are the creative juices of the best and brightest in our society devoted to constructing a world where economic and racial barriers are overcome and creative work is available for all. Instead, the gap is widening between the haves and the have-nots, and one of the primary forms this gap takes in our world is in terms of education and technology. The recent U.S. involvement in the Gulf War provides ample proof of this. In that war, we discovered the tremendous resources, technology, and sophistication that one country could amass to carry out a military campaign of dubious justification. But this vivid display of money, power, and ingenuity wrapped up in the American flag and focused toward the preservation of selfish interests in the Middle East lies in stark contrast to the lack of resources and inventiveness that this same nation is willing to direct toward the education of inner-city children. As Jonathan Kozol says,

> We know what works. We're just not willing to pay the bill. Even President Bush knows Head Start works, but he says we don't have $5 billion to provide it for every child who needs it. But somehow we found $50 billion to restore the emirate of Kuwait to his throne. Which is more important to America? (26)

As human creativity is increasingly directed toward selfish rather than communal ends, we will continue to have bombs that are smarter than our children, and we can expect a spirit of competitiveness and greed to persist in pitting the poor against the affluent in the battle for education, jobs, and a future.

Grace as the First and Last Word in the Human Predicament

It would be possible to take the dimensions of freedom, community, and creativity characterized in this chapter and interpret them as if they were merely natural characteristics of human existence. In a sense, they are natural characteristics. They go with the territory of what it means to be a human being. And yet the Christian must affirm that the qualities of freedom, community, and creativity are first and foremost graced qualities. In other words, to the extent that we are, indeed, free, social, and creative, that is purely by grace. It should not be surprising, then, that Christians choose to talk in terms of our creation in the image of God rather than in merely naturalistic terms when describing the human predicament.[2] A faith that the deepest dimensions of our very being are products of grace allows us to believe that we are a truly good creation despite obvious and daily evidence to the contrary. This faith also requires us to interpret the corruption, violation, and oppression of our created goodness as something more than sheer human inevitability. It is instead sin.

---

2. Ultimately I believe that the distinction between natural and supernatural in this context is misleading. It perpetuates a failure to recognize God in every and all experience and tends to cause us to look for God's presence only in unique, unrepeatable, or unexplainable experiences.

So it is finally impossible to talk about the human predicament in terms of (1) its created goodness, (2) its subsequent corruption, and (3) its potential redemption, without recognizing that (1) grace is what makes us human in the first place, (2) grace is refused and violated by all of us (we are all sinners), and (3) grace is what ultimately redeems us. Grace is the first and last word when talking about the human predicament. Grace is the first and last word, therefore, when talking about Christian ministry.

So what is grace? How does it make us human in the first place? How is it refused and violated by us? How does it redeem our fallen condition?

Grace is, simply, the presence and activity of God in the world. Grace is God's pure unbounded love for all of us. If we are genuinely free, that is because God is present and active in our every experience, providing us liberating options. If we are genuinely communal, that is because God is present and active in our every experience, giving us not only Godself, but God's entire creation for relationship. If we are genuinely creative, that is because God is present and active in our every experience, providing us novel aims that lure us into a new future beyond the mere repetition of the past. To reject God's options, presence, or aims is to reject grace and, thus, to reject God. But grace, for all that, never ceases ... because God does not cease being God. God is always present and active in any and every experience whatsoever. Grace is, as John Wesley described it, prevenient—it is always present and active, it runs ahead of us, it stays with the conversation, it restores and redeems.

But just as important as our affirmation that God is always immediately present and directly active in any and every experience is our affirmation that God's presence and activity is also mediated indirectly through our presence and activity.[3] Nothing could be more important for our understanding and practice of ministry than recognizing the distinct link between these two types of God's activity. If God's presence and activity is not limited to God's own immediate presence and direct activity but includes also our presence and activity, then we are indeed agents (or ministers) of God's grace to the world and to one another. We are God's body—God's hands, God's feet. And what God is up to in the world as discovered decisively in Jesus of Nazareth is meant to be reflected in and through our lives and ministry.

All this means that the image of God as a gift of God's grace is the source, mode, and aim of Christian ministry. First, just as we ourselves have experi-

---

3. Schubert Ogden makes this distinction as follows:

> The agency of God as the Creator and the Redeemer and also the Savior pertains in each case to two closely related but nonetheless distinct types of divine action: first, that which is immediately and directly God's own action, whether as the Creator of all things, or as the Redeemer thereof, or as the Savior of men and women; and, second, that which is only mediately or indirectly God's action, since it occurs only through one or more of God's creatures or in cooperation with their own immediate and direct action (1988: 2).

enced liberation, so our ministry must be undertaken in freedom and for the sake of freedom. Ministry is not image-of-God ministry if it is coerced or if it is performed out of guilt or compulsion. Freedom must be the mode of our ministry just as surely as it is the origin and aim of our ministry. Second, just as we have been reconciled with God and one another, just as we have been initiated into a new covenant community, so also our ministry must be undertaken in community and for the sake of community. Ministry is not image-of-God ministry if it is undertaken as a lone ranger. Community must be the mode of our ministry just as surely as it is the origin and aim of our ministry. Third, just as we have been made a new creation in Christ, so also our ministry must be undertaken creatively and for the sake of creativity and hope. Ministry is not image-of-God creativity if it is inflexible or if it lacks vision and novelty. Creativity must be the mode of our ministry just as surely as it is the origin and aim of our ministry.

Ministry, in sum, has a kind of three-fold character: it is a response to grace, it is a participation in grace, and it is an offer of grace. Through Christian ministry, the work of the restoration of the image of God begun in us is extended to the world. God's compassion becomes our compassion. God's solidarity with victims becomes our solidarity with victims. We too take sides. We too stay with the conversation. We too run ahead and are present with those who suffer and despair. This is the audacious and yet humbling reality that is image-of-God ministry and the calling of every Christian today.

3

The God of Compassion

We began our theology of compassionate ministry by exploring what it means to be human—to be graced with the qualities of freedom, community, and creativity that comprise the image of God. But already it becomes clear that the question of who we are as humans is inseparable from the question of who God is. Even though we have no real context for imagining ministry or ourselves as ministers apart from the foundational question of who we are, the question of who God is still retains a certain priority and urgency. This is true for at least two reasons. In the first place, answers to the questions of who God is and what God wants shape and define our understanding of who we are. After all, if we are indeed created in God's image, it might pay off to be clear about who God is. In the second place, the answer to the question of who God is also shapes our understanding of ministry by providing its source and hope, its origin and aim. Take, for example, compassionate ministry. Let's face it; compassion is not one of our most spontaneous and natural inclinations as human beings. Compassion is intentionally entering into community with those who suffer and working on behalf of their liberation. But suffering is not something we consider normal persons to be naturally drawn toward. As civil as we human beings have at times learned to be toward one another, it is finally God that we must rely upon as both the source and the hope of an effective and liberating practice of compassion.

In keeping with the circle between theology and ministry, we must explore the question of who God is by interfacing what we believe with what we do. It is only by clarifying and fully reflecting on the relationship between the two, rather than hiding or neglecting that relationship, that we can take positive steps toward bridging the gap between faith and practice, thought and life, theology and ministry. Once again, this dynamic circle challenges us to move in two directions simultaneously.

In the first place, we must move from theology toward ministry. How we understand and imagine God is critically important for how we envision ministry and go about its practice. If, for example, we imagine God as a unilateral and uninfluenced lawgiver or judge who proclaims an arbitrary set of moral rules, keeps record of offenses, and punishes offenders, we should not be surprised if ministry becomes rather legalistic and oppressive. Ministry, in this view, will most likely be both imagined and practiced as a form of obeying rules and keeping commandments. Ministry will bring liberation all right, but it will be primarily a liberation from God—specifically, from God's wrath.

Or perhaps we imagine God as the supreme controlling power who determines every detail of the world and already knows the outcome of any and every act of freedom. (Is there really such a thing as freedom then?) If this is the theology out of which we operate, we should not be astonished if ministry becomes slavish, uncreative, and protective of the status quo. Life, in this view, is the simple unfolding of a predetermined plan. Human freedom and creative participation in that plan are minimal, if not absent altogether.

It is also possible to conceive of God as a divine goodie-giver who rewards the obedient with prosperity, success, power, and health. If this is our starting point, we should not be amazed if ministry as compassionate suffering-with-victims is replaced by a pseudo-ministry that is turned in on itself, insulated and isolated from suffering to the greatest extent possible.

Or if God is envisioned as sentimental love—a softy who makes no demands and bends to every pressure—we should not be shocked if ministry tends to disregard issues of justice, obedience, and discipleship, being reduced instead to encounter groups, ski trips, and Christian family nights at Disneyland.

Our theology definitely informs and shapes our practice. We will explore that side of the circle in more depth at the end of this chapter. But if the interdependence between how we understand God and how we go about envisioning and practicing ministry implies a path from theology toward ministry, so also that interdependence implies a path moving in the opposite direction from practice toward theory, from ministry toward theology. Traveling in this direction is not familiar territory for most of us and requires careful examination.

To Know God Is to Do Justice

Arriving at an adequate understanding of the human predicament is something far different from arriving at an adequate understanding of who God is. In the previous chapter, we attempted to grasp what it means to be human at the intersection of theological insight, practical experience, and social-scientific investigation. We could rely not only on the Genesis creation accounts but also on our common human experience and, especially, the experience of the poor and the marginalized. But whereas human existence has an empirical dimension, accessible to us through practical and public exploration, how do we even begin to encounter or come to know an invisible God?

Throughout history a variety of answers have suggested themselves to this question. Some of the more usual claims are, for example, that we come to know who God is by reading scripture, by praying, by meditating, or by going to church. Others feel quite confident that God can be known just as adequately, and perhaps even more intimately, in the primal experience of nature —in the encounter of the majesty of the mountains, in a spectacular sunset, or maybe by sitting next to a quiet stream. A strong case can also be made for the ability of human reason to take what we experience at any and every level and move toward an understanding of who God is. God is, after all, present and active in all experience. Certainly, the whole tradition of philosophical, or natural, theology has historically relied on precisely this confidence in human reason and experience.

Without denying the appropriate role of any and all of the above in our knowledge of God, we must not overlook a distinct and persistent notion in scripture as to what it means to know God. This recurring trend is by no means exhaustive of the variety of talk about God that we find in the Bible, but it does constitute a powerful and consistent pattern that can serve as something of a key for us in understanding who God is. One of the most uniform impressions we receive from reading the Bible is that there is a critical distinction to be made between knowing God and knowing about God. This distinction is not airtight, and it does not always operate in the same way, but it is thoroughly characteristic of the biblical witness. Usually the distinction is made in the form of a warning that those who know about God are not always those who genuinely know God and vice-versa.

On the one hand, there are those human beings who claim to know God. They can cite scripture to satisfy any occasion, pray spontaneously if the situation requires, and are unparalleled when it comes to making a joyful noise to the Lord. On the other hand, there are others who make no such claim and who perhaps consider themselves marginalized from the religious mainstream. They may even view the trappings of religion as obsolete, if not downright repulsive. In general, however, the witness of scripture consistently refuses to equate knowing God with the first group and often treats the second group as if they can see their way to God more clearly than the others (see Matthew 21:31–32). As Robert McAfee Brown states,

This notion, so strange to us—that "knowing God" is a matter of deed rather than word, that one could affirm God without saying God's name or deny God while God's name was on one's lips—is not strange to the Bible. (1984: 69)

Jesus puts the matter this way: "Not everyone who says to Me, 'Lord, Lord,' will enter the kingdom of heaven; but the one who does the will of My Father who is in heaven" (Matthew 7:21). According to Jesus, it is by "fruits" that we distinguish the company of those who know God, and judgment of others on any other basis is hypocritical and misleading. Indeed, whenever Jesus is either asked point blank about what it takes to be saved, or whenever he specifically considers the question of what it is that distinguishes the saved from the unsaved, strong parallels to this distinction between knowing God and knowing about God begin to surface.

In one situation, for example, Jesus is asked by a lawyer what it would take to inherit eternal life. By way of response, Jesus clarifies what the law means by saying that we should not only love God with all our heart, soul, mind, and strength, but also our neighbor as ourselves. This he does by telling the parable of the good Samaritan. The obvious twist that Jesus weaves into the parable is that there are those, such as the priest and the Levite, who know an impressive amount about who God is and who even devote their whole lives to the worship of God. They, however, passed by on the other side of the wounded man on the road. The Samaritan, on the other hand—despite his "bad theology"—felt compassion on the wounded man when he saw him. The Samaritan alone stopped and cared for the man, and so it was he rather than the God experts who proved to be the genuine neighbor to the wounded man. Jesus answers the question of eternal life with a case study on compassion.

In a second instance, Jesus finds himself asked bluntly by a rich young ruler, "What shall I do to inherit eternal life?" As in the previous situation, Jesus affirms the keeping of the law and the commandments. Jesus goes on, however, to spell out the implications of what this means, and we find that salvation becomes a matter of selling possessions and distributing them to the poor. Jesus goes on to invite the young man to follow him—a summons to take up Christ's own lifestyle of compassion and simplicity.

On yet another occasion, Jesus specifically addresses himself to the question of distinguishing between those who genuinely know God and those who do not by telling a judgment parable where God is seated on a throne while the nations of the world are gathered before him (Matthew 25:31–46). It is then and there, claims Jesus, that the criteria for distinguishing the sheep from the goats will be the following surprising ones:

> For I was hungry, and you gave Me something to eat; I was thirsty, and you gave Me drink; I was a stranger, and you invited Me in; naked and you clothed Me; I was sick, and you visited Me; I was in prison and you came to Me. (Matthew 25:35–36)

This is quite a startling set of criteria for those of us who have been taught to place priority on other gauges of measuring one's knowledge of and relationship with God! But in case we fail to gather the full revolutionary intent of the parable, Jesus makes clear that the truly shocking nature of the judgment scene is found not only in the criteria by which sheep-hood is determined, but also in the fact that both the sheep and the goats are surprised to discover their true identity. Neither the sheep nor the goats realized what their life activity had counted for or how it had either succeeded or failed in knowing God. For Jesus, it is the practical atheist, and not necessarily the theoretical atheist, who most certainly does not know God.

If, by way of example, we were to apply this insight to political contests, we might say that the candidate who claims to be Christian or "born again," or who even represents a so-called Christian majority is not necessarily the most genuinely Christian candidate. Rather, the candidate who, like the good Samaritan, exhibits concern for the wounded and practices compassion for the poor is the one whose activity is a genuine example, even if unconscious or implicit, of knowing God.

The question of what it means to know God is answered elsewhere in scripture in ways that either echo or anticipate what Jesus says. James, for example, mocks those who claim to have faith but who fail to care for the poor in distress: "You believe that God is one. You do well; the demons also believe, and shudder" (2:19). Here again, sheer knowledge about God can never suffice for a living faith that, as James affirms, gives our brothers and sisters clothing, daily food, and "what is necessary for their body." Even the demons have their theology straight, but a theology that doesn't make a difference in the lives of people who are hurting is worthless. John makes much the same point when he writes,

> Beloved, let us love one another; for love is from God, and everyone who loves is born of God and knows God. The one who does not love does not know God; for God is love. (1 John 4:7–8)

A claim could hardly be more straightforward—for John, it is impossible to know God apart from one's neighbor:

> Those who do not love their brothers or sisters who they can see, cannot love God who they have not seen. (1 John 4:20, *translation mine*)

Of all the biblical texts that impress upon us the intrinsic relationship between compassionate activity and knowing God, perhaps the most compelling is found in Jeremiah 22:13–16. In this passage we find Jeremiah, like any good prophet, hard at work reprimanding the king. This time it's because the king is building a new luxury palace complete with expensive paneling and painted with bright and gaudy colors. Beyond the sheer fact that the palace is excessive, it is also being built by unjust means. The king is refusing to pay his workers and is exploiting those at the bottom for his own personal gain:

> Woe to him who builds his house without righteousness
> And his upper rooms without justice,
> Who uses his neighbor's services without pay
> And does not give him his wages,
> Who says, "I will build myself a roomy house
> With spacious upper rooms,
> And cut out its windows,
> Paneling it with cedar and painting it bright red."

As if this attack weren't harsh enough, Jeremiah goes on to compare the king with his popular father, Josiah, now deceased, who had been a reformer and a passionate defender of the poor:

> Do you become a king because you are competing in cedar?
> Did not your father eat and drink,
> And do justice and righteousness?
> Then it was well with him.
> He pled the cause of the afflicted and needy;
> Then it was well.

Jeremiah now puts a decisive question to the king, referring to his father's practice of doing justice and righteousness for the poor and oppressed:

> "Is not that what it means to know Me?"
> Declares the Lord.

Though put in the form of a question, the answer is obviously "Yes." To know God is to practice justice and to take up the cause and defense of the poor and the marginalized. To know God is not the mere repetition of religious rituals, the keeping of rules, the practice of worship, or the assent to orthodox creeds or biblical propositions. To know God is to do justice.

Now the point of all of this is not that doing justice or showing compassion has some kind of magical power that results in new and otherwise unattainable information about God popping into our heads. The point is that knowing God is not primarily information about God at all, even though it does include a kind of understanding or confidence that can only be termed "faith." In today's world where information is power and where the predominant model of education is an infusion of data, the revolutionary truth of the scriptural witness is that knowing God is not, first and foremost, the accumulation of information, but rather an active commitment to a particular practice that centers on such elements as compassion, love, caring, and justice.

The implications of this notion of knowing God are significant for ministry. If I am in need and I go to a ministry site for assistance, it is not the pictures of Jesus in the hallway, or the cross on the steeple, or the Christian music playing over the receptionist's radio that makes that ministry, or the ministers who serve there, godly or even Christian. Quite simply, it is the effectiveness and faithfulness of that ministry in carrying out God's justice and compassion that allows me to qualify that ministry as a Christian ministry. In social-service circles, this insight is especially crucial. I find that Christian agencies and churches often try to distinguish the social services they render to needy people from those rendered by so-called secular institutions. Desperate to find or create some distinguishing marks and finding none, they may resort to religious trappings. Usually this means employing some variety of external paraphernalia to extend an image of Christianness to the public eye. What a shock it might be some day if we were to find out that the biblical insight contained in Matthew 25 is applicable not only to individuals but to institutions—that Christian organizations were so busy being Christian they failed to be just, compassionate, or human. And how equally shocked we might be to find out that in God's eyes many of those secular institutions that never garnered one conversion to Christ, placed one Bible in a sack of groceries, or required a single homeless person to listen to a sermon before providing food and lodging were nonetheless counted as God's friends. They may not have been explicit about God but they will have been human and therefore godly toward their neighbors. According to the biblical witness, it is this latter group who may be rightly said to know God!

Knowing God: The Conversion to Compassion

Now undoubtedly some will say that all of this sounds very close to works-righteousness. This, of course, is the great phobia of Protestants, and today it is not uncommon to find virtually any call to radical Christian practice labeled as an example of works-righteousness. The difficulty, however, is not that much of the biblical material sounds like an example of works-righteousness. The difficulty is that much of the biblical material is an example of works-righteousness, at least if we understand the word "works" correctly.

What the Bible offers us is something significantly more than a call to be more compassionate to the poor. Compassion is much more than something that most or even all Christians ought to get around to doing. Rather, the practice of compassion is somehow essential to knowing God, and not simply in some abstract, theoretical way, but in what can only be called a saving way. But, then, do scriptures such as Jesus' judgment parable in Matthew 25 or Jeremiah's claim that "to know God is to do justice" contradict the classical Protestant doctrine of "justification by faith and not by works"?

To begin with, we should acknowledge that the idea of "justification by faith and not by works" is far from unambiguous even in the biblical witness itself. On the one hand, Paul claims that human beings are "justified by faith apart from works of the Law" (Romans 3:28). James, on the other hand, states that human beings are "justified by works, and not by faith alone" (James 2:24). Could anything be more contradictory?

The confusion here has to do with how we understand the word "works." When Paul addresses himself to the subject of salvation, or justification, he typically opposes faith to the "works of the Law." These last three words, however, make all the difference in separating Paul's subject from James's subject. Paul's point is not that salvation comes from some absence of activity —some passive acceptance of God's gift of grace. As Paul says, in quoting the prophet Habakkuk, "the righteous [person] shall live by faith" (Romans 1:17, cf. Habakkuk 2:4). Faith is not the opposite of activity. It is, as Paul here affirms, a way of living and acting. Faith is not the opposite of works; it is a particular way of doing works. Law, however (or what Protestant reformer Martin Luther battled against as a system of merit), is an alternative mode of doing works. Really, the question never even boils down to whether salvation is by and through activity, life, or works. It always is. The crucial question is whether our activity, life, and works are by faith or for merit. Do we engage in compassionate ministry to earn salvation? Or do we engage ourselves, rather, as an act of faith, an act of response to grace that has been freely given by no merit of our own?

The answer, of course, is the latter and it is this common ground on which both Paul and James stand, even though their arguments move them in different directions. Paul is arguing against salvation by merit. James is arguing against any misunderstanding of Paul that would somehow separate faith from activity (and, specifically, compassionate activity directed toward the poor). As long as we view faith and works as competing against one another or as two opposite and contradictory paths to salvation, we will fail to see the truth of their mutuality and interdependence. We are not justified by faith alone without works, and we are not justified by works alone without faith. It would even be wrong to say that we are justified by a faith which subsequently expresses itself in works. Faith is the attitude that we bring to our activity, that transforms it and makes it human, thereby also making it image of God activity and, in God's eyes, justified or righteous activity. If we take into account the biblical witness as a whole, we must finally say that our lives, actions, commitments, and works finally justify or condemn us, precisely insofar as they are carried out in faith or unfaith, with compassion or with hostility, in solidarity with victims or insulated and isolated from human need.

The upshot of the foregoing is that the decision with which each of us is confronted by the God of Jesus is a faith decision—or, better, a decision to live by faith. But this decision is not some abstract acceptance or rejection of salvation understood as a private and interior experience or a guarantee of heaven. This decision, because it is a decision to live, has content and meaning now, in history. It is a decision about a way. It is a decision about a faith that is constituted by activity and commitment. The critical decision to which we are called by God in Jesus is fundamentally a decision to convert to compassion. We are called to a leap of faith that is a conversion from inauthenticity to authenticity, and it is a transformation of lifestyle, allegiances, and commitments, or it is nothing at all. It is a conversion to compassion as a way of life— a fundamental commitment to taking sides, being a neighbor, feeding the hungry, giving drink to the thirsty, inviting in the stranger, clothing the naked, visiting the sick and the imprisoned, setting the captive free, liberating the oppressed, and doing justice.

Does this mean, then, that practice takes the place of theory, or that what we do is more important than what we think about God? In one sense, yes. But in another sense, it is impossible to deny that people of God have always based their understanding of the kind of commitment and action to which God has called us on a clear vision of who God is. On the one hand, what we do shapes and determines what we think. On the other hand, what we think and believe shapes and determines what we do. So, for example, the people of Israel consistently understood themselves to be called forward by the God who had led them up out of Egypt, having liberated them from the oppression of the Pharaoh. In fact, the basis for the fundamental laws of their life and practice— the Ten Commandments—is to be found in their common memory of who God is:

> Then God spoke all these words, saying,
> I am the Lord your God, who brought you out of the land of Egypt, out of the house of slavery.
> You shall have no other gods before me.
> You shall not make for yourself an idol, . . . (Exodus 20: 1–4)

Here we see theory guiding action: "Remember who God is and what God has done; then, live like this: . . ."

So too, the demand of the Hebrew prophets for righteousness and justice is premised on who they understood God to be—a God who cannot tolerate inequality, violence, corruption, and dishonesty. It is knowledge of God's character—knowledge about God—that drives the prophets to demand a change in personal habits and social structures. Nowhere is this more true than in the case of a particular prophet named Jesus, whose entire life, teaching, and ministry was premised on his understanding of who God is.

The point, then, of emphasizing the priority of knowing God over knowing about God is not to rule out the latter in favor of the former, as if they were opposed to each other, but to affirm that knowing God through the activity of compassion and justice is the key, the starting point, and the context from within which any genuine knowledge about God can take place. In effect, what we have here, once again, is a circle. At times, the Bible affirms that to be compassionate and to do justice is to know God. In other instances, the Biblical witnesses clearly rely on what they know about God's character and purpose as the most fundamental motivation to their becoming engaged in compassionate activity in the very first place. On the one hand, we cannot merely start off with a database about who God is and then simply apply that knowledge to our own setting in various forms of ministry. It is only by placing ourselves squarely within a ministry of compassion, justice, and caring that we know God in the first place and can then go on to know more about God. On the other hand, however, once we have come to know about the God who does not ride fences, but who takes sides, the God who is the defender of the poor and the oppressed, we are challenged to live and move in response to that knowledge and to express what we know concretely in terms of ever-new and liberating forms of ministry.

In the end, there is no avoiding the circle. The practice of compassion leads to knowledge of God. Knowledge of the compassionate God of the Bible compels us to be engaged in the practice of compassionate ministry. But this compassionate circle is no contradiction disguised as a paradox. Nor is it a theoretical riddle that paralyzes and numbs. It is a circle that emancipates our minds and our actions and makes ministry effective and dynamic. To convert to compassion is to leap into this very circle—a leap that makes possible a liberating interdependence between thought and life, theory and practice, theology and ministry.

The God of Jesus: The God of Compassion

I have not tried to undercut the theoretical importance but only to underscore the practical urgency of answering the question of who God is. And for the Christian, the decisive answer to that question is to be found in the histor-

ical encounter with Jesus of Nazareth. It is here that we find the understanding
of God that is normative for guiding our practice of ministry. According to the
apostolic witnesses, it is the life and ministry of Jesus that finally give concrete
and definitive meaning not only to who God is, but also to what God desires.
Brazilian theologian Rubem Alves beautifully captures this truth in his book, *I
Believe in the Resurrection of the Body*:

> Sometimes we would like to know what God is made of. To know his
> sacred substance. And many pages of theological books and catechisms
> have been written to describe the marvelous properties of God's flesh:
> spirit, invisible, omnipotent, omniscient, omnipresent. And with words
> like these we write essays on sacred anatomy and physiology.
>
> Waste of time. The Christians discovered that this man, Jesus of
> Nazareth, is God's answer to the question "Who are you?" And he answers
> us, not with a treatise on anatomy/physiology, but by telling us about his
> desires. God is love. And he tells us about his dream of love. He places it
> alive, among us. Jesus of Nazareth is God's desire. He is his choice. A love-
> lier, more beautiful, more delightful thing there can not be. (33)

Affirming that Jesus is God's answer to the question "Who are you?" does
not mean, of course, that God has never been present at any other time or
place than in the person of Jesus of Nazareth. On the contrary, God is present
in all of creation and throughout human history. The life and experience of the
people of Israel bear impressive witness to that fact. And Paul, in his speech to
the Athenians on Mars Hill, insists that God is alive and at work even outside
the Jewish and Christian faiths, albeit anonymously. The Christian, however,
claims that God is present in Jesus in a unique and decisive way, that Jesus
sums up and makes explicit what is always and everywhere implicit: namely,
who God is and what we are therefore called to be and to do. Thus, if we wish
to discover the truth of who God is and what God desires (both of which are
absolutely foundational for a theology of compassionate ministry), we must
pay close attention to the historical encounter of the apostles with Jesus of
Nazareth. And when we do just that, we discover a God of compassion who is
(1) a God of solidarity, (2) a God who graciously takes sides, and (3) a God of
surprise and novelty. We should not be surprised that each of these qualities
points to the three dimensions of the image of God in which we are created—
community, freedom, and creativity.

Solidarity: The God of Community

If Jesus is God's answer to the question "Who are you?" then what we first
discover when we look to Jesus is that God is a God who is *Immanuel*, "God-

with-us" (Matt. 1:22–23). This is the good news of the Christian story: God fully tastes of our most intimate sorrows and our most outrageous joys. Solidarity with the human predicament, then, is one of the most fundamental, defining characteristics of the compassionate God of Jesus.

So far as ministry goes, we often forget the elementary but indispensable path of simple presence. In Jesus of Nazareth, however, God is present. In the book, *Compassion*, authors Donald McNeill, Douglas Morrison, and Henri Nouwen remind us,

> In a time so filled with methods and techniques designed to change people, to influence their behavior, and to make them do new things and think new thoughts, we have lost the simple but difficult gift of being present to each other. . . . Simply being with someone is difficult because it asks of us that we share in the other's vulnerability, enter with him or her into the experience of weakness and powerlessness, become part of uncertainty, and give up control and self-determination. And still, whenever this happens, new strength and new hope is being born. (14)

The God of Jesus especially identifies with the struggles and concerns of the outsider, the nonperson, and those whom the world considers insignificant. This God suffers with the hurting and, for that very reason, is to be discovered precisely among them. But God's identification with hurting people, it must be emphasized, is more than merely being nice or softhearted. It is a passionate and powerful movement of emotion and feeling from deep within. Interestingly, the very word for compassion used over and over in the New Testament means literally "to have one's guts wrenched." If the life and ministry of Jesus is any clue to the character of God, then God's compassion is hardly superficial or passing. It is a gut-wrenching and deep-seated combination of tenderness and intensity.

Despite all this, God's nature as social and related has, throughout history, consistently been ignored or rejected in favor of a picture of God as essentially aloof, unrelated, and absolute. The damage this one-sided portrait of God has inflicted on our understanding of compassion is inestimable. Compassion has been reduced to an alien charity dropped into situations of suffering from outside and from above rather than a sympathizing and suffering presence with those who agonize and a solidarity that heals from below. It's puzzling to know why Christians, of all people, would cling to such a distorted picture of God. The Genesis creation account ought to be enough to convince us that God is a social God—that God loves and desires relationship. If that's not enough, the history of God's covenant relationships throughout human history reinforces that conviction. Indeed, in God's covenant activity, mere relationship is converted into genuine partnership. But if that's still not enough to convince us, the life and ministry of Jesus leave absolutely no room for doubt on the matter. God's way of being related and social is so intensified in the Christ-event that one must finally move beyond words like relationship and partnership in order to recognize it as solidarity. Why then, do we continue to imagine God as unrelated, unchanging, and absolutely transcendent?

On the face of things, I suppose, it sounds like a compliment to God: to be perfect is to need nothing, to be self-sufficient, unchanging, immovable. But these attributes are one-sided, and our usage of them (to the exclusion of other more relational attributes) only reveals how steeped we are in the legacy of Greek philosophy (Plato and Aristotle) rather than the biblical witness to God which culminates in the life and ministry of Jesus of Nazareth. For example, while there is a sense in which it is true to say that God lacks for nothing and therefore needs nothing, there is another sense in which it is just as true to say that God is enriched by the world and depends upon it for the character of divine activity in the world.

The classical Greek assertion of God's essential independence from all creation is an enormous distortion of God's character as discovered in Christ. For example, since when, even on our own imperfect scale of valuing, do the qualities of self-sufficiency or independence, taken by themselves alone, define the highest degree of perfection in an individual's character? Is not the ability to receive from others and the ability to relate adequately to others an important constituent in one's overall character? Perfection includes not only independence, but dependence; God is not only the perfect giver, but the perfect receiver—always present and sympathizing.[1] God is perfectly related to all that is, and is thus perfectly and essentially social. It is this twin ability, both to receive and to give, both to suffer with and to heal, both to hear the cry of the oppressed and to offer liberation, that characterizes the God of compassion and defines the compassion of God. If compassion has failed to play a central role in our understanding of God as well as of Christian ministry, perhaps that is precisely because of our failure to affirm this fundamentally social nature of God.

The compassionate nature of God as communal is, of course, amply witnessed to in scripture. Indeed, one of the most basic definitions of God is simply that "God is love" (1 John 4:8). There can hardly be a more relational and social term than "love." To use it either of God or ourselves is to claim that we are beings related to other beings in more than an external or superficial way. To say that God does not, however, need to be love or that God could be

---

1. Perhaps no one has influenced contemporary thought with this simple insight in as compelling a way as the philosopher Charles Hartshorne. See *The Divine Relativity: A Social Conception of God*, New Haven: Yale University Press (1948); *A Natural Theology for Our Time*, LaSalle: Open Court Press (1967); and *Creative Synthesis and Philosophic Method*, Lanham: University Press (1970).

otherwise is to challenge the heart of the Christian gospel—namely, that in Jesus Christ we discover who God really is. Period.

Love, however, is not some abstract or mushy quality. It is a way of being related to and conditioned by others. Scripture affirms not only that God is social and conditioned by others (contrary to the classical theological tradition), but supremely so. So then, when we think of God's holiness, for example, we ought not to have in mind either a geographical distance or a transcendence of relationship. Rather, God is "super-relative," as Charles Hartshorne says. God is the one individual who not only makes a difference to all things, but to whom all things make a difference.

We should, of course, make it clear that the notion of being social, or communal, while literally applicable to both God and human beings, is radically different for God than for us. The same would be true were we to compare God's capacity for compassion with our capacity for compassion. God's relatedness—and, so, compassion—is boundless and unlimited, while ours is fragmentary and limited. God's solidarity with others is completely responsive and healing, while ours is never completely empathetic and tends to be mixed with self-interest. But the difference between God and humans, when stated in this way, only serves to intensify the fact that we are, indeed, created in God's image, however finite is our own capacity for relationship. The difference between God and humans, when stated in this way, also serves to underscore our dependence on God for whatever measure of authentic compassion can characterize our lives—compassion that knows no bounds, is supremely empathetic, and is perfectly responsive to need.

In Jesus, then, we discover who God is and, at the same time, what compassion is. And the God of compassion we discover is (1) supremely sympathetic and (2) supremely inclusive. The first has to do with the quality of God's compassionate solidarity—complete understanding of human need and suffering precisely as God's own. The second has to do with the extension of God's compassionate solidarity—for all, even the enemy, and especially the outcast.

Taking Sides: The God of Freedom

If Jesus is God's answer to the question "Who are you?" then what we secondly discover when we look to Jesus is that God is a God who takes sides, who works for human liberation and community and against oppression and slavery. For most of us, our earliest experiences in life are our most formative ones, especially our initial experiences of our parents. How my mother or father related to me, what they expected of me, and what they themselves thought of life all shaped and formed me in countless ways that I can never escape or deny. So also, for the people of Israel, their earliest experiences of God molded their theology, worship, customs, and culture in a number of ways to which they constantly looked back for strength, comfort, and challenge. The most important of those experiences was, beyond the shadow of a doubt, the exodus—the historical event of liberation from the powers of oppression in Egypt.

So significant was this event in the life of the Israelites that it became indelibly impressed upon their corporate self-understanding; it became a kind of mental screen through which they remembered their past, interpreted their present, and projected their future. It is the event of exodus that, in an initial and inescapable way, defines who God is for the people of Israel. It is the event of exodus that is the indispensable watershed event of history from which the very identity of a whole nation of people emerges and to which that same nation of people looks back when pondering the meaning of their existence.

In the exodus story, another dimension of God's compassion comes to the surface: listening. The Israelites found themselves in Egypt under the oppressive domination of the Pharaohs. And while, month after month, hardship, affliction, and injustice were heaped upon the Israelites by the Egyptians, the misery of the Israelites did not go unnoticed:

> And the sons of Israel sighed because of the bondage, and they cried out; and their cry for help because of their bondage rose up to God. So God heard their groaning; and God remembered his covenant with Abraham, Isaac, and Jacob. And God saw the sons of Israel, and God took notice of them. (Exodus 2:23–25)

Listening, however, is transformed into action for the compassionate God of Israel. Rather than sit idly by while the oppressors continued their injustice and persecution, God took sides in order to deliver the Israelites from their bondage. Moses was sent as the instrument of liberation, and after a great ordeal the long-sought liberation was achieved.

These are the bare facts of the story. When it came to interpreting the exodus event, however, and allowing it to give meaning to the existence of the people of Israel, this event of liberation from oppression became the lens through which an entire people viewed themselves, their mission, their worship, their ethics, and even the actions of other nations. Indeed, what is perhaps most interesting about the influence of the exodus event on the people of Israel is the way it colors and influences even their understanding of creation itself.

For many Christians today, however, our context distorts the message of the exodus story. Christians who live in relative comfort and affluence are familiar with the story and tend to read it with a view to its portrait of a God who is a supernatural and powerful sovereign, a God who will not let the forces of evil keep his chosen ones in bondage. That is why the magical plagues and the parting of the Red Sea become the favorite portions of the story. They prove that God is Lord even over nature.

The view from below, on the contrary, cannot seem to separate God's spectacular power from the very earthly, political, and economic realities that permeate the entire exodus story. God's miraculous power over nature is not what is of primary importance. What is most significant is the fact that God is a God who takes sides in situations of economic oppression. God is not just a supernatural being with an extraordinary bag of magic tricks. God is a God who is not aloof, but intimately concerned with the very earthly and natural predicaments that people in bondage face every day. And perhaps most importantly, if God is for the children of Israel, God is against the Pharaoh. God is a God who takes sides. This is the message that the poor and marginalized around the world hear in the story of exodus today. It is a message of hope and of liberation. The message of exodus is not just one more extraordinary Bible story; it points to the fact that God is not neutral where suffering takes place; that God enters into the suffering of the exploited and forgotten; that God stands against those who serve in Pharaoh's court. So here we discover another dimension to compassion—not only to recognize suffering and to suffer with the sufferer, but also to work for liberation from that suffering.

We find this same exodus theology reflected in other Hebrew writings, especially the Psalms, the worship book of God's exodus people. God is a God who is tuned in to the struggle and takes sides in that struggle:

"Because of the devastation of the afflicted, because of the groaning of the needy, Now I will arise," says the Lord; "I will set [them] in the safety for which [they long]." (Psalm 12:5)

God's compassion is the confidence in which those who are systematically forgotten and trampled on can feel secure:

O Lord, Thou hast heard the desire of the humble; Thou wilt strengthen their heart, Thou wilt incline Thine ear to vindicate the orphan and the oppressed. (Psalm 10:17–18)

This strident message—that God's compassion is not passive or sentimental, but a compassion that takes sides—somehow gets lost in the translation of the biblical message heralded by Christians today, whether from the pulpit, in hymns and books, or even in our own political arrangements. One gets the impression that two different Bibles are being read—a Bible for the materially comfortable and a Bible for the materially poor. The "Magnificat" of Mary in Luke 1:46–55 is a prime example of how the God who takes sides has unconsciously been shuffled to the margins of our Bibles. Every year, in thousands of churches throughout the First World, the story of Mary, the mother of Jesus, is tenderly woven into Christmas pageants and Christmas sermons everywhere. We know Mary as the meek and mild mother of our savior who responds to the angel messenger with the words:

> My soul exalts the Lord,
> And my spirit has rejoiced in God my savior.
> For he has had regard for the humble state of his bondslave.

But for impoverished peasants in Latin America, undocumented immigrants working quietly for slave wages in the United States, or homeless persons who daily roam the streets of our inner cities, the song of Mary is something much more. Through the eyes of the poor, Mary's proclamation does not stop with these first few lines and is far from harmless and tender. It is, perhaps, even revolutionary:

> God has done mighty deeds with his arms; God has scattered those who were proud in the thoughts of their heart. God has brought down rulers from their thrones, and has exalted those who were humble. God has filled the hungry with good things; and sent away the rich empty-handed.

Somehow Mary's song, when heard from the perspective of a jobless single mother who, along with her three little girls, has just been evicted from her house, points to a God whose most essential quality is not the supernatural ability to part the sea or make a virgin pregnant, but rather a suffering love that is not above and beyond the fray and that genuinely takes sides.

We may say, then, that the God of the Bible is a compassionate God—a God who enters into solidarity with those who suffer and who works to accomplish their healing and liberation. Compassion is not a neutral charity, inattentive to the social arrangements between the givers of the charity and the receivers of the charity. The biblical notion of compassion includes and is inseparable from the struggle for justice. If it is really true that God loves everyone, then God demonstrates that love by taking sides for the exploited, rather than remaining impartial. Desmond Tutu, Anglican bishop of South Africa, puts the matter this way:

> If you are neutral in a situation of injustice, you have chosen the side of the oppressor. If an elephant has his foot on the tail of the mouse, and you say you are neutral, the mouse will not appreciate your neutrality. (Brown, 1984: 19)

If God was discovered by the people of Israel to be a God who takes sides in situations of oppression, it should not be surprising that the original witnesses to Jesus of Nazareth understood that here again God was taking sides, even at the cost of Jesus' reputation and, finally, life. The Gospel of Luke, for example, records that Jesus gave his first sermon in his home town of Nazareth. It was here that Jesus set forth his evangelistic mission that had so recently been illuminated by his experiences of baptism and temptation. Jesus, in this sermon, clarifies his allegiances and pinpoints those who are to be the special focus of his ministry. When getting up to speak, Jesus reaches for the scroll of Isaiah and reads the following words as a kind of "inaugural address":

> The Spirit of the Lord is upon me,
> Because he anointed me to preach the gospel to the poor.
> He has sent me to proclaim release to the captives,
> And recovery of sight to the blind,
> To bring liberation to those who are oppressed,
> To proclaim the favorable year of the Lord.
> (Luke 4:18–19, *translation mine*)

Luke records that Jesus' home-town crowd was impressed with him and that they began to remind themselves that he was Joseph's son—one of their own! But to be sure that his hearers understood what he was trying to communicate, Jesus goes on to provide commentary on the text by mentioning two incidents that turned out to be quite disturbing.

Jesus first recalls that during a famine in Israel, the prophet Elijah was sent with help, not to the Israelites, God's chosen people, but to a widow from Sidon, a far northern country. Then there was also the time, so Jesus mentions, that during a plague the prophet Elisha was sent with healing—again, not to the Israelites, but to Naaman, a Syrian. The very idea that God would identify himself with worthless foreigners rather than the chosen ones was too much for the crowd to handle. Luke reports that the synagogue where Jesus was preaching swelled with outrage and that Jesus was escorted by a frenzied mob to a nearby cliff where he narrowly escaped with his life. The crowd found it unthinkable that God would grant favor to nonbelievers while leaving out those who had been entrusted with his message, ministry, and mission. It was more than they could bear to contemplate.

What we find here again is that the God whom Jesus so decisively discloses is a God who takes sides with the oppressed and who also, as Jonah discovered, defies being easily identified with the comfortable, the religious, or the majority. We should ask ourselves if Jesus' words, cited in Luke, are as abrasive and upsetting to us today as they were in his own context. If they are not, perhaps we have read the Bible through eyes that filter out the harsh and even irritating message of Jesus, neutralizing it so that it doesn't call us to change our allegiances or to rethink our own mission and purpose in life. Or perhaps, if they are not, it is because we, the readers, are very different from the people in Jesus' home-town synagogue. Maybe we are so committed to the poor, the captive, the blind, and the oppressed that for us to hear that Jesus identified his mission with their cause generates no real irritation in us. Possible? Perhaps. Probable? Not really.

God is a God who takes sides. This means not only that God desires freedom, but that God is free. In other words, the origin of God's freeing activity is God's own freedom. It is important for a theology of compassionate ministry to affirm God's own character as free, especially in light of our previous assertion of God's character as social. In our world, freedom and sociality, autonomy and responsibility, liberation and community, are often pitted against one another as if they were mutually exclusive. Economic debates between capitalism and socialism have especially fueled the fire at this point. Capitalists are accused, not unfairly, of exalting unrestricted freedom while disregarding social concern and community responsibility. Socialists are accused, not unfairly, of pressing for the common good and for social welfare at the expense of individual conscience and creativity.

This tension between freedom and community has the potential for wreaking havoc on our understanding of who God is and, by extension, our understanding of compassion. Our tendency is to emphasize either freedom or community in such a way as to eliminate the other or else simply to assert the two in a contradictory way, disguising the contradiction by calling it a paradox. But freedom and community need not be opposed to one another, whether in our understanding of God, ourselves, or ministry. What we discover throughout the biblical witness, but focally in Jesus, is the truth that, while God enters into community and solidarity with those who suffer, experiencing with complete intensity of feeling their pain and grief, God's freedom to act on behalf of sufferers is never ruled out or overwhelmed. In other words, God's sociality does not undermine God's freedom. God's compassion, while reliable, is completely gracious: it is a gift. Thus, to borrow Jesus' parable, while the loving father is in no way insulated from the prodigal son's predicament, the father is neither paralyzed nor totally determined by the prodigal's course of action. The father still has room to act freely, creatively, and redemptively. Freedom, as defined by God's presence and activity in Jesus of Nazareth, is fundamentally a graciousness toward creation rather than an independence from creation.

Furthermore, just as we influence God without robbing God of freedom in response to us, so also God influences us while not frustrating our own freedom. God, of course, influences everyone and everything, while our influences are much more radically limited in scope and intensity. Our influence upon God is real, though slight, while God's influence on us is great, though it does not override our freedom. God's providence must ultimately be understood in this way, I believe: not as a coercive power that dictates the course of events, but as God's own persuasive influence in every event.

This complementary relationship between freedom and sociality, between liberation and community, is an absolute necessity for the practice of compassionate ministry. Authentic compassion begins with solidarity. It enters into the suffering of another with genuine empathy, vulnerability, and concern. But the compassionate minister is not overcome by this suffering nor wholly determined by it. She remains free and brings something to the experience of suffering that is not derived from the experience itself. She brings a vision and a hope. She sees the possibility of liberation and community. She sees the space for creativity and novelty. And, thus, while fully participating in the pain of the other, she brings faith and healing, emancipation and promise. Compassion is simply not compassion without this dimension of freedom. That is why compassion must never be understood either as a command to be obeyed or as a mere tool to accomplish other allegedly more important activities like church growth or evangelism. Compassion, as Jon Sobrino recognizes, is

> a specific form of love: a love manifest in a praxis that arises from unjust suffering inflicted on the other so as to eradicate it, and seeks no other reason for doing so beyond the fact that the suffering does indeed exist. Nothing else exists prior to compassion in order to motivate it, and nothing exists beyond compassion so as to reject it or relativize it. (90)

Compassionate ministry, then, is suffering with others (a ministry of community), but it is also and always a response to that suffering (a ministry of liberation). An adequate compassionate ministry can never allow one side of this equation to elbow out the other. Neither can an adequate compassionate ministry simply slap ministries of community and ministries of liberation side by side with no connection or bond. On the one hand, liberation is never Christian liberation if it does not imply solidarity with victims. On the other hand, community with fellow-sufferers is never Christian community if it does not imply a holy dissatisfaction with and intense commitment to transform situations of despair, hopelessness, and indignity.

In Jesus, then, we discover who God is and, at the same time, what compassion is. And the God of compassion we discover is (1) supremely liberating and (2) supremely gracious. The first has to do with the aim of God's compassionate taking of sides—the restoration of human dignity, alleviation of human suffering, and emancipation from every form of oppression. The second has to do with the origin of God's compassionate taking of sides—the uncoerced freedom for the world that persuades rather than conquers, that empowers rather than overpowers.

Surprise and Novelty: God as Creative

If Jesus is God's answer to the question "Who are you?" then what we thirdly discover when we look to Jesus is that God is a God who is always up to something new and whose expressions of compassion catch us by surprise in ever-fresh and creative ways. In the recent novel, *Jurassic Park*, mathematician Ian Malcolm constantly tries to call attention to the unpredictability of the universe, especially large, complex systems in nature. Malcolm—as a scientist and mathematician—is confident, of course, that human beings can predict with a high degree of certainty the regular movements of objects according to linear equations. So for example, we can fire a rocket toward the moon, and it will actually reach its destination as predicted. Malcolm, however, is a student of chaos theory, which draws attention to the irregularity and unpredictability of complex systems such as weather (or dinosaur theme parks!) that operate with nonlinear dynamics. Here the slightest differences in initial conditions of two otherwise similar weather systems, for example, have repercussions that create two entirely different results. Malcolm says, "The shorthand is the 'butterfly effect.' A butterfly flaps its wings in Peking, and weather in New York is different" (Crichton: 74).

Despite the hyperbole of the butterfly illustration, the real findings of nonfictional chaos theory do draw attention to the impact of subtle actions and conditions on other actions and conditions. Our world is incredibly complex and interrelated. For those of us who throw into the equation a belief in genuine human freedom (i.e., that we human beings are not merely conditioned by outside forces and conditions, but always retain a measure of creativity in our responses to those forces and conditions), the scientist or mathematician who describes reality in purely empirical or physical terms hasn't even begun to scratch the surface with regard to the high degree of unpredictability or chaos in our world. The butterfly flaps its wings by pure instinct, but human creativity and freedom throw an even greater monkey wrench into the machinery of both natural and social processes. One can never predict when we will flap our wings, so to speak. To complicate matters even more, there are those of us who want to throw into the equation the creative freedom of a God who interacts not simply with some beings, but with every being. Now you have a complexity and unpredictability that boggles the mind.

In fact, chaos is a rather poor name for the fact that all creation retains some measure of creativity, freedom, and unpredictability, despite the recurring patterns and rhythms that lull us into thinking just the opposite. Whether on a sheerly physical level or on an intellectual, moral, social, or spiritual level, it is fascinating how novelty and creativity always have a way of asserting and reasserting themselves, notwithstanding the regularity and redundancy at every level of life. Thus, for example, on the level of physical science, even though energy operates according to the law of entropy, whereby it is constantly being degraded and diffused into increasingly less usable forms, there are nonetheless those appearances of new concentrations of energy that defy entropic dynamics. Or again, on the level of morality, politics, and social organization, there is obviously a universal trend toward taking the easy road—the path of least resistance and the path of what is most simple and immediate. Nevertheless, one must always account for history's recurring moral, political, and social giants, whether in the form of a Mahatma Gandhi, a Martin Luther King, Jr., a Mother Teresa, or lesser-known giants who unpredictably violate all that we have been taught about human behavior as being simply conditioned or even determined by our circumstances, culture, and upbringing. Or, finally, on the level of human intellectual history, though the propensity is always toward reductionism, oversimplification, and overgeneralization, how do we account for those flashes of insight and bursts of genius that soar above our landscape in persons such as Plato, Pasteur, or Einstein?

All of these examples point to the reality of creativity and novelty at every level of existence. And while this is especially true of human beings who, as we have already seen, are creative (and destructive) in virtually every dimension of life—work, sexuality, art, play—it is first and foremost true of God in an even more radical and limitless way. But then this is just another way of saying that we are created in God's image. And just as it is true that God is creative, so it is true that we are also. Of course, even if we can affirm that both God and human beings create, there is still a radical asymmetry between the way God is creative of us and the way we are creative of God. God is creator throughout all time and is creative of literally everything whatsoever. In other words, God is an ingredient in the becoming of every entity and provides an element of novelty to all that is. Human beings, on the other hand, do create, but the scope of our contribution to others is severely restricted. Because of the obvious limitations on our own ability to impact and make a difference to others, we are creative of only some others. God, however, is creative of all others.

In Jesus of Nazareth, God has surprised us! In fact, even though we can believe with our minds that God is a compassionate God, actually to experience God's compassion blows us away. This was, for example, the case with Jonah. Jonah knew that God was a compassionate God, slow to anger and quick to forgive, but he was still surprised to actually witness God's creative, relenting,[2] and redeeming activity in history. As Jesus says in John's gospel, "The wind[3] blows where it wishes and you hear the sound of it, but do not know where it comes from and where it is going" (John 3:8). God is reliable, but reliably surprising, creative, and new. Furthermore, those who are born of this wind, or spirit, are characterized by just that kind of surprising creativity.

Over and over, in the life and ministry of Jesus, the compassion of God surprises us with something new. It violates our common sense and turns our standard ways of responding to one another upside down. We look for God in a mansion or a palace; we get a manger instead. We look for a ruler; we get a servant. We look for a hero; we get a convicted criminal. We look for power; we get a cross. God's mode of liberation, God's mode of community, is always amazing and often disturbing. So, again, if we recall the story of the prodigal son, the fact that the father welcomes his son home with such a great celebration, despite the son's offensive behavior, is surprising and unexpected. The older son, of course, wants justice, by which he means retribution. The father's compassion, however, transforms mere retribution into a creative justice that forgives even as it redeems.

It is important to understand, then, that solidarity and taking sides, community and liberation, are the central ingredients for understanding God's compassion as discovered in Jesus of Nazareth. However, without finally mentioning surprise and novelty as the mode of God's creative compassion, we lock God in a box and tragically undercut our own effectiveness and redemptiveness in a complex world. It is this notion of God's creativity, in fact, that helps us conceive of God in a way that moves beyond patriarchy, with God understood solely in male terms like "king" or "father." God's way of creating is ongoing and sustaining, not merely a once-and-for-all decree by an independent, aloof sovereign. God creates through tender, all-embracing, and motherly love as well.

Wherever God shows up on the scene, suffering with victims, taking sides, and bringing healing and restoration, God's compassionate activity and presence is never an alien, preplanned, or fixed principle for any and every circumstance. It is a creative response to the situation at hand. That is why law never quite captures the heart of God's compassion. That is why, as the Apostle Paul affirms, "letter kills and the spirit gives life." Even and especially the Bible, if taken woodenly and literally, kills. Jesus expresses precisely the creativity of divine compassion when he challenges the nominal religiosity of the Pharisees

---

2. God changes God's mind!

3. A play on the Greek word *pneuma* which, like the Hebrew word *ruach*, can mean "spirit," "breath," or "wind."

in words that today would have the religious Right labeling him a humanist: "The sabbath was made for humans, not humans for the sabbath" (Mark 2:27). If there is any shred of truth to the butterfly effect, especially when that truth is deepened to include human and especially divine creativity and freedom, then any ministry which fails to respond to the rich complexities of every moment—no matter how grand or expensive that ministry may appear to outsiders—will become little more than a Jurassic Park, doomed to failure, operating with strictly linear equations, and ultimately self-destructive.

Finally, we must recognize that there is always a double movement in the creative dimension of God's compassion. On the one hand, God's compassion is iconoclastic: always defying the accepted way of doing things and always resisting institutions and structures that would ritualize compassion or wrap it up in neat once-and-for-all packages. On the other hand, however, God's compassion is ever-creative of new structures, new "wineskins," new ways of doing things, and ever-inventive of new forms for the expression of compassion. A dry, institutionalized compassion is as destructive as an abstract and formless compassion is useless. The ultimate example of this truth is, of course, Jesus of Nazareth—God's compassionate surprise package. God does not simply say, "I empathize with you." God experiences our experiences with us ... in the flesh.

In Jesus, then, we discover who God is and, at the same time, what compassion is. And the God of compassion we discover is (1) the God of criticism and protest and (2) the God of imagination and invention. The first has to do with the critical quality of God's compassionate creativity: discontent with the stale and the rigid, always surprising and novel, never precalculated or confined. The second has to do with the constructive quality of God's compassionate creativity: always transforming the old into the new, always responding to the world with unpredictable but effective grace.

4

Jesus

The Compassion of God

If God is a God of compassion, then according to Christians, Jesus is the compassion of God. As Jon Sobrino says,

> The primordial compassion of God becomes historical in the practice and message of Jesus. Jesus' "compassion for the crowds" was not a merely occasional attitude in his life but one that shaped his entire life and mission, shaped too his vision of God and the human person, and brought him to his final destiny. (89)

Jesus is our window to discovering the center of God's character and desires. Jesus is our window to discovering that God is a God who is with us, a God who takes sides, a God of new creation.

But perhaps the window metaphor is not entirely faithful to the witness of scripture, because Jesus is there presented not only as the one through whom we have discovered who God is but as the one through whom we have also discovered what we ought therefore to be and do as human beings. Perhaps the image of Jesus as a two-way mirror would be more appropriate. In other words, a more than an ordinary significance is claimed for Jesus of Nazareth because he unites the questions of who God is and who we are in a way that gives genuine meaning and purpose to the way we lead our lives. This chapter explores the question of how we might understand Jesus' significance as the link between who God is and who we are, especially with regard to the way we imagine and practice ministry.

Throughout the history of the church, the Christian struggle to understand the significance of Jesus has classically been reduced to a question of who Jesus is in himself, or in the abstract, and has revolved around two fundamental assertions about his person: (1) Jesus is fully God and (2) Jesus is fully human. In other words, christology has boiled down to a description of Christ's "innards"—an exercise in keeping divine nature and human nature compressed and held together in the one person of Jesus "without confusion or change, without division or separation."[1] The link between God and human existence, then, has typically been imagined in terms of a link between two natures inside the person of Jesus.

In attempting to keep these two natures together and balanced, the church has performed all types of mental gymnastics and sophisticated philosophical arguments, labeling as heresy any view of Jesus that overemphasized one of these assertions while playing down the other. On the one hand, Christians have affirmed that in Jesus of Nazareth we discover God acting decisively to redeem humanity. Thus, Jesus is fully God. On the other hand, Christians have affirmed that in Jesus we have discovered the true human being, the model and measure of authentic humanity. Thus, Jesus is fully human. While, in the church's long history, the last of these—the full humanity of Jesus—has typically been neglected and discounted in favor of a portrait of Jesus as superhuman or as a God dressed up in human disguise, Christian faith has generally been consistent in recognizing that central to its witness is the scandalous notion that perfect deity and perfect humanity are discovered in the one person, Jesus of Nazareth.

But we fail to comprehend just how scandalous Christian faith truly is as long as we consider the significance of Jesus only in the abstract as some kind of mixture of human and divine essences, natures, or substances (whatever those could possibly be). The first problem with such an approach is that it requires us to begin with a preconceived idea of what divine nature is (something all-powerful, all-knowing, beyond change, beyond suffering) and then try to squeeze that nature into Jesus. This usually never really works very well, though, and violates the central Christian claim that it is precisely in and through Jesus that we discover what God is like in the first place. At least part of the scandal of Christianity is that Jesus defies and challenges most of our assumptions about who God is. Specifically, Jesus on the cross is the epitome of everything that runs counter to our classical notions of deity. The apostle Paul certainly recognized this truth and claimed that the cross is the central scandal of Christianity. On the cross God is revealed as a God who suffers. On the cross, Paul says, we see God's weakness and foolishness (1 Cor. 1:18ff).

The second problem with the classical approach to Jesus is that the scandal of Christianity is typically presented as the interface of deity with a generic

---

1. As the Chalcedonian formula states it.

humanity. But the humanity of Jesus is not just any kind of humanity. It is suffering, impoverished, and victimized humanity. When considered from the perspective of those who suffer and are oppressed in our world, the scandal of Christianity is far more scandalous than classical theology has led us to believe. From below, the scandal of the incarnation is not simply that the "Word has become flesh," but that where we would expect the Word to become royal, powerful, and prestigious flesh, the Word has become poor, powerless, and suffering flesh. As McNeill, Morrison, and Nouwen put it,

> Not only did [Jesus] taste fully the dependent and fearful condition of being human, but he also experienced the most despicable, and horrifying form of death—death on a cross. Not only did he become human, but he also became human in the most dejected and rejected way. (26)

Let's face it. The humanity of Jesus bugs us. But what really bugs us is the poverty and suffering of Jesus. Jesus' poverty and suffering contradict our standard notions of divinity in a way that his being human never does. And so while we glibly affirm the divinity of Jesus in our theology, sermons, and hymns, we find it much more difficult to know what to do with Jesus' manger, homelessness, poverty, or cross. In fact, we ultimately look for the day when Jesus will return to earth with the stuff that real divinity is made of: power, glory, authority, and dominion. Yet the scandal of Christianity is precisely the opposite. In and through the compassion of Jesus, God is revealed precisely as God. In and through Jesus' identification with those who suffer and his acceptance of the cause of the poor as his own cause, we hear the very heartbeat of God. Jesus' suffering is not something that an otherwise powerful and sovereign deity had to go through. It is the revelation of who God is, and it is our own path for the recovery of the image of God.

Whatever we can or cannot know about Jesus' own faith, what he believed, or what he actually said, we do know what the apostles said was his way. He was a person who washed the feet of others; he was a person who associated with prostitutes, the diseased, the lowest classes of society; he was a person who openly conversed with women in public, thereby breaking all rules of social and religious convention; he was a person who put human need before religious tradition; he was a person who put people ahead of scripture and love ahead of letter; he was a person who chose the road of the servant, along with the suffering, agony, and pain that this path included. He brought about peace when tempers flared, and when common sense would have dictated revenge, Jesus taught forgiveness. Jesus always comes as unexpected news to those of us who live in comfort. Jesus was a street person. He had no home, no job, no steady income. Jesus was poor. It's important to let this sink in. Jesus did not simply minister to and visit poor people. He was poor. He looked at the world through their eyes. He stood up for their cause and sided with them in their struggles. This is the character and activity of God that we discover in Jesus. This is why Jesus is none other than the very compassion of God.

In reflecting on the significance of Jesus for our lives, we would do well to consider two fundamental claims about him discovered in the biblical witness: (1) Jesus was born in a manger, lived and died homeless, without material possession or title, cast his lot with the oppressed, impoverished, and outcast of society, and was executed among common criminals after being brutally tortured; and (2) in Jesus, God is perfectly and truthfully revealed and the path of salvation is decisively disclosed.

The classical approach to christology merely advances these two claims side by side as if they had no relationship to one another. The view from below, however, ponders these two claims and asks if they are simply coincidental. Is it mere happenstance that Jesus is the King of Kings and Lord of Lords and at the same time the one who had nowhere to lay his head? Or is there some intrinsic connection between the two?

I submit that the real challenge of christology is in appreciating the way that the compassion of God is related to human suffering in and through the life and ministry of Jesus, rather than deliberating over the union of abstract divinity and abstract humanity inside the person of Jesus. Furthermore, it is precisely the former option which holds promise for a theology of ministry. While refusing to be preoccupied with who Jesus is in and of himself (either in terms of his metaphysical status or inner psychological makeup), we are free to focus on the concrete problems of human living, working, playing, and loving for which Jesus was understood to be significant in his own day, and for which he is equally significant today.

Jesus and the Compassionate Kingdom

The place to begin in determining the significance of Jesus for Christian ministry, then, is not with meditations on his preexistence, trinitarian status, or divine-human equilibrium. Rather, we must begin with the first witnesses to Jesus and their context, their hopes, their struggles. It is they who tell us of his significance for their lives. It is they from whom we can draw out that significance for our own lives. Of course, a good reason for beginning with these earliest witnesses is simply that we have nowhere else to begin! We have nothing directly from Jesus himself—no videotape, no sound recordings, no writings. We do not know with certainty how Jesus understood himself, for example. And even when Jesus appears in the gospels as the one who is preaching or ministering, we must remind ourselves that it is not Jesus, but followers of Jesus, who are proclaiming, from their own context decades later, what Jesus said or did. Thus, even what are commonly known as the synoptic gospels (Matthew, Mark, and Luke), while certainly our most historically reliable sources for reconstructing the original witness of the apostles, can hardly be considered historical biographies as we understand that phrase today. The gospels are first and foremost a witness of faith to Jesus' significance rather than what we might today call historical reporting. When we stop to think about it, we can readily understand why. The decisive events of Jesus' crucifixion and resurrection exploded with such force in the lives of his followers that, in looking back over Jesus' life, they could not help but interpret him in the light of these events. Statements made by Jesus or actions performed by Jesus took on a whole new meaning and were often reported with the new meaning already attached. Thus, we should not be surprised by the fact that the synoptic gospels, as a genre of literature, are comparable to no other literature at the time. And in the case of John's Gospel, as the vast majority of New Testament scholarship recognizes, the distance between theological reflection and historical reporting is even more pronounced. John's Gospel, written almost a century after Jesus' death, is theologically biased, as John admits, "that you may believe that Jesus is the Christ, the Son of God; and that believing you may have life in His name" (John 20:31). John follows through on this promise, and the picture of Jesus he paints is remarkably different from those painted by Matthew, Mark, or Luke. Furthermore, when we turn to other New Testament documents, such as those written by Paul, we find reflection on the significance of Jesus that is even further removed from what Jesus actually said or did and instead is focused almost solely on who Jesus is as Lord, Savior, or Messiah.

We need not, however, view the New Testament gospel writers as obstacles to our understanding of the significance of Jesus simply because they fail to detail the life of Jesus with the kind of historical accuracy we crave today. On the contrary, these witnesses become absolutely essential for us if we will remember, first, that their words are a response to the call to faith discovered in Jesus and, second, that their response becomes for us, in turn, a new call to faith (Marxsen: 146). As we reflect on the significance of Jesus for them and for their context, perhaps we can extract some meaning for ourselves.

It is difficult, of course, to provide a concise, undisputed summary of what the earliest witnesses took to be most important about Jesus. By means of literary criticism, however, New Testament scholarship has been somewhat successful in reconstructing some of the fundamental elements of the earliest proclamation about what Jesus said or did, prior to those later reflections on who he was which appear after the influence of the crucifixion and resurrection. One of the earliest and undisputed summaries of Jesus' teaching and ministry is that which is recorded in Mark 1:15.

Time is up! The kingdom of God is at hand. Turn around and exercise faith in the good news. (translation mine)

This short verse, when amplified by other key elements in Jesus' ministry and preaching, can serve as a useful tool for initiating our reflection on the significance of Jesus for our lives and ministry, and especially for the recovery of the image of God (creativity, freedom, and community) in which Christian existence and ministry finds its aim and origin.

Creative Participation in the Kingdom of God

The most striking feature of this short verse in Mark is undoubtedly its reference to the kingdom of God, which is generally understood to be the central and unifying proclamation of Jesus' ministry.[2] Juan Luis Segundo believes the term is a loaded term, full of political content, and deliberately employed by Jesus to elicit political reaction (1985: 88–89). Indeed, it is rather difficult to imagine how Jesus could have consistently used the phrase without being conscious of its political overtones. But whether Segundo is wholly correct or not, it is clear that the apostles understood Jesus' use of the word "kingdom" to have profound meaning for their own context. It signaled a new state of affairs being ushered in that demanded nothing short of radical change and conversion on the part of those to whom it was proclaimed.

But how do human beings participate in this kingdom? Jesus' answer to that question contains a double movement. In the first place, the kingdom is a gift—something to be received by human beings and not the product of human effort or striving. We must receive the kingdom as a little child (Mark 10:13–16), and how the kingdom sprouts up and grows, we do not fully know (Mark 4:26). At the same time, however, the gratuitousness of the kingdom does not mean that the kingdom simply works automatically apart from human freedom or creativity. The irony of the kingdom is that receptivity does not mean passivity. Precisely because the kingdom is an earthly kingdom (Matthew 6:10), its gracious origin does not rule out, but only affirms, a high degree of causality and creativity on the part of human beings who live in the kingdom. We might say that receiving the kingdom and actually participating in the kingdom, while distinct, are inseparable matters. John Wesley, in answering the question, "Does not [God's]

---

2. As Norman Perrin states,

    The central aspect of the teaching of Jesus was that concerning the Kingdom of God. Of this there can be no doubt and today no scholar does, in fact, doubt it. Jesus appeared as one who proclaimed the Kingdom; all else in his message and ministry serves a function in relation to that proclamation and derives its meaning from it (54).

working thus supersede the necessity of our working at all?" puts the matter this way: "First, God works; therefore you can work. Secondly, God works, therefore you must work" (511). Creative participation in the kingdom of God is both a gift and a demand.

But even if human actions both condition and are conditioned by the kingdom, it is still God's kingdom that is understood by Jesus' witnesses to be breaking in. Indeed, as Segundo notes, because God is the force behind the kingdom, human participation in the building of the kingdom is freed from the oppressive fear and burden of trying to earn salvation or entry into the kingdom. Jesus, therefore, means for us existence as project rather than existence as test (1987: 90ff). When we are confident that God is the source of our salvation, we are free to live our lives creatively as a project of love, quite apart from the anxiety and fear that come from relying on our own efforts. The central significance of Jesus, then, is that all calculation and laboring for our own salvation is ruled out. And because they are ruled out, there is nothing to fear. Salvation is no longer about passing the test; it is about life lived here and now, life lived abundantly and creatively, as coworkers together with God in God's project of universal liberation and community.

When it comes to our understanding and practice of ministry, the implications of the inbreaking of the kingdom and our role in it can hardly be overestimated. Jesus confronts us with the possibility of creative participation in the kingdom of God. This means, firstly, that Christian ministry stands against any and every form of paralyzing apathy. Even though we can be confident in leaving all care about tomorrow until tomorrow (Matt. 6:24–34), it is the doing of God's will rather than the mere utterance of the words, "Lord, Lord" that is authentic participation in the kingdom (Matt. 7:21).[3] Apathy, of course, is essentially a faith that there is nothing we can do—that things must simply be put up with. As a resignation to the present state of affairs, apathy is the worst and perhaps most prominent form of practical atheism. Jesus confronts our apathy with the possibility of the kingdom of God, the possibility of real novelty, both in terms of our own individual lives and in terms of the transformation of our world. Thus, Jesus' preaching of the kingdom of God is the signal of as well as a summons to a new state of affairs. Things can be different

---

3. Paul's statement that verbal confession results in salvation (Romans 10:9–10) is either a blatant contradiction of what Jesus says here and elsewhere (Matt. 15:8), or must be understood as dealing with the subject in some other context or at some other level of meaning. It seems rather clear that Paul is dealing with the subject of verbal confession in the context of his own preaching ministry and also the equality between Jew and Greek when it comes to salvation. In other words, anyone to whom the gospel is addressed and who will respond to it can be saved, not merely those who have the law of Moses.

and, indeed, are different because the kingdom of God has arrived. Business as usual does not have to be put up with; therefore, business as usual must not be put up with. There is hope.

The second implication of our creative receptivity of the kingdom is that, while apathy is invalidated, Christian ministry must never be confused with sheer self-reliance. Ministry in the kingdom of God means that human creativity is liberated and enhanced, but that does not mean that life is to be lived entirely on our own terms, with our own methods, and on our own timing. Thus, Christian ministry must always avoid mere busy-ness—a fixation on sheer activity which results in a preoccupation with matters of how to rather than what for. So also, religious piety in ministry, regardless of how legalistically intensified, is excluded as of no worth whatsoever (Mark 7:1–23). Again and again, Jesus confronts those who think that the kingdom of God is established by escalating religious activity, following tradition, or relying on their own efforts and accomplishments. On the contrary, the kingdom of God is not found where one might typically look or where God-experts might point (Luke 17:20). It is in the midst of those who have the faith to recognize it. Thus, ironically enough, absolute and unconditioned human autonomy is actually destructive of human creativity. The kingdom which Jesus is understood to be ushering in confronts us with upside-down values that run contrary to conventional wisdom and common sense, but which actually emancipate human potential and capacity. God's ways are not our ways, even though they can be.

Here then is the central proclamation of the kingdom which Jesus announces. Freedom from ourselves—from apathy, fear, anxiety, and self-reliance—is freedom for creatively loving others, understood as the historical project of the kingdom of God. Kingdom-ministry calls people to a conversion, but this conversion is not understood as a ticket to heaven or as entrance into a lifeboat, so to speak. Conversion to the kingdom of God is the liberation of human creativity for the sake of a new community on earth. And nothing could be more revolutionary for our understanding and practice of ministry than this movement, as Segundo puts it, from existence-as-test to existence-as-project. Kingdom-ministry, in short, is fundamentally geared toward the recovery of our authentic humanity, not its negation or desertion. And that authentic humanity is a humanity which, as we have seen, has been created in the image of God—an image of creativity and novelty. The practice of Christian ministry today, then, must be creative and flexible in its attempts to move beyond the ever-increasing tendencies toward barrenness or apathy, on the one hand, and destruction or unrestricted autonomy, on the other. Both of these tendencies threaten our existence in Christian hope.

The Proximity of the Kingdom: Liberation Community

If the first element of the proclamation and ministry of Jesus is his insistence on the divine origin of the kingdom fused with his insistence on human agency and creativity in that kingdom, the second element is his characteristic insistence on the proximity of the kingdom of God, expressed in phrases such as "Time is up!" and "The kingdom of God is at hand." It is this proximity of the kingdom of God that has enormous consequences for how Jesus' original witnesses understood his significance for their lives. Thus, it is certainly not Jesus' pre-existence or triune status that is so interesting to the first witnesses, it is rather what happens in their world now that, in Jesus, the kingdom of God has arrived! Consider, for example, Jesus' response to John the Baptist's query, "Are you he who is to come, or shall we look for another?" In answering this question, Jesus turns John's question about who Jesus is into a question about what takes place when the kingdom is here—in other words, its functions (cf. Marxsen: 148):

> the blind receive sight and the lame walk, the lepers are cleansed and the deaf hear, and the dead are raised up, and the poor have the gospel preached to them. (Matthew 11:2–6; cf. Luke 7:22–23)

What is clear is that it is precisely these liberating functions that are recognized in the minds of Jesus' interpreters as the signs of the times. The liberation of the blind, lame, lepers, deaf, dead, and poor signals something new. They confirm to all who have eyes to see that the reign of God has arrived. Those who recognize the connection between these liberating functions and the proximity of the kingdom, but who do not stumble over the one who is performing these functions, are considered "blessed" (Matt. 11:2–6).

In the minds of Jesus' original witnesses, however, not only are the liberating functions of Jesus' ministry understood as signs of the proximity of the kingdom, so also is the new way of being in community that Jesus proclaims We are asked, for example, to go the extra mile with those who ask us (Matt. 5:42) and to recognize everyone as our neighbor (Luke 10:29–37). Because no one can earn or merit the kingdom of God, not only do the poor enjoy a special place of honor in the kingdom, sinners are invited to fellowship as well. Peacemaking also finds a fundamental role in kingdom community, and so patterns of retaliation and retribution are condemned and excluded (Matt. 5:9, 38ff). The proximity of the kingdom of God creates a new way of being in community that combines justice, equality, compassion, and peace.

In order adequately to interpret the significance of Jesus for our lives and ministry, then, we must incorporate into the previous question of what role human beings have in the kingdom (creative reception) the critical question of what takes place when the kingdom of God arrives—namely, liberation and community.

Liberation

In the first place, the freedom which is the result of the proximity of the kingdom is a freedom that is as broad and as comprehensive as human existence itself. That the apostles understood Jesus to be not only a forgiver of personal sins but also a social liberator is, I would argue, beyond question. One need only observe the contrast between the apostles, on the one hand, and those who rejected Jesus, on the other. The professionally religious of Jesus' day looked for signs—proofs of divinity—and Jesus refused to give them any. The followers of Jesus, on the other hand, consistently interpreted Jesus against the backdrop of what concretely enslaved people in their daily lives: poverty, physical disability, social exclusion, and so forth. Thus, while it is true that the apostles understood Jesus' activity to be the very activity of God, what made that activity so interesting in the first place was precisely its function in terms of concrete, historical liberation for people on the underside of human history. The implications for Christian ministry are tremendous.

First, that the proximity of the kingdom of God spells concrete human liberation for the oppressed means that Christian ministry stands against any dualism that would pit this-worldly struggles against other-worldly hopes. We are to pray for the kingdom of God to come "on earth as it is in heaven;" not in heaven after earth is gone. The coming of the kingdom does not mean negation of or escape from the world. The presence of the kingdom is known precisely because of its functions in the world. It is, of course, clear that the liberating presence of the kingdom may never finally be reduced to any one concrete sociopolitical option or ideology. That does not mean, however, that kingdom-ministry may somehow remain above any particular sociopolitical options or that the church should refrain from lending its voice and support to concrete sociopolitical measures that creatively serve the values of the kingdom. In the first place, the church has a sociopolitical influence whether it likes it or not, even if that influence is the merely default influence of protecting the status quo. The church has a voice. The church has a historical presence. And neutrality is generally complicity with the way things are.

The second implication of the liberating proximity of the kingdom is that Christian ministry must stand against any dualism that would pit sociopolitical concerns against so-called spiritual concerns. In other words, the compassionate kingdom is fundamentally holistic. Jesus simply does not, in practice, carve human beings up into dimensions of "body" and "soul." While Jesus is consistently represented as one who cares about who and what a person truly is—regardless of that person's exterior trappings or facades—he nonetheless ministers to the physical as well as to the spiritual frailties of those he encounters, and he bids his followers to do the same. Indeed, from looking at the judgment parable found in Matthew 25, it appears that ministering to merely physical needs is not only acceptable, but finally the primary criterion for participation in the kingdom.

In Jesus, the kingdom of God is at hand. There can be no more excuses, no more pointing off into the clouds, no more ducking into synagogues or churches to avoid the world and draw closer to God. The good news of the kingdom is the good news of human liberation. The significance of Jesus, by making explicit that the ground of all liberation is God, is that we find ourselves challenged not only to understand ourselves as free, but to structure our lives and ministry accordingly, both in the service of this freedom and against any dualistic tendencies which threaten our existence in Christian freedom.

Community

In the second place, the community that is the result of the proximity of the kingdom is a community modeled on the very forgiveness and acceptance extended to us by God in Jesus of Nazareth. Here again, we are drawn to several important implications for ministry. In Jesus, we are challenged, first, to understand ourselves as objects of God's supremely sympathetic and all-inclusive love and, second, to respond to that love by structuring our lives, our practice, and our ministry in accordance with that love through authentic Christian community. Thus, in the first place, to understand ourselves as the object of God's love—to know that whatever else happens, our lives unfailingly contribute to the divine life—gives to our lives and ministry a new meaning and sense of abiding significance. What we do matters. In the second place, to know ourselves to be the object of God's unconditional love is to be free to love others as God has loved us. This means that our love must, insofar as possible, be fully sympathetic and without bounds. Obviously, our relationships are finite, and our ability to sympathize with and include others is radically different from that of God. Nonetheless, we are genuinely created in the image of God as communal. Our lives, if they are to be authentic and meaningful, must express themselves in sympathetic, unbounded love—in a word, "compassion." In this way, and this way only, can we move beyond the ever-increasing tendencies toward selfishness and individualism, on the one hand, or domination and subordination, on the other, both of which threaten our existence in Christian love.

Conversion: The Demand of the Kingdom

If the kingdom of God calls for our creative participation in it, and if the arrival of the kingdom of God brings with it both liberation and community, there is nonetheless a straightforward demand that is the basis for both. Again, Mark 1:15 serves as our starting point. Jesus' proclamation that the "kingdom of God is at hand" is followed by his summons to turn around ("repent," "change your ways"), and this is connected with his command to "exercise faith in the good news." In other words, Jesus' announcement of the proximity of the kingdom includes with it a call to radical change and faith on the part of those who hear that announcement. But not everyone hears this call to conversion in the same way; indeed, it is not directed by Jesus to everyone in the same way.

Throughout the gospel accounts of Jesus' activity, we discover that Jesus regularly relates the functions and consequences of the kingdom to two groups: (1) those who suffer and are impoverished, for whom the kingdom is automatically good news and (2) those who are comfortable, wealthy, and powerful, for whom the kingdom is automatically bad news—even though it may, of course, become good news. The relationship between the kingdom of God and the two groups is evidently not identical. As Segundo points out, while it is the values of the second group that turn the gospel into bad news, it is the situation of the first group that causes them to see the gospel as good news.

> The kingdom also comes to change the situation of the poor, to put an end to it. As the first Beatitude tells us, the poor possess the kingdom of God. That is not due to any merit of theirs, much less to any value that poverty might have. On the contrary, the kingdom is theirs because of the inhuman nature of their situation as poor people. The kingdom is coming because God is "humane," because God cannot tolerate that situation and is coming to make sure that the divine will be done on earth. (1985: 107)

Even though in Jesus of Nazareth people find themselves face to face with a love that is boundless and therefore the basis of Christian community, this love must nonetheless be expressed in terms of a special concern for the poor because of their situation. But this partiality would be impossible if it were not rooted in God's impartial and boundless love. It is in genuinely understanding that we are all boundlessly loved by God that we find ourselves called to make a place in the human community for those who are marginalized and oppressed. Ironically, it is in the very fact that Jesus took up a ministerial preference for the poor that we understand him to be God's offer of salvation for all, even the rich. In other words, here again, the poverty and the messiahship of Jesus are not merely compatible; they presuppose each other.

Jesus' message and ministry leave no room for doubt that, for many, the arrival of the kingdom is not automatically good news. What is called for is precisely a conversion to understanding the liberation of the oppressed as good news. In opting for the poor, then, Jesus not only makes clear what happens when the kingdom of God "is at hand"—namely, liberation and community— he also makes clear the conditions under which one may enter that kingdom— namely, conversion to the good news of the kingdom.

This means that Christian ministry is directed to all—both rich and poor. It is ministry to all because the kingdom of God comes for all. That does not mean, however, that Christian ministry is directed to all in the same way. As Segundo rightly concludes, only for the poor is the coming of the kingdom at first "a cause for joy"; and, "according to Jesus, the dividing line between joy and woe produced by the kingdom runs between the poor and the rich" (1985: 90).

We can say, then, that Jesus' evangelistic call to conversion takes two distinct forms. On the one hand, as directed toward the rich—those who are secure in their political power and economic comfort at the expense of the powerless-ness and discomfort of others—Jesus' good news of the kingdom comes as a woeful event. This group of people, caught up in the insidious mechanics of oppression, can only react with fear and skepticism to the coming of the kingdom. There is no avoiding the negative implications of Jesus' beatitudes. The full go away hungry; the rich go away empty. Jesus' evangelism to this group takes the form of undermining their ability to determine the will of God through legal considerations and focusing their minds instead on what is humanizing. The conversion that Jesus demands of this group is a conversion from the security of the letter of the law (a most oppressive form of security) to the liberating insecurity of having to opt for the poor. In essence, being in tune with the poor and their interests will open them up to who God is, what the law and the prophets really have to say, and, inevitably, to who Jesus is himself. As Rosemary Radford Ruether says, "Jesus addresses this message particularly to the poor, not in order to exclude the rich, but in order to make clear to them the conditions under which they will enter the kingdom" (17). With regard to the rich, the call to conversion is a demand to orient their lives toward a God of boundless love and in doing so to orient their lives toward the poor. Such a transformation obviously requires a thoroughgoing reversal of vision and values.

On the other hand, as directed to the poor—those to whom the gospel is, in a sense, naturally addressed—Jesus' good news of the kingdom comes as a message of liberation and inclusion in human community. The poor do not need to be converted to that fact. In fact, it is very difficult to find any similarity between the rhetoric and practice of contemporary Christian evangelism and anything that Jesus said or did to the poor. What is scandalous in Jesus' evange-lism is that God does not place moral or religious conditions on the poor in order for them to enjoy the coming kingdom. And this is precisely because God's love is compassionate. As Segundo says, "God does not pass judgment on a human being who is not yet truly human" (1985: 140).

All this does not mean that there is something romantic about poverty. Poverty is destructive. The very heart of Jesus' message, however, is that poverty must cease wreaking havoc on human life and that the inhuman treatment of the weak and the oppressed must come to an end. This is the news that is auto-matically good news in a situation of poverty and oppression. Therefore, with regard to the poor, the call to conversion is a demand to understand themselves as artisans of their own humanity and forgers of their own future, despite what they may now believe or have been led to believe in the past. Jesus calls the disinherited to understand themselves as inheritors of the kingdom; but of course this is not an easy task. Today, as in Jesus' day, the poor suffer not only materially, but ideologically from a kind of social fatalism. In our own day, that fatalism is all the more unyielding by virtue of its addiction to other-worldly hopes that, as Karl Marx rightly observed, serve as an opiate to subdue any revolutionary ambitions the poor might have and that keep the status quo quite secure and unthreatened. But the poor are called to the risky and coura-geous task of recovering their own true humanity—a task of self-creation which is nonetheless possible only by the grace of a liberating God.

What we have here is a two-fold evangelism to which Jesus calls us as his disciples. Both types of evangelism are valid forms of kingdom-evangelism, but the common denominator of each is its contribution to the humanization of both rich and poor. While ministry to the rich and ministry to the poor take different forms, both begin with a call to conversion and both end in our creative participation in God's liberation community. The authentic liberation of the dehumanized is simultaneously the liberation of the one who has dehu-manized others. James Cone summarizes this conviction in the following three statements:

First, the work of Christ is essentially a liberating work, directed toward and by the oppressed.

Second, Christ in liberating the wretched of the earth also liberates those responsible for the wretchedness. The oppressor is also freed of his peculiar demons.

Third, mature freedom is burdensome and risky, producing anxiety and conflict for free [people] and for the brittle structures they challenge. (1969: 42)

Kingdom or Community?

One of the challenges of remaining faithful to the Christian witness found in scripture is how best to communicate the understanding expressed in Jesus' use of the phrase "kingdom of God." Jesus' use of the phrase signaled something profound in the minds of Jesus' hearers: a new state of affairs being ushered in, bringing liberation and community and requiring conversion and change on the part of those to whom it was proclaimed. The question, however, is whether the phrase "kingdom of God" signals that same kind of meaning and demands a similar conversion for us today. "Kingdom" is not exactly a contemporary word, in the sense that very few of us today have a grasp of what it would be like actually to live in one. It is a concept from a bygone era—an era to which virtually none of us wishes to return. For all of its shortcomings, we like democracy; and the idea of a monarch who unilaterally controls the affairs of state, creates and enforces legislation, commands the military, and provides for the welfare of the people has lost whatever attractiveness it may at one time have had. And yet "kingdom" is how Jesus expresses his understanding of a state of affairs where God's will is done.

Of course, even though Jesus uses the word "kingdom," it is also true that Jesus does not himself approach God as a king (though he does refer to God as a king in a few parables). Rather, he prefers the word "father." There is something about the word "king," even in Jesus' own day, that doesn't adequately portray the God of compassion. So what do we do with the phrase, "kingdom of God"? How must the words change for the meaning to remain the same? In the first place, we want to eliminate the obviously patriarchal and oppressive overtones of the notion of a kingdom—overtones which violate so much about what we discover through Jesus to be true of God as compassion. Feminist Hispanic activists and theologians Ada María Isasi-Díaz and Yolanda Tarango wrestle with this difficulty and offer their own substitute:

> There are two reasons for not using the regular word employed by the English Bible, kingdom. First, it is obviously a sexist word that presumes that God is male. Second, the concept of kingdom in our world today is both hierarchical and elitist—which is also why we do not use reign. The word kin-dom makes it clearer that when the fullness of God becomes a day-to-day reality in the world at large, we will all be sisters and brothers —kin to each other. (116)

Similar to such a suggestion is Martin Luther King, Jr.'s own use of the phrase "beloved community" to describe the kingdom of God.

But as valuable as such suggestions undoubtedly are in affirming the mutuality that is central to Jesus' understanding of the kingdom of God, how do we retain the explicitly political and material connotations that the word "kingdom" unquestionably carries? My suggestion is that, while the word "community" does emphasize the elements of relationship and participation which are so central to life in the kingdom of God, the word "liberation" adds the dimension of social, political, and spiritual transformation that the coming of the kingdom brings about. In other words, the kingdom of God might well be understood today as a liberation community—a state of affairs where human beings creatively participate with God as brothers and sisters together in the holistic restoration of human dignity, purpose, and meaning.

Undoubtedly this phrase will also have its own shortcomings and limitations, not the least of which, perhaps, is its inadequacy in expressing the truly global proportions of God's will in our lives and world. The word "community," after all, is typically used to refer to a particular or localized group of people who have much in common. To employ it in imagining something as inclusive and far-reaching as the kingdom of God may be stretching its meaning a bit. Or perhaps not! Is it really that difficult to speak meaningfully of the entire human community? Is it really that hard to see the various nations and peoples of the world increasingly linked together by an inescapable network of forces and relationships? Do we not already perceive that what happens in one corner of the globe has ongoing repercussions for what happens in the rest of the globe? Perhaps imagining the kingdom of God as a liberation community is not really that far removed from our capacities after all.

Furthermore, if the kingdom of God can be imagined as a liberation community, then perhaps it is not impossible to recognize the church as a sign, or sacrament, of this new creation and as, thus, a legitimate instance of liberation community itself. To speak of the church as a sacrament of liberation community and, thus, as a liberation community itself, is to speak of the church as both model and agent of liberation and community. A sacrament both points to something beyond itself and participates in that to which it points. Thus, while the church, as sacramental agent of God's liberation community, may never be strictly identified as the exclusive representation of what God is up to in the world, there is a sobering sense in which the church is indeed the live model on earth of what God is always and everywhere up to. As long as the church refuses to idolize itself as the sole locus of liberation and community in the world, it need not fear or retreat from its responsibility of being a flesh-and-blood sacrament of liberation and community to the world. While the church is never the liberation community, it is always called to be a liberation community.

Compassionate Ministry as Humanizing Ministry

Jesus of Nazareth gains a decisive significance for us today when recognized as the offer of a restored humanity—the recovery of the image of God. We have seen that the original witnesses to Jesus understood this offer as the inbreaking of the kingdom of God: a new order on earth that we receive and in which we are creative participants, a kingdom that both liberates and restores, a kingdom that is the gift and demand of community. In Jesus, it is clear that this offer of creative participation in God's liberation community is grounded in the very presence and activity of a compassionate God: a God who is with us, who takes sides against injustice and inhumanity, and who surprises us with ever-new and creative possibilities for our lives. In Jesus, we discover who God is, and we discover what we are therefore called to be: human.

Now to say that God in Jesus wants us to be human may sound rather point-less. We could really do very little else! It's like saying that God wants Los Angeles to be a city, or that God wants the Atlantic to be an ocean. These things are simply so. We are, after all, human! But when we look closely at our world—when we discover that every two minutes a woman is raped and that every eigh-teen seconds a woman is beaten by the man she lives with—we realize that we are not very human at all. When we remember the dates of August 6 and August 9 and recall that by the end of 1945, 140,000 people had died in Hiroshima and 70,000 in Nagasaki, we are forced to conclude that we are not very human at all. When we examine the quality of life in the inner cities of our world and acknowledge the large-scale unemployment, homelessness, and squalid housing conditions that permeate our ghettoes and barrios, we must admit that we are not very human at all. Indeed, given the way we habitually dehumanize one another, we could just as well conclude that our existence is the expression not so much of being human, but of being inhuman.

But if Jesus means anything for us, it is that despite our inhumanity toward one another, we are invited to be human—indeed, we are called to be human. And in Jesus of Nazareth, of course, not only are we invited and called to be human, we are actually confronted with the path to becoming human: the path to redemption, transformation, and re-creation in God's image. That path is the path which Jesus identified as the kingdom of God and which I have been referring to as the path of liberation community.

Christian ministry begins with our own positive response to this summons to become more fully human and with our own participation in the human-izing process identified by Jesus. From there, authentic Christian ministry goes on to extend this summons and this path to other human beings, both person-ally and corporately. In other words, Christian ministry has the audacity to claim that its character and praxis is an extension of God's character and praxis. And it is precisely our faith in Jesus as the Christ that allows us to be so presumptuous. Christian ministry is always more than sheer activity; it is faithed activity. It is born out of a confidence in the God of compassion discovered in Jesus of Nazareth and it is shaped and structured by a loyalty to that same God. This ministerial praxis is a humanizing praxis precisely because it originates in and is aimed at the restoration or re-creation of true humanity (the image of God) in each of us and in all of us.

Much of the remainder of this book is devoted to suggesting just how compassionate ministry as a humanizing ministry might be imagined, if it is to remain faithful to the historical encounter of the apostles with Jesus, and if it is to become relevant to the concrete challenges and opportunities of contemporary human existence—especially as those challenges and opportunities are presented to us in the life and experience of the poor, the suffering, and the dehumanized of our world. Before moving on, however, we may summarize the significance of Jesus as the one in whom we discover the gift and demand of humanizing praxis by noting how, in the thought of the apostle Paul, each of the three dimensions of the image of God (freedom, community, and creativity) is restored in and through our becoming, as Paul puts it, "in Christ."

In what follows in this chapter, then, we will turn from the historical Jesus of the synoptic gospels to the Christ of the Pauline writings. We are, of course, talking about the same Jesus in both, but while the synoptic gospels are more concerned with what Jesus said and did—specifically, his call for a conversion to and creative participation in God's liberation community—Paul is more concerned with who Jesus is as Lord and Savior and what it means to live in Christ.

When we move from the words of the gospels to the words of Paul, we are first struck by the relative absence of any reference to what Jesus actually said or did in his lifetime. And yet, there is no way to avoid the fact that, in all that Paul says, Jesus is still clearly the subject. Even though Paul's letters were written earlier than any of the gospels, and are thus closer chronologically to the life of Jesus, Paul's approach to the significance of Jesus seems much further removed from the actual historical figure of Jesus. Whereas, for the gospels, the day-to-day struggles, issues, and politics of Israel's religious and cultural life provide the framework for interpreting Jesus' significance, Paul's thought is aimed at a variety of contexts throughout the Roman Empire. Paul's thought appeals to a broader range of human experience and interprets the significance of Jesus in a more universal and history-encompassing framework. While Matthew, Mark, and Luke focus primarily on what Jesus said and did in such a way as to establish that Jesus should therefore be understood as the Christ, Paul begins with Jesus as the Christ and focuses more on what it means for any human being to live in Christ.

The phrase "in Christ" and its equivalents, "in Christ Jesus" and "in the Lord," occur no less than 132 times in Paul's writings. They are not found at all in the synoptic gospels. The phrase is a uniquely Pauline way of describing the almost mystical intimacy that exists between Christians and the resurrected Christ. Paul's notion of being in Christ is something like

> a sphere or environment or element in which a Christian lives, as a bird in
> the air, a fish in the water, or the roots of a tree in the soil. (Vincent: 4)

The notion here is similar to the "putting on" of Christ like a garment (Gal. 3:27) that Paul imagines Christian baptism to be.

We would be misled, however, if we reduced Paul's talk about being in Christ to Christian initiation rituals or to certain religious or mystical experiences of union with Christ—what we might call close encounters with the resurrected Jesus. Being in Christ has to do with an entire way of living and being that includes not only a new way of understanding ourselves but also a new way of acting toward our neighbor. Being in Christ is not something magical or merely private. It is participation, both personally and corporately, in Christ's sufferings and joy, in Christ's mission and future, in Christ's way. It is a life lived in response to the God we discover in Jesus.

As we explore Paul's thought, although his theology is certainly a step removed from the historical encounter of the apostles with Jesus, we can still detect how his vision of being in Christ dovetails with the significance attributed to Jesus by those same early witnesses. Paul interprets the life and experience of living in Christ in terms of a fundamentally new liberty, a fundamentally new creation, and a fundamentally new community. The three are interdependent and interwoven in Paul's thought. To be free in Christ is to be free from futility and barrenness and free for community in our life project of making faith effective on a daily basis.

A New Freedom in Christ

First of all, for Paul, to be in Christ is to be free. Few individuals make this point as strongly as Richard N. Longenecker in his introduction to Paul's thought, Paul, Apostle of Liberty. With regard to the phrase "in Christ," Longenecker says, "Here, then, is the controlling concept for Paul's teaching regarding liberty. Christian liberty is constituted only 'in Christ'" (170). On the one hand, what most sets Paul apart from the Stoics of his day, says Longenecker, is his insistence that the path to liberty is not freedom from ignorance as one progresses down the enlightened and self-centered path of knowing oneself. On the other hand, what most sets Paul apart from the Jewish rabbi of his day is his insistence that the path to liberty is not to be found in a blind subjection to the law either (160–161). Rather, for Paul, authentic liberty is a freedom from sin that comes from being in Christ.

But what is meant by this word "sin," and why is freedom from it so central to Paul? Just as important for our purposes here, what at all does freedom from sin have to do with Jesus' announcement of the inbreaking of the kingdom of God and our summons to creatively participate in that kingdom? We have seen that the dynamics of the kingdom of God are very earthly, political, social, and even economic. The kingdom of God is about liberation from injustice and oppression: it is about the possibility of genuine human community here and now, the possibility of forgiving enemies, the possibility of lifting up the down-trodden, the possibility of fully including the marginalized of society. Has Paul now shifted us to a religious plane that is above and beyond the social, political, and economic realities with which we are daily faced? Is salvation primarily a spiritual matter between the individual and God that may, at best, only have implications for our daily struggles and projects in life? Or should we, perhaps, simply add on Paul's more spiritual gospel to the more down-to-earth gospels of Matthew, Mark, and Luke? Perhaps salvation from sin is something that has to happen along with liberation from injustice and poverty?

The answers to these question have profound implications for how we imagine and go about practicing Christian ministry. If salvation from sin occurs on a personal-spiritual-religious plane, while liberation from injustice and poverty occurs on a social-physical-political plane, then, as a church, we are faced with the question of how Christian ministry is to be divided between the two planes, if it all. (One may, of course, conclude that only one of these planes is of direct concern to Christian ministry.) But if salvation and liberation are not two distinctly different processes, and if they do not occur on two different planes of human existence—if Paul's theological rhetoric about freedom from sin in Christ is but a different way of talking about the conversion to creative participation in the kingdom of God which Jesus came preaching—then the church's question of how to understand and practice Christian ministry must be radically rethought and restated. The reduction of Christian ministry to a choice of evangelism or justice, prayer or politics, is thrown out the window just as surely as is a dualistic sandwiching of evangelism and justice, prayer and politics. In other words, perhaps the choice is neither either/or nor both/and; perhaps it is something else altogether.

While Paul's way of interpreting the significance of Jesus is certainly broader and less down-to-earth than the more historical approaches of Matthew, Mark, and Luke, we do ourselves, Paul, and the gospel of Jesus itself a great disservice by contrasting too sharply the religious-spiritual dimensions of salvation, on the one hand, and the political-historical dimensions of salvation, on the other hand. Paul is not talking about a type of redemption that floats above or is only one aspect of our daily existence and from which we merely draw socio-ethical implications. Just as sin is historical, psychological, political, social, and economic, so too is salvation always historical, psychological, political, social, and economic. To talk about a spiritual dimension to life, as I have already argued, is not to talk about one particular domain of life; it is to talk about all dimensions of life together, or as a whole.

Thus, sin is not a spiritual matter that requires a spiritual cure—faith—if either sin or faith is taken to refer to a human dimension or posture that is removed from our mundane world of senate bills, currency exchange rates, trade policies, and factory closings. Sin is, however, a spiritual matter that requires a spiritual cure—faith—if both sin and faith are understood as referring to human attitudes and postures that pervade every dimension of our lives and have a direct bearing on all of our relationships.

Juan Luis Segundo offers a compelling interpretation of Paul's thought at this point. Segundo holds that, for Paul, sin and faith are contrasted with one another as measures of "the gap or distance that is always there between what a human being intends and what he or she actually performs or accomplishes" (1986: 145–146). Thus,

> The effect of Sin is to put greater distance between the two [intentions and results], so that human beings find their own actions incomprehensible and unrecognizable. The effect of Faith is to put less distance between the two, so that the works and deeds of human beings are somehow restored to them as their own, at least to some extent. (146)

If Segundo is on target here, then, for Paul, sin is what robs human dignity to the extent that it distorts and hinders the creative exercise of our freedom. Sin dehumanizes. Our activity becomes no longer ours. It is born out of fear and slavery, subject to forces and aims that are alien to us. Just as the law, which was supposed to act as a tutor for the Jews (Gal. 3:23ff), became an end in itself to which their actions became enslaved, so also the church and even the Bible can become alien overlords for Christians, keeping us in bondage rather than liberating our own creativity and God-given humanity. Thus, sin corrupts the image of God in us. It turns freedom into slavery, creativity into futility, and community into alienation. It should not be surprising, then, that in Paul's writings, sin shows up almost as if it had a life of its own. It seems to have a universal enslaving power over human beings that takes our intentions (our faith) as we try to implement them and distorts them so that, "that which I am doing, I do not understand; for I am not practicing what I would like to do, but I am doing the very thing I hate" (Rom. 7:15).

Of course, it would be easy to overemphasize this sense in which sin is an impersonal and almost alien dynamic in our lives. It is undoubtedly true, even for Paul, that sin is a path we freely choose. But, in reading Paul, and especially the Epistle to the Romans, it is difficult to avoid his insistence that sin is something "we are all under" (3:9), something that "reigns" in us (5:21, 6:12), something to which we "go on presenting the members of our bodies" as "instruments" (6:13), something that is our "master" and to which we are "slaves" (6:14–20), something to which we are "sold into bondage" (7:14), something we can be "freed from" (6:7–22, 8:2) or "die to" (6:10–11), something that "deceives" and "kills" us (7:11), and something which operates by its own law within us (7:23). Just as arresting, along these lines, are Paul's words, "So now, no longer am I the one doing it, but sin which indwells me" (7:17) or his statement, "But if I am doing the very thing I do not wish, I am no longer the one doing it, but sin which dwells in me" (7:20).

So then, while we certainly do commit individual sins, for Paul, it is essential to recognize that sin is structural (both on a personal level and on a corporate level). It is bigger than all of us and operates independently from any one of us. It has become part of the system, built into the very mechanisms of our daily existence. A good example of this would be racism. Racism, of course, is a sin, but it is difficult to lay our finger on it as a simple and intentional act—"a willful violation of the known law of God," as the classical definition of sin puts it. Racism in America, for example, is deeply entrenched not only in our institutions, our legal system, our political process, and our business practices, but also in our own individual lifestyles and personal relationships. It sometimes seems as if it has a life of its own. And yet, although it is structural, sin is not merely outside of us, operating on its own; it is also very much within us, taking advantage of our own instincts, or as Paul puts it, "desires" and "cravings" (cf. Rom. 1). We are "accomplices" to sin (Segundo, 1986: 174). In fact, the very effort to deceive ourselves and others of our complicity with sin is what produces the hypocritical attitudes to which, ironically enough, religious persons are especially prone (cf. Rom. 2). But, then, this just goes to show how sin operates at every level of our existence, is personal and yet corporate, willful and yet structural, generated by us and yet inherited by us. How this whole process works can be illustrated by taking as an example the relationship between contemporary Christians in the United States and the devastated inner cities which those same Christians drive around and past regularly. The problems of the inner city—unemployment, crime, violence, deterioration, overcrowding, drugs, gangs, economic exploitation, and substandard education, only to name a few—are hardly sins in a narrow, individualistic sense that one could easily point to or ask a handful of primary culprits simply to quit doing. They represent complex systems of structural injustice, evil, escape, and exploitation; in other words, they represent sin, alive and at work as an impersonal force in the world.

As the Christian church in the United States has progressively abandoned the inner city physically, politically, economically, and spiritually, it has operated by a kind of mass dynamism toward security, comfort, and wealth. Each member of every Christian church in America did not individually decide that the church should abandon the city, but it has happened nonetheless. And so now the church finds itself in a situation where it is less and less conscious of and, to a certain degree, less impacted by urban poverty and deterioration. The church has in many respects actually become a middle-class church with a dangerous distance from the poor. As the church now begins to shift its focus away from material and economic suffering and from social and structural injustice, at least two transformations take place. First of all, the church begins to become more preoccupied with the psychological suffering of the middle class. Issues related to stress, burnout, negative thinking, guilt, despair, or anxiety begin to top the list of sermon topics and group Bible studies (none of which are entirely inappropriate in and of themselves for consideration in the church). Secondly, ethical behavior in the church becomes further and further removed from matters of social responsibility or structural injustice and poverty. Morality now becomes private piety defined, negatively, in terms of the avoidance of a list of particular individual vices and, positively, in terms of a general decency, civility, and appropriate display of religious activity, such as attending church, making monetary contributions, praying publicly before meals, and serving on church boards and committees.

Having lost virtually any sense of culpability for the destruction of the city or responsibility for its welfare, the church in America has become much like those to whom Paul addresses himself in the second chapter of Romans: increasingly turned inward, supposing their own legalistic piety to be a shield from sin and judgment and a cause for "glorying." The tragic results of treating religious performance this way, as a wage paid for salvation, are, first, the way it causes us to feel personally at ease and, second, the way it provides a basis for our passing judgment on others, especially the inhabitants of the inner city themselves, for their poverty, crime, drugs, and overpopulation. Reinhold Niebuhr recognized this hypocritical attitude of the middle class toward the poor when he wrote:

> The middle class tries to make the canons of individual morality authoritative for all social relations. It is shocked by the moral cynicism, the tendency toward violence and indifference toward individual freedom of the [poor]. . . . The middle classes believe in freedom, but deny freedom when its exercise imperils their position in society; they profess a morality

of love and unselfishness but do not achieve an unselfish group attitude toward a less privileged group; they claim to abhor violence and yet use it both in international conflict and in the social crises in which their interests are imperilled; they want mutuality of interest between classes rather than a class struggle but the mutuality must not be so complete as to destroy all their special privileges. (1932: 176–177)

The height of this audacity is when the middle-class church sends its missionaries to convert the poor of the inner city to its own private brand of suburban holiness.

The point here is neither that the church is entirely to blame for the conditions of our inner cities today, nor that the dispossessed of society are somehow less sinful than the wealthy and comfortable (though much could be said about the relationship between the wealthy and the poor as the relationship between sinner and sinned-against). The point is that no amount of moral righteousness on a personal level can ever balance out the glaring omissions of our responsibility on a social and structural level. A tragic example of this principle is the way conservative Christians today focus incredible amounts of energy combatting what they take to be a grievous personal sin in the life of others—namely, homosexuality—while at the same time themselves practicing Ezekiel's definition of sodomy on a social level:

Behold, this was the guilt of your sister Sodom: she and her daughters had arrogance, abundant food, and careless ease, but she did not help the poor and needy. (16:49)

To the extent that we Christians find ways of excusing, denying, or neglecting our own participation (whether consciously or unconsciously) in structural sin and injustice, while focusing on what we take to be the sins of others, not only do we simply deceive ourselves, we further intensify, as Paul puts it, the way we are offering "the members of our body as instruments of unrighteousness" (Rom. 6:13). Here is the irony that Paul establishes so clearly throughout his writings: it is the very process of trusting in our own moral excellence and inner purity that over and over proves itself to be sin's greatest accomplice.

Is there any way out of this constant need to add up our works for salvation without giving up on activity altogether? Is there any way to pull out of a preoccupation with our own righteousness without falling backward into a cloud of apathy and pessimism? And how, if at all, can the cycle of sin, sinning, deception, and hypocrisy be transformed into a life that is liberated, liberating, and loving?

There certainly is, for Paul, a freedom from the tyranny of sin that faith in Christ brings to our daily activity. But we should never mistake Paul's use of the word "faith" for some merely passive acceptance of the gift of salvation. We are, as Paul says, "created in Christ Jesus for good works" (Eph. 2:10). In Paul's mind, just as in Jesus' preaching, a liberating faith is both a gift and a demand. Faith is the structuring of our entire lives (politically, economically, and psychologically) as a lived response to the character and activity of the God discovered in Jesus of Nazareth. Thus, if the God we discover in Jesus is a God of compassion, our lives will never be truly human and therefore free unless structured by this very quality of compassion.

For Paul, just as sin is understood as a loss of freedom, the work of Christ is to set us free from this enslaving power, from this "law of sin and of death" (Rom. 8:2). This is what Christ does, not by magically removing us from the world of tough social relationships, political decisions, and ongoing personal choices, but by reconstituting us toward that world, by offering us a whole new way of responding to and constructing our world. Christ frees us by offering us the possibility of a faith that understands our living not as an effort or a test to merit salvation, but as a lived response to a caring, compassionate God who is also alongside us and at work with us. This freedom does not mean that sin no longer exists. On the contrary, precisely becasue it is a structure deeply embedded in the systems and institutions of human existence on our planet, sin continues to cause death by taking advantage of our faith and distorting it. Paul is confident, however, that the gap between our intentions and the results of our activity can be narrowed, that we can be liberated from sin's alienating and destructive grip on our lives, through our re-creation in Christ.

A New Creation in Christ

There is only one cure for the dehumanization that both causes and is caused by sin, and that is rehumanization: the recovery of our "vocation" to be human (Freire) both individually and collectively. For Paul, such a humanizing process is not merely a possibility; it is a reality. Indeed, the person who is "in Christ" has become "a new creation" (2 Cor. 5:17).

Faith in Christ accomplishes this new creation, but not by some supernatural transformation of our wills, intellects, or bodies. We do not become new creations by means of genetic alteration, nor are we suddenly whisked away from the concrete world of structural sin and injustice. Faith, as Paul uses the term, means entrusting our lives and our destiny to the God discovered in Jesus. In so doing, we are liberated from the temptation to seek security in the law, the church, the Bible, or other human beings and are thereby freed to be fully and creatively loyal to God. Our actions are returned to us as ours. We become once again the creators we were created to be. And the result of this freedom is that we are made fully alive (Rom. 6:11, 1 Cor. 15:22), having been emancipated from the kind of guilt and condemnation (Rom. 8:1) that paralyzes, robs, and misdirects human creativity.

Freedom and creativity, then, are closely related and interconnected in Paul's thought. To be free in Christ is to be free for creatively leading one's own life. Thus, freedom from is also freedom for. But this freedom, along with the possibilities and responsibilities it unleashes, can be frightening for those who are used to seeing the world in black and white, those who prefer the security of having others tell them what is right and what is wrong, what is lawful and what is not lawful. For Paul, however, "all things are lawful" (1 Cor. 6:12). True, "not all things are profitable," but it is precisely the task of creative freedom to discover just what is and what isn't profitable. The only criterion we are given is the criterion by which Jesus himself judged human actions—namely, what serves to make us more fully human.[4] Thus, radical freedom in Christ does not undercut human creativity and responsibility but thrusts it upon us. The one who is in Christ is no longer subject to the law or other external authorities but is instead given the heavy responsibility of placing any and all authorities in the service of human beings.

To single out one example, we should not be surprised that in the New Testament alone we receive mixed signals about the Christian's relationship to governing authorities with no one clear rule for how this relationship should be understood predominating over the others. In one context, Paul deals with a specific situation in the community at Rome and preaches a strict obedience to government (Rom. 13). Peter and the apostles, in another context, insist on obeying God rather than humans (Acts 5:29). In still another context, on the lips of Jesus himself appear the classic words, "Render to Caesar the things that are Caesar's, and to God the things that are God's" (Mark 12:17). When we pause to ask ourselves if there is anything that is not God's, however, it is clear that Jesus' instructions are not a clear-cut solution for any and all situations. The problem, of course, is that we are often tempted to relinquish to Caesar many things that are due only to God. Furthermore, we know that Caesar is often tempted to want to play the role of God and thereby to claim our complete allegiance. Christians today, just as in the days of Jesus or the apostles, must sort these matters out for their own context. That is the responsibility of Christian maturity. But, of course, the responsibility of being human can be quite frustrating for people who want

---

4. So, for example, Jesus is presented as one who bends the law in the service of human hunger and healing (Matt. 12:1–13) and exposes those who bend the law away from human need (Mark 7:1–13). He is presented as one who contrasts the religious excellence of the Pharisees with the more important qualities of justice, compassion, and faithfulness (Matt. 23). He is presented as one who casts off religious and social convention when necessary (John 4:7–27) and as one who is even willing to override the explicit instructions of scripture in favor of forgiving others (John 8:1–11).

carefully circumscribed rules for their own lives and a good amount of control over others' lives.

It is no wonder that Paul's notion of the liberty that we have in Christ (Gal. 2:4) was so radical and upsetting to those of his day. As Segundo recognizes,

> it so destroyed the religious security of Paul's contemporaries and fellow believers that many of them preferred to return to the bondage of the law. The new "liberty" forced them to think about things for which they had previously had prefabricated answers. (1984: 337)

New creation in Christ is always risky and adventurous. We are created for creativity! The temptation is always to choose dehumanizing security and rigidity over humanizing liberty and flexibility. But while our freedom in Christ can never avoid the tremendous responsibility of learning this creativity and flexibility—while often experiencing failure in just that task—we are nonetheless secure in our knowledge that whatever happens, nothing can separate us from God's boundless love for all of us discovered in Christ (Rom. 8:38–39).

A New Community in Christ

New creation in Christ can easily be misunderstood as a purely private matter between the individual and God—the re-creation of human liberty one individual at a time, piece by human piece—and this without regard for the millions of others who are daily frustrated in their attempts to lead life without even the smallest shred of human dignity. This misunderstanding is, in part, a natural consequence of the very personal and intimate nature of Christian faith and the conversion that is required in order to live by faith. No one can make our most important decisions in life for us. But this attitude is also the destructive by-product of a rank individualism that permeates Western culture and that is quite foreign to the mindset of Jewish/Christian writers such as Paul. As Longenecker says,

> the Apostle could never envisage a Christian who could rejoice in the personal aspect of being "in Christ" without likewise accepting the corporate and social nature of that relationship. (167)

In other words, the new creation and new freedom discovered by faith in Christ takes place in and calls for a new community in Christ. The attempt to become more human individualistically actually works against our humanization and is really only another form of dehumanization.

Of course, it stands to reason that if we are created in the image of God together, and if we sin together, we are also saved together. If anything is clear in Paul's writings, it is that Christian faith is a corporate faith and that the experience of being in Christ is the experience of being "one body" and "members one of another" (Rom. 12:5). It is for that reason that some, such as Rudolf Bultmann, tend simply to equate Paul's talk about being in Christ with belonging to the Christian church (I:311). In this interpretation, Paul's use of the phrase "in Christ" does not so much refer to personal communion with Christ as it is an ecclesiological formula, another way of talking about our corporate life in the Church.

But even if we insist on retaining a personal dimension to Paul's notion of being in Christ, and even if we are unwilling to interpret that notion along with Bultmann in a wholly corporate sense, there is no denying that to be in Christ is to be constituted as a human being in a fundamentally new way toward our neighbor. New community goes with the territory of new creation. Indeed, Paul's writings are flooded with intuitions about the character of this new community in Christ.

So, for example, to be in Christ means that any and all oppressive barriers to full and universal human community are done away with. "There is," as Paul insists, "neither Jew nor Greek, there is neither slave nor [free], there is neither male nor female; for you are all one in Christ Jesus" (Gal. 3:28). Neither circumcision nor uncircumcision mean anything for those who are in Christ. On the contrary, the only thing that matters is "faith working through love" (Gal. 5:6).

This equalizing force easily becomes an abstract and vague unity of Spirit in the contemporary life of the church, whereby Christians find it possible to remain segregated from one another on the basis of skin color and ethnicity while nonetheless affirming their so-called spiritual brother- and sisterhood. Here again, sin, salvation, and the corporate life of the church are too often interpreted in terms of this empty and destructive use of the word "spiritual." So, we can talk about spiritual unity without ever having actually to practice getting along with our neighbor. We can talk about spiritual brotherhood without ever having our prejudices challenged or transformed. We can talk about being spiritually in Christ without ever having to shape our communities concretely in terms of the values and allegiances that Christ proclaimed. In reality, then, the spiritual becomes for us a kind of ideological mechanism that allows us to be holy in our own minds and yet perverse in our concrete relationships with one another. For Paul, however, being made alive in Christ means that peace is a reality between racial groups (Eph. 2:14–15) and that this means not merely a transformed understanding, but a transformed "walk" (Gal. 5:25).

A good example of the concrete way that our new creation in Christ is to be fleshed out can be found in Paul's emphasis on the special care that must be taken for weaker members in Christ's new community. This kind of care can hardly be legislated in a timeless way for every situation. That would go against Paul's fundamental theological premise of the freedom and creativity that come with being in Christ. Special care for the weak, however, is no more an abstract and ambiguous notion for Paul than it was for the early church, which, as recorded in the book of Acts, selected seven deacons to ensure that the weaker members of the community were cared for (6:1–6). For Paul, every member of the body is equally important and necessary, but to those members who are deemed "less honorable" or who appear unsightly is to be assigned a "more abundant honor" (1 Cor. 12:22–23). Paul demonstrates this attitude concretely not only in his collection for the poor (Gal. 2:10), but also in his advice with regard to brothers and sisters who have "weaker consciences" (1 Cor. 8). Paul sees no contradiction between maintaining the notion of equality and unity, on the one hand, and yet exercising preferential treatment for the weak and poor, on the other hand. Paul's gospel really does not depart from Jesus' gospel at all on this point. The gospel can be for all only if a special effort is made to include those who are pushed to the margins.

The bottom line for Paul throughout his writings is this: in Christ we find a tremendous new freedom and giftedness, a newly restored humanity. But this new creation is not to be used selfishly or without regard for those who suffer. Freedom must be used creatively and responsibly in the service of all, especially the weak. In this way, Paul lays the foundations not only for understanding Christian ministry as humanizing ministry, but for understanding the church as the sacrament of the human. The church both models and mediates the human. The church reflects image-of-God humanity not only in terms of its own internal structure and organization but also in terms of its understanding and practice of ministry in the world.

5

The Church as a Liberation Community

In Jesus of Nazareth we are confronted with the possibility of being human. We encounter this possibility as something that is more than a merely ordinary possibility for our lives, but as a gift and a demand rooted in the very character of God. The possibility of being human—of being restored in God's image as free, communal, and creative—is not just *a* possibility for our lives, but *the* possibility for our lives. We can truthfully claim Jesus to be the Christ because it is in him that we discover decisively and explicitly who God is and what we are therefore called to be and to do as human beings.

By way of describing the actual content of what it is we are called to be and to do in Jesus Christ, I have relied on several phrases, each of which is only a different way of saying the same thing: we are called to creative participation in God's liberation community; we are called to humanizing praxis; we are called to compassionate ministry; and we are called to recovery of the image of God. In this chapter, we will explore the content of this calling a bit more and thereby begin to imagine what the church might look like as a liberation community and what the ministry of the church might look like as compassionate, humanizing ministry.

The Church: Models and Metaphors

How we imagine the church has a direct bearing upon how we understand and do ministry. In a sense, the church is ministry, and our particular vision of the church can work either to enslave us or liberate us when it comes to being the church and carrying out that ministry. Perhaps that is why Jesus and his original interpreters employed such a rich variety of metaphors and models (salt, light, body, bride, temple) when speaking about the community that we have come to call "church." Of course, imaginative models have their limitations, but in bridging the gap between theory and practice they can be quite effective—either for good or for bad. Models and metaphors of the church can be effective in keeping the church turned in on itself, focused on self-preservation and self-righteousness. Models and metaphors of the church can also be effective in liberating the church from itself and for God and the world. In the first case, the church becomes another effective instrument in the arsenal of dehumanizing forces in the world; indeed, it baptizes that arsenal and provides it a sacred cloak. In the second case, the church becomes a sacrament of the human: a model and agent of the recovery of the image of God.

Consider, for example, some common but rather inadequate metaphors and models of the church. It is sometimes said that the church is like a great ship. The captain is Jesus, the wind is the Holy Spirit, and the rudder that guides the ship and keeps it on course is the Bible. The church offers us a safe passage across the stormy seas of life and delivers us safely to our final destiny: heaven. There may, indeed, be some merit to such a metaphor, but there are undoubtedly some severe limitations. In the first place, there are no passengers in the church of Jesus Christ. We must ask whether or not the ship metaphor perpetuates a misunderstanding in this regard, encouraging a model of ministry that makes dormant passengers out of most of us. In the second place, the ship metaphor fortifies a disastrous tendency always present in the church: identifying itself with the wood, concrete, and steel that keeps the church afloat. The church is challenged in every age to resist believing that its own existence or ministry is somehow finally dependent on the quality of the brick and mortar that serve as its vehicle.

Another metaphor for the church is *army*. Instead of Uncle Sam, it's Jesus who wants you! The advantages of this metaphor are obvious. The church must be aggressive, well trained, and on the move. There is a sense in which the church is, indeed, engaged in battle. But here again there are critical limitations. For one thing, the mission and methods of the church are vastly different from the mission and methods of an army. The church does not seek to conquer or destroy, but to transform and redeem. The church, while most definitely engaged in a power struggle, does not struggle for a kind of power that puts us one up on others, but instead relies upon a new and creative power that humanizes and restores others. The church seeks to persuade by giving itself rather than by overpowering and dominating others. A second and even more unfortunate consequence of the army metaphor is the model of leadership presupposed by its top-down chain of command. According to Christ, leadership begins at the bottom; the greatest is the one who is the servant. A church that takes seriously its call to challenge rather than mimic the world's hierarchical patterns of domination and subordination may very well find it difficult if not impossible to imagine itself consistently as an army.

There are a variety of other metaphors that Christians have relied upon to help them envision the mission and purpose of the church. Many of these metaphors are only implicit in the life and theology of the church. We won't find anyone defending them, but these implicit metaphors represent powerful images by which the church understands itself and carries out its ministry. For example, the church is often imagined and even functions as a kind of *drama*. On one particular day of the week an audience comes together and passively observes a handful of actors on a stage performing. This is called going to church. As another example, the church is imagined, even if only unconsciously, as a building. And while nowhere in the New Testament does the word "church" ever refer to a physical location, our everyday language suggests that the metaphor of church-as-building is deeply ingrained in our thinking. So, for instance, we ask, "Where did you go to church yesterday?"

Often the church seems like a business. The gospel is a product to be sold and bought into, and so the church concentrates its efforts on elaborate methods of marketing its product and training its sales people. Incarnational Christianity is replaced by tactical and gimmicky Christianity. The most damaging effects of this metaphor manifest themselves when churches actually begin to compete with one another, selling themselves and their programs as if they were little more than competing brands of green beans in the neighborhood supermarket.

At other times, the church conceives of itself as something like an amusement park. The idea is to be bigger, better, and more fun than the next church, so that we can attract people. It is difficult to overstate the power of the concept of attraction in the current theology and ministry of the church. The insidious preoccupation of the contemporary church with comfortable and beautiful facilities for the purpose of attracting the community (read wealthy) is genuine proof of this. In other words, Christian churches today are all too often more preoccupied with getting people from the community in than they are with getting themselves out into the community.

Finally, the church is sometimes imagined along the lines of a hospital. The church is, after all, a place where healing can happen. The major problem with this image, however, is that in a hospital there is one group of people (an elite minority) who are doctors and another group of people (the vast majority) who are patients. But in the church of Jesus Christ, we are all both; there can be no neat distinction between active and passive ministers, between those who are the ministers and those who are the ministered to. We are all to be, in Henri Nouwen's phrase, "wounded healers."

As weak as most of these metaphors are in imagining the church, there are, of course, some very strong and positive biblical metaphors with useful implications for Christian ministry. In the first place, the community that we call church is, as Jesus says, like salt. Just as salt heals and preserves even as it stings and burns, so also the church is to be an agent of social revolution and liberation while being, at the same time, an instrument of reconciliation and peace. The image of salt is also appropriate for understanding the church as a change agent (seasoning) in the whole of that to which it is added. Once salt has been added to food, we can't separate it from the other ingredients the way we pick mushrooms off a pizza if we don't like them. So also, the church, while distinguishable from the world, must never separate itself from the world. Even though the Greek word for church, *ekklesia*, means "the called out," that calling refers to the church's distinctive mission, values, and function in the world, but never to some segregated sphere of existence. The church always faces the challenge to distinguish itself from the world without thereby separating itself from the world.

A second metaphor that Jesus uses to describe his followers is the metaphor of light. As we increasingly discover the way the metaphors of light and darkness perpetuate racist attitudes both consciously and unconsciously (light = good, dark = bad) in religion and culture, we must approach this metaphor with some caution today. Nonetheless, the community of people who are constituted by Christ's proclamation of the kingdom of God and the conversion demanded by it is a community that sheds light on (in other words, makes explicit) who God is and who we therefore ought to be. The church shoulders the same praxis of illumination carried out by Jesus of Nazareth, "the true light which, coming into the world, enlightens every [one]" (John 1:9).

Perhaps the most helpful and intentional of the New Testament metaphors for church is the body metaphor used by the apostle Paul. For Paul, a number of implications follow from the notion that the community of Jesus' followers is like a body. As with the physical body, every member of the church has an essential function and is gifted for the effective performance of that function. Individual members of the church, as with individual members of the body, must recognize their limits and defer to other gifted members for some roles. When one member gains honor, honor is gained for all. When one member suffers, all are involved in the suffering. And, of course, as Paul insists, special care must be taken for weaker members. We search in vain to find a more adequate metaphor to portray the church as a community.

Paul also uses the metaphor of *household* to describe the church. This image was especially appropriate to Paul's own culture, made up as it was of numerous extended family units that served as the basis for the house church network of early Christianity. Another metaphor, this time employed by the apostle Peter, is that of a priesthood (1 Peter 2:5,9). For Peter, the followers of Jesus are a chosen people comprising a kind of transnational nation. These chosen people, like a priesthood, represent the needs of the world to God and, at the same time, mediate God's salvation to the world. The Protestant stress on a priesthood of believers finds its roots in this metaphor, though, as Robert Banks observes,

> Protestants have tended to spiritualize and individualize it, conceiving each believer as his or her own priest to another believer rather than focusing on the corporate calling of the body of believers vis-à-vis the world around them. (27)

The origins and history of Christianity, then, are packed with images, metaphors, and models of how the church and its ministry might be imagined. Often these imaginative models have paved the way for revolutions not only in the church's collective conscience, but in the practical and institutional realities that give expression to that conscience. What is required today is just such a model of the church and of Christian ministry—a model which attempts to incorporate the truth of the various New Testament metaphors, but that is also responsive to the unique crises of freedom, community, and creativity in which contemporary human beings find themselves.

In our present context, I propose that the church is best understood as a liberation community. On the one hand, the church is a liberation *community* —a body of individuals who understand themselves as on the way to becoming more fully human as they are restored in the image of a compassionate God. On the other hand, the church is a *liberation* community—a body of Christians who have likewise banded themselves together in the service of compassionate, humanizing praxis in the world. In this body there is no authentic liberation without community, just as there is no authentic community without liberation. Furthermore, both liberation and community describe not only the internal structure and dynamics of the life of the church, but also its outward mission, purpose, and relationship to the world. While the church is distinct from all other humanizing and liberating activity in the world, it is not, for that reason, the exclusive path of becoming human. The church is instead a sacrament of the human to the world. In other words, what is always and everywhere present in the world—namely, the possibility of being human through God's transforming grace—is re-presented visibly and effectively in the church and its twin ministries of liberation and community.

The Experience and Ministry of Liberation

The word "liberation" has been used in recent years by theologians, terrorists, and even a President of the United States to describe his intentions in sending troops into war.[1] Liberation essentially means freedom, but the two words are hardly synonymous. We might, for example, speak of a soft drink as sugar-*free* but we would probably not speak of it as sugar-*liberated*! Liberation is best understood as a freedom from some injustice or captivity. It usually includes dimensions of a power struggle. Liberation is freedom from oppression.

Defining liberation as freedom from oppression, of course, requires that we clarify what we mean by the word "oppression." I remember feeling as though I was oppressed recently when the largest man in the state of Texas sat next to me in an airplane, but that is not exactly what oppression means. Oppression is perhaps best understood as any power or force that prevents a person from becoming fully human and thus fully reflective of the image of God. Forces of oppression are precisely forces that rob human dignity because they rob human freedom, human community, and human creativity. To oppress others is to dehumanize them.

The problem with such a broad definition of oppression, however, is that it applies to virtually everyone. That may not seem like a problem at first. After all, we are all oppressed in some sense, aren't we? We may concede that there is a sense in which we are all oppressed (Paul himself treats sin as a dehumanizing force in every human life). The consequence of this flattening out of the definition of oppression, however, is that we mask the vast difference between the kind of oppression that results from dehumanizing others (being involved in, responsible for, or benefiting from the oppression of others), on the one hand, and the kind of oppression that results from being dehumanized by others, on the other hand.

So, for example, there is an immeasurable difference between the oppression of an impoverished Filipino prostitute, sold daily by her pimp to satisfy the U.S. military personnel that for years have occupied her island, and the oppression experienced by a white, teenage daughter of a Xerox executive in Pasadena, California, whose main concern is whether her credit card is dangerously close to its limit as she stands in line waiting to purchase some new blue jeans—blue jeans produced at slave wages and imported from the Philippine Islands.

Dehumanization, as Paulo Freire admits, "marks not only those whose humanity has been stolen, but also (though in a different way) those who have stolen it" (28). And yet the failure to understand the relationship between the oppressor and the oppressed, between the victimizer and the victim, is a tragic mistake that disguises oppression even as it perpetuates it. The rapist may be experiencing an intense social and psychological oppression that drives him to commit his monstrous crimes. But do we really want to say that his hurt is no different from the hurt of his raped victim? The failure to understand the rela-

---

1. George Bush: "The liberation of Kuwait has begun!"

tionship between oppressor and oppressed provides an excuse and source of solace for the oppressor. The oppressor hides behind the statement, "We are all oppressed," employing it (even if only unconsciously) to mask, perpetuate, and excuse oppression. To refer to everyone without qualification as the "oppressed" or "the poor," as Gustavo Gutiérrez says, "is to play with words—and with people" (1973: 290).

The church is the community of those who understand themselves as in the process of being restored in the image of God and who have united themselves against the forces of oppression in the world, including their own complicity in those forces. The ministry of the church, therefore, embraces not only its own process of being liberated (and, so, a consistently self-critical attitude), but its participation in the liberation of others. This ministry is compassionate ministry because, as a particular praxis, it is the authentic response to the character and activity of a compassionate God—a God who enters into solidarity with those who suffer, graciously takes sides on their behalf, and brings about a new creation in both the victim and the victimizer.

I would suggest three levels at which the compassionate church must respond to situations of oppression and suffering in our world with the experience and ministry of liberation. The three levels interlock and overlap with one another. Furthermore, they represent the holistic character and mission of the church only when they are interfaced with the experience and ministry of community to be explored later in this chapter. The three levels of the ministry of liberation are charity, empowerment, and justice.

Charity

At its most basic level, liberation is an act of charity. It is freely opening our hands to the poor and the hurting even though they "will never cease to be in the land" (Deut. 15:11). It is food, clothing, shelter, medicine, and financial support. It is, as James implies, observing "a brother or sister without clothing and in need of daily food" and coming to his or her assistance (1:14ff). It is, as in the parable of the good Samaritan, showing compassion on the beaten man, bandaging up his wounds, and taking care of him (Luke 10:30–35).

Of course, charity as a response to human need is not simply identical with authentic Christian compassion. Charity can be a cheap, painless, and even condescending substitute for liberating involvement with those who suffer. Just because the Rotary Club shows up once a year at Thanksgiving to feed the hungry or just because I write a check every month to support a relief organization does not mean that either they or I have demonstrated genuine compassion, even though we have probably exhibited some form of charity. This kind of charity is often little more than an attempt to relieve our feelings of guilt, establish credit for ourselves in the wider community, or make us feel good because of our kindness and decency toward our fellow human being.

But simply because charity can be distorted does not mean that it should be rejected altogether. Charity really can be an avenue toward the restoration of the image of God—in both the giver and the receiver of charity. Given the context in which we find ourselves today, where increasing numbers of people lack even the bare minimums for living life humanly—much less leading it with dignity—charity is an essential first step toward eliminating poverty and oppression. But not all forms of charity are equally compassionate. Taking our cue from the compassion that is the character of the God discovered in Jesus, we can identify compassionate charity as resident, committed, and creative.

Resident Charity

Just as God is a God of solidarity with victims, so authentic charity can never be an alien charity—a charity that is insulated and isolated from human suffering and that drops in from the outside. Compassionate ministry does indeed begin with charity, but it is a charity born of patient listening, genuine vulnerability, and a dependable presence with victims. Only in this way can the charity offered be an appropriate response to the need it confronts. And only in this way is there the possibility (though never the guarantee) that we will avoid attitudes of condescension and feelings of superiority in our charity.

Adopting a resident rather than an alien charity is more easily talked about than done. It means that those who take seriously the call to compassionate ministry must constantly ask themselves how their own lifestyle either augments or diminishes their ability to identify with those who are hurting. This self-critical reflection is difficult in the first place because it is much easier to throw stones at others than to keep focused on our own lifestyles. We are easily tempted to point out the inconsistencies in our neighbor's lifestyle rather than in our own. It is difficult in the second place because legalism is always lurking around the corner, ready to turn the life and joy of compassion into a rotting corpse lying in state for public display. Just because resident charity takes one form in my life does not mean that it will take the same form in your life. It is difficult in the third place because it often seems virtually impossible to identify fully with some kinds of hurt and suffering. How, for example, does a white male identify with the racism experienced by an African-American female in the United States? How do those of us who do not have AIDS identify with the death sentence experienced by those who do?

Here, as much as at any other point, resident charity requires the ability not only to be present, but to listen. The extent to which an individual can actually become vulnerable will vary from situation to situation. But although it is all too easy to be present without listening, it is impossible to listen without being present.

Charity That Takes Sides

If God is a God who takes sides with the victim and against the victimizer, authentic charity can never be a neutral charity. Oppression is the result of forces and powers that dehumanize. The practice of compassionate charity prods us to look beyond the mere symptoms of poverty and suffering to their root causes in unjust social structures and to the way the suffering and poverty of the many interlocks with the comfort and privilege of the few. Just because the Pharaoh gives Christmas baskets to the children of Israel each year makes it no less difficult for them to make bricks without straw.

Again, we find ourselves forced back to the priority of commitment in compassionate ministry, and here I mean the kind of commitment that entails a specifically political commitment. Compassionate charity entails political commitment because oppression has to do with power, and politics—like it or not—is the realm where balances of power are fought and decided. It is in this sense of the word that Jesus himself can be understood to have had an explicitly political significance for his original witnesses. In their understanding, there was no separating good news for the poor from bad news for the rich, both of which were incorporated into Jesus' gospel of the kingdom. From the perspective of his followers, Jesus' compassion for and preferential treatment of the socially ostracized made political enemies of those with vested interests in keeping social structures just the way they were (interestingly enough, the religious establishment).

Thus, it was not Karl Marx who first discovered the reality of class conflict, nor is taking sides with the poor and the suffering in order to participate in their liberation a modern invention. From Christ's birth in a cow shed to his execution, naked and suffering, on a cross, Jesus is portrayed in the gospels as one who took sides with the outcast. So also, the early church portrayed itself as (Acts 4:32–35), and continually challenged itself to be (James 2:15–16), imitators of this commitment—not only in terms of outward ministry (the poor as preferential recipients of charity, cf. Gal. 2:10), but also and especially in terms of the very internal makeup, organization, structure, and worship of the church itself (Acts 6:1–7, James 2:1–9).

How this kind of committed charity can supersede and replace an allegedly neutral charity in terms of concrete compassionate ministry requires creativity rather than legislation. But it most definitely stands opposed to all forms of charity that simply bestow food, clothing, shelter, or money on the poor without taking sides politically against policies that oppress and enslave them in cycles of dependency, or that withhold from them desperately needed relief, empowerment, justice, and opportunity. James Cone, writing about the white person who is happy to provide charity to black people but who is uninterested in taking sides in the war against racism, says:

But he is still white to the very core of his being. What he fails to realize is that there is no place for him in this war of survival. Blacks do not want his patronizing, condescending words of sympathy. They do not need his concern, his "love," his money. It is that which dehumanizes; it is that which enslaves. (1969: 27–28)

Here we see a hint of another real danger that is hidden in charity. Bestowers of a neutral, alien charity actually require unjust social arrangements to perpetuate their charity. Charity can become addictive and can actually serve as a tool of control over suffering people—a means of keeping them dependent on the good will of the righteous in society. Committed charity, on the contrary, begins with a critical self-examination and a lifelong suspicion about the social, political, and economic arrangements between the givers and the receivers of charity —a suspicion that simply because the givers of charity have chosen to be generous, they have not thereby ceased to serve in Pharaoh's court altogether. Authentic charity drives toward empowerment and justice. As Paulo Freire puts it,

True generosity consists precisely in fighting to destroy the causes which nourish false charity. False charity constrains the fearful and subdued, the "rejects of life," to extend their trembling hands. True generosity lies in striving so that these hands—whether of individuals or entire peoples— need be extended less and less in supplication, so that more and more they become human hands which work and, working, transform the world. (29)

Creative Charity

Just as God is a God of surprise and novelty, so authentic charity can never be a rigid or prefabricated charity—a pile of precalculated social programs created in a university laboratory or a denominational headquarters office and subsequently distributed among the poor and the marginalized. "Just add water!" Creative charity means finding innovative and fresh ways to treat the hungry, the elderly, the alienated, the diseased, and the marginalized as human beings on a daily basis.

Creative charity is especially difficult for churches who decide to get on the compassionate ministry bandwagon and so throw compassionate ministry into the ecclesiastical mix as an interesting side show. Too often, there is little vision, commitment, solidarity, vulnerability, theology, or imagination involved in such endeavors—just more stale food pantries and tattered clothing closets that end up perpetuating attitudes of dependence on the part of the receivers of charity, and attitudes of superiority on the part of the givers of charity. What is missing is compassionate creativity.

In essence, there can be no specific model or models of compassionate ministry to be imitated or repeated from one context to the next. Churches, denominations, and other organizations that pursue compassionate ministry from the top down typically end up making compassionate ministry comprehensively condescending. What is really needed for an authentic compassionate ministry is a vulnerable and listening presence, a holistic spirituality, a faithful and credible theology, and a wild imagination! In the end, not even charitable donations make the ultimate difference. A single act of creative solidarity with victims is worth a thousand dollars flown in from the outside.

It's easy to offer theological critiques of denominations and ecclesiastical structures. In many ways, they're slow-moving targets. On a strictly personal level, however, creative charity is difficult even for those individuals who have devoted their whole lives to compassionate ministry. Having understood and responded to Christ's call to compassion, the practice of living among and siding with those who suffer remains far easier than the continual opening up of ourselves to newness and creativity in our ministry programs and plans. With each new face, we already know the story we will hear once again. The phone call at night will mean another shooting, another break-in, another person in jail needing bail money. It's easy to become hardened and anesthetized. The pressure to distribute basic services such as food, housing, or medical care to increasing numbers of people translates effortlessly into mass programs of prepackaged, impersonal charity. And charity, like any other human activity is an easy target for manipulation and automation.

The dynamics of suffering, poverty, and oppression in our world are such that new, creative solutions must always be imagined and implemented. A holistic spirituality of compassionate ministry can undoubtedly help in this regard. It is precisely the dualism between the spiritual and the material that often keeps our creative impulses so far removed from the practical realities in which they are meant to be immersed. This dualism is more than just the distance between our right brain and our left brain, between the pragmatic and the imaginative. It comes down to a gap in our theology. If, in our theology and imagination, the physical can be neatly distinguished from the spiritual, with the former having incomparably less worth than the latter, there is really no way that something like creative charity can ever result. Rigid patterns of charity will only breed attitudes of insensitivity and callousness on the part of the giver of charity, and feelings of dependency, hostility, and indignity on the part of the receiver of charity. As our practical ministry structures become animated by imagination and vision, however, they are transformed into something fresh, alive, and dynamic. As the children of Israel discovered, allegiance to God is more like an outrageous roller coaster than a lifeless museum tour. Charity is genuinely liberating and compassionate only when it is allowed to reflect God's novelty and dependable creativity moment by moment.

Empowerment

While compassionate ministry within a liberation community begins with charity, the bulk and core of its energy must be directed toward the empowerment of people who are trampled on and forgotten, so that they may determine their own destiny and forge their own future. Thus, there is a good measure of truth in the axiom that "what poor people need is not more money but more power." Of course, in our world, money is power. The point, however, is that true economic power is more than simply having money flow through our hands. Empowerment at every level requires a degree of ownership, a voice, and an ability to direct our life-projects with dignity.

While charity aims at providing many of the basic physiological necessities for living a human life at all, empowerment aims at enabling others to lead a human life with dignity. Empowerment is concerned that individuals be energized to break out of cycles of dependency and helplessness and to move toward self-determination and responsibility. Without the dimension of empowerment in compassionate ministry, charity becomes little more than a band-aid and can even serve as a force in the further entrenchment of poverty and dependency.

Power, of course, can be downright frightening, especially when too much of it is in the hands of those who use it selfishly or ignorantly. In the words of Lord Acton, "Power tends to corrupt and absolute power corrupts absolutely." Yet it is impossible to live our lives at all without power. Power is just as present in the use of a bulldozer as it is in a personal decision. Indeed, a decision can be ultimately more powerful than a bulldozer, since it determines where and when the bulldozer is used in the first place. As Reinhold Niebuhr suggests, we only need to compare the relative importance of priest and soldier throughout history to appreciate this fact (1943:II:20).

Power operates on a number of different levels and should never be simply equated with sheer force or compulsion, however much the latter may be appropriate in using power. So, for example, when we talk about power politics, as Paul Tillich points out, we aren't talking about a type of politics that is unique in that it involves the use of power. All politics requires power, just as does all religious activity, all education, all business, all sexuality. What we really mean when we use the term "power politics" is a form of politics that is characterized by a distorted and manipulative use of power (1954:8).

It is essential to recognize that the role of power in human living is all-pervasive and multidimensional. The church may at times find itself believing that concern for the shape of power relations as well as the proper use and distribution of power are matters which lie outside of its own proper sphere of interest, duty, or influence. The church may even become deluded as to its own use of power, regarding itself as somehow operating on a level that is a step removed from the dirty world of power. Nothing could be further from the truth. If the ability to live requires power, then the ability to lead life humanly—to be restored in the image of God—requires power all the more.

So, to take only one example, if recovery of the image of God in our lives includes the recovery of authentic community both with God and with our neighbor, and if the church's primary function and mission in the world is to be a sacramental agent of this recovery to the world, then the church must necessarily thrust itself into the business of shaping how power is exercised in community. Power is meaningless and empty apart from its relationship to other powers. In fact, it is only insofar as one bearer of power encounters another bearer of power that power becomes real at all (Tillich 1954, 41).

But if the church as a liberation community lifts its voice and mobilizes its resources in the arena of power, this must never be for its own selfish aggrandizement in society. With regard to power, the church is not so much interested in getting more for itself. It is interested, first, in using power to insure that human beings have the basic necessities for survival. It is interested, second, in the empowerment of the powerless. It is interested, third, in just power relations that will safeguard the free, creative, and responsible expression of power. To the extent that the ministries of charity, empowerment, and justice all involve the acquisition, distribution, and expression of power, these ministries are not for the church's well-being or perpetuation. The church exists as sacramental agent rather than exclusive guarantor in the process of humanization that Christians call salvation.

Empowerment as Development

At a basic level, the church may use its voice and energies to provide a variety of developmental ministries. These ministries can serve to empower individuals and communities by providing them the resources and tools to take control of their own destinies and to break out of brutal cycles of dependency and depreciation. Some of these ministries take the form of educational and literacy programs, job creation, job-skills training, job placement, homeownership creation, cooperative farming, economic development, and even community gardening. Whatever the services being provided, however, development ministries typically attempt to empower by fostering responsibility in the lives and neighborhoods of those to whom they are directed. The church's ministry of empowerment attempts to train and educate individuals while providing them opportunities they might not otherwise have.

There is simply not enough space here to detail specific blueprints or delivery systems for such development ministries. For one thing, development in one community will probably be considerably different from development in another community. So much depends on the context, needs, population, and resources available in a particular community. During the Savings and Loan bailout of the late 1980s, for example, my own community in inner-city Fort Worth, Texas, was able to acquire over one hundred houses by donation over a three-year time span. We then went to work funding the rehabilitation and sale of those houses at little or no interest to low-income families. The homeownership program continues to be successful in redeveloping an impoverished neighborhood as well as bringing pride and responsibility to individual new homeowners. But ask me how to do the same thing in southern California, where the least expensive piece of property could well buy one whole block full of houses in Fort Worth, and I'll probably look at you with a blank stare on my face. The precise form that development ministry takes must be community-specific.

One feature of development that is not community-specific is the danger of paternalism and colonialism that comes with it just as with charity. Even though development intends to serve as more than a band-aid on human problems, it can easily become an alien, uncommitted, and rigid form of social control that perpetuates injustice and dehumanization among the poor. For some time now, third-world theologians have been especially critical of first-world development efforts in their countries and communities. These efforts, by typically failing to attack the root problems of social injustice, inequality, and top-down decision making often simply leave poor communities even further dependent on the wealthy.

"Development," after all, is an ambiguous word. Think, for example, of a beautiful park with large shade trees and a stream flowing through it. Now imagine a suburban housing development taking it over, filling in the stream, cutting down the trees, and building hundreds of look-alike condominiums packed into every square foot. Is this really development? By whose definition? What is the goal of development? When it comes to poor people and their communities, if development means simply acquiring skills apart from the more fundamental issues of freedom, justice, and creative self-determination, we have truncated, if not falsified altogether, the integral human liberation intended for us by God and witnessed to throughout scripture. God did not send Moses to develop the Israelites into more educated and highly skilled workers for the Pharaoh. Development means little apart from an overarching context of human liberation.

Soul Power

While compassionate empowerment will undoubtedly include efforts to provide the dispossessed with the material power to make their own way in life—job skills, literacy, employment, a diploma—it must nonetheless also include a deeper empowerment of the mind and spirit—an empowerment of the soul! In using the word "soul" here, I do not have in mind the soul of Greek philosophy—an enduring, immortal substance that is imprisoned within the body during its relatively short stay on earth and is freed from its physical captivity at death. In this view, the soul is a fundamentally distinct and, in principle, separable component of the human person—a nonphysical essence inside every human body. And though I am well aware that the mainstream of the Christian tradition has operated with this kind of dualism between body and soul, there is nonetheless an alternative view of soul that is typically Hebrew rather than Greek and considerably more characteristic of the biblical witness as a whole. In this view, my soul is the totality of who I am at any and every moment—my body, mind, spirit, life, relationships, will, and heart taken together in their entirety—in other words, my self. "Soul power," understood from within this holistic vision of the self, is an empowerment of persons at the depths of their existence—at the center and core of who they really are.

It is often difficult to recognize just how deeply embedded are slavery, alienation, and paralysis in those who are oppressed by society's imbalances and injustices (and, it may also be added, though in a different sense, in those who benefit from those imbalances and injustices). Thus, there is an internalized oppression—a consciousness or attitude that perpetuates or recycles oppression from within. This internalized oppression, as feminist theologian Sharon Welch describes it,

> is being shaped by the values of the oppressor. It leads oppressed people to see themselves as they are seen by the oppressor—as less intelligent, less moral, less valuable. It leads oppressed people to act like oppressors even in our work for social change, instituting our own hierarchies, using power over each other. (177)

Paulo Freire describes this phenomenon as "the fear of freedom" which leads the oppressed to internalize the oppressor and adopt the oppressor's values and guidelines for behavior (31).

Oppression at this level is deep-seated and pervasive, the consequence of long histories of subjugation and humiliation reinforced daily in cultural and religious institutions, language usage, economic and political policies, educational practices, and cultural norms. Internalized oppression is more than just a mental problem that more information could somehow fix. And it is more than a religious problem that converting oppressed peoples to Christianity could instantly correct. What is needed is a spiritual revolution that is not merely superficial or partial, but is a life-long process of renewal and transformation that takes place at the core of our being, and that includes literally every aspect of our existence. What is needed is a revolution of the soul.

In attempting to understand this revolution of the soul and to imagine a way in which the church as a liberation community can participate in the ministry of spiritual empowerment, I would like to draw on two somewhat diverse sources—the method of conscientizing, or consciousness raising, of Brazilian educator Paulo Freire on the one hand, and the emphasis on empowerment by the Holy Spirit of the American holiness movement in the late nineteenth and early twentieth centuries, on the other hand. Both sources, I believe, contribute something important to the development of a truly human and, at the same time, spiritual empowerment.

Freire's famous book, *Pedagogy of the Oppressed*, has become something of a handbook for theological reflection in third-world countries and for the development of the base community churches that have exploded onto the scene by the tens of thousands in those same countries. These relatively new "base community" churches are small grass-roots communities of Christians who meet together regularly for worship and bible study, for reflection together on daily life, work, and politics, and for organizing themselves to resist oppression and to struggle for justice.

Freire's method of literacy training among the poor is unique in several respects, not the least of which is its emphasis on dialogue rather than the depositing of data when it comes to education. The primary aim of this method, however, lies in its encouragement of learners to analyze their situation and to move toward action and transformation. Because it not only teaches the poor how to read, but challenges them to grasp their own condition and to do something about it, Freire's method is controversial and has been perceived as subversive in many world areas. Freire himself calls this process of empowerment *conscientização* (in Portuguese), or "conscientization." We can, perhaps, speak of it simply as consciousness raising.

The purpose of consciousness raising is to assist the oppressed in understanding objective reality and themselves as subjects of that reality. If concrete forms of oppression really do have a way of distorting the consciousness, values, and attitudes of the oppressed, then it should not be surprising that the oppressed share with the oppressor a particular view of reality as the way things are and as the way things must be. A first step in transforming a situation of oppression is in coming to see it for what it really is and in understanding one's own potential role in making things different. For the one who ministers with the oppressed, this requires entering into a genuine dialogue— that is, respecting each other's right to name the world. There can be no dialogue where one party wants to dominate others with its own brand of naming, whether that is wealthy naming, white naming, academic naming, or even Christian naming. The poor are not objects. And as important as it is for the oppressor to cease treating them as objects, liberation can only begin when the oppressed themselves understand that they are not objects and that their reality is not fixed, necessary, or unchangeable. Things can be different.

In Freire's mind, the one who is sincerely interested in working with the oppressed to achieve their liberation and empowerment must start by attempting to understand the objective situation of the oppressed as well as the latter's awareness of that situation. This kind of understanding requires more than a few casual conversations—it probably takes months and maybe even years. It includes, first, a rigorous investigation of "limit-situations" in which the oppressed find themselves and which function as seemingly insurmountable barriers to their liberation. It is in these limit-situations where liberation can begin. In the North American context, an example of a limit-situation might be the distressing lack of job skills that increasingly characterizes what can only be called an underclass in our society. This lack of even the most basic skills essentially locks out the poor from anything other than the most menial and dehumanizing work.

Consciousness raising takes place as the oppressed are challenged to think about themselves and their situations in more than the simplest and most provincial terms. Liberating education, according to Freire, should not be envisioned as banking—in other words, as the depositing of information into other people's heads. Rather, it is constituted by posing problems to customary interpretations of life. In ministering with the oppressed, one must never discard their interpretations of reality as being mistaken or infantile. Their interpretations must nonetheless be challenged and subjected to critical reflection. According to Freire, one way of carrying out this critical reflection includes asking who it is that benefits from certain limit-situations and who, on the other hand, is being "negated and curbed by them" (92), thereby exposing the situation of oppression for what it is. So also, by posing problems to customary interpretations of reality, critical reflection attempts to make the oppressed aware of the oppressor housed within themselves.

Critical reflection is not the end but only the beginning of the process of consciousness raising for Freire. Critical reflection goes hand in hand with action to yield praxis—"reflection and action upon the world in order to transform it" (28). For Freire, action and reflection occur simultaneously; indeed, Freire even allows that critical reflection is action. What Freire wants to avoid, however, is any dichotomy whereby "praxis could be divided into a prior stage of reflection and a subsequent stage of action" (123). But liberating action will never take place until the oppressed are able to get a handle on the limit-situations they face. Then they can move toward their own liberation. And make no mistake, the oppressed must themselves move toward liberation—as subjects, not objects. No one can liberate another person. A minister can, however, play a crucial role in the empowerment of others through consciousness raising.

Now admittedly this whole process of consciousness raising sounds a bit far removed from the experience of spiritual empowerment with which some of us from more traditional Christian backgrounds grew up. For one thing, Freire's method was born in Brazil, in a context characterized by poverty on a massive scale, where hundreds of thousands of children were not in school and adult illiteracy was figured at rates as high as 60 to 70 percent. But simply because Freire does not use familiar religious jargon does not mean that the liberation he envisions is somehow less spiritual than that of traditional Christianity in North America. In fact, in dealing with oppression by going to the very core of our existence—our minds, consciousness, values, perceptions of reality—we might ask whether Freire has not perhaps come closer to what Christians ought to mean by soul power. (Many traditional and explicitly religious interpretations typically focus on obtaining a particular sacred experience regardless of the concrete socio-economic factors that characterize the human predicament.) If the spiritual renewal and vigor expressed in the rapid growth and proliferation of base community churches in Latin America[2] is any indication of the relevance of Freire's method to a Christian ministry of liberation, we have some grounds for concluding that authentic Christian empowerment can perhaps only be truly spiritual when it is first human and earthy.

Yet perhaps Christians do want to say more about the ministry of spiritual empowerment than we discover in Freire's method of consciousness raising taken simply on its own terms. Freire, himself a Christian, would undoubtedly claim that his contribution is not meant to be a theology of ministry, however well it may serve toward that end. But what is the "more" that we want to say?

It is here that I find the contribution of the holiness tradition in which I was raised to be important and even complementary to Freire's work in helping us to frame a holistic approach to spiritual empowerment. It is not coincidental that, for all practical purposes, empowerment has been taken as synonymous with being spirit-filled in the holiness tradition. Indeed, the hinge that often connects the two is the scripture, "you shall receive power when the Holy Spirit has come upon you" (Acts 1:8). But though I am thankful for my tradition, it is rather tragic that it has tended to interpret this empowerment either in a strictly religious-cultic sense that has mostly to do with appropriate demonstrations of fervor in public worship, or in a rigidly private-moral sense typified by such practices as, for example, avoidance of the motion-picture theater. Sitting through endless sermons, bible studies, and summer camps while growing up, I never remember empowerment by the spirit having spillover implications for such worldly concerns as racism, the plight of the poor, urban decay, or the war in Vietnam.

---

2. It is estimated that there are as many as 80,000 base communities in Brazil alone (Hebblethwaite: 37).

As I began to study the roots of the holiness tradition, however, I discovered that the link between being spirit-filled and being empowered had not always been forged in the suspiciously sanitary way with which I had grown up. The insulated and sterile version of spiritual empowerment I inherited was in many respects the consequence of plucking the flower of holiness from its social roots among the poor and dispossessed of society and transplanting it into a middle-class, suburban environment where all roads lead to the mall. I discovered that for female (it would not be an exaggeration to call them feminist) holiness preachers of the late nineteenth and early twentieth centuries, being spirit-filled meant being empowered to overcome gender stereotypes and sexist limitations placed on them both by the church and by society. It is sometimes shocking to read their radical (even by today's standards) testimonies and autobiographies that bear witness to this understanding. I also discovered that many other prominent spirit-filled Christians during this same period understood spiritual empowerment to mean participation in acts of civil disobedience, organized rebellions, and activist crusades for radical social and political reform.

I learned that spiritual empowerment for these "holy rollers" meant participation in renewal activities for burned-out districts in the inner city and in antislavery activities such as the underground railroad.[3] The founder of my own denomination—a denomination which came into existence during this same period—had his own way of interpreting empowerment by the Holy Spirit within his original vision for the fledgling church:

We want places so plain that every board will say welcome to the poorest. We can get along without rich people, but not without preaching the gospel to the poor. We do not covet the fine churches of our neighbors; we only long after a richer anointing with the Holy Ghost, that we may be committed to reach the poor and the outcast, for whom some care so little but for whom our Redeemer lived and died. Let the Church of the Nazarene be true to its commission; not great and elegant buildings; but to feed the hungry and clothe the naked, and wipe away the tears of the sorrowing; and gather jewels for His diadem.[4]

Now returning to the book of Acts in the wake of my new discoveries, I began to see the story of the early church's spiritual empowerment in a new light, as the story of, among other things, the church's struggle against racism. The social and political dimensions of the story had always been there, but I had been conditioned to see only the private and religious dimensions of the

---

3. One of the best sources for exploring this legacy is Donald W. Dayton's *Discovering an Evangelical Heritage* (New York: Harper & Row, 1976).

4. Phineas F. Bresee, in a 1899 editorial in *The Nazarene Messenger*.

story. As I began to read the book of Acts again, it seemed that at almost every juncture where the Holy Spirit showed up, the church was being empowered to cross some new political or racial line that had been drawn either by religion or society. It seemed more and more that power, in the book of Acts, was a power for authentic Christian community and not merely a private power for individual piety. Even the central event of Pentecost itself ceased to look like just a big camp meeting and instead resembled something more like a social and economic revolution. For these first Christians, empowerment by God's Spirit even led them to sell their property and possessions in order to share the proceeds with the poor. They had experienced the fullness of the Spirit, and they came to the conclusion that they should also live in that fullness and share it with others. They came to the conclusion that the meaning of Pentecost, in Jürgen Moltmann's words, is that "there is enough for everyone."

> This is what the experience of the Spirit of fellowship means. . . . In him the divisions between people and our enmity towards one another are overcome. The oppression of people by other people stops. The humiliation of people by other people comes to an end. The estrangement of one person from another is swept away. Masters and servants become brothers. Men and women become friends. Privileges and discriminations disappear from human society. We become "of one heart and soul." (130)

In other words, spiritual empowerment is a transformation of one's entire being (one's soul), with tremendous significance for both our private and our social existence, for both our worship and our economics. It is an empowerment that yields a sharing community, and because this sharing community is a spiritual community, it is a thoroughly worldly community. Carmelite missioner Carlos Mesters provides an example of how the poor in some of the Brazilian base communities are reading the Bible and reflecting on the church's theology in a fresh way, while at the same time giving the word "spiritual" a new meaning:

> Some time ago Pope Paul VI delivered an address in which he warned priests not to become overly preoccupied with material things. He urged them to show greater concern for spiritual things. One farmworker in Goiás had this comment: "Yes, the pope is quite right. Many priests concern themselves only with material things, such as building a church or decorating it. They forget spiritual things, such as food for the people!" (209)

Did this farmworker misunderstand what the Pope really meant? More than likely, yes. Did this farmworker misunderstand the pentecostal meaning of the words "spiritual" and "spirit"? I think not. On the contrary, he grasped the holistic, earthy, and human characteristics of the spiritual.

The question today is whether the church as a liberation community can shoulder this praxis of consistently calling itself and the world it serves to just such a holistic empowerment. It is by no means an easy task. The church must first venture out of its sacred compounds and into a thoroughly secularized world. And it must do this in hope of its own liberation as much as for the liberation of the world. Perhaps it is finally in the world that the church can most authentically encounter the Spirit of life, the Spirit that genuinely makes a difference in how we treat employees and not merely how high we wave our hands when singing hymns. Perhaps it is in the world that the church can find the voice to invite those who have come to accept their enslavement by others to move toward healing and freedom by opening themselves to God's re-creating Spirit. So also, perhaps it is in the world that the church can find the voice to call those who have come to accept their enslavement of others to move toward repentance, here again, by continually opening themselves to God's re-creating Spirit.

Undoubtedly, soul empowerment is not something that happens accidentally. It requires decision, even conversion. But it does not, for that reason, happen once-and-for-all as a singular event or as a magic deliverance from deeply ingrained patterns of domination and subordination. Empowerment of our spirits by the Living Spirit really does require something like the life-long process of consciousness raising to which Freire points. The church, rather than understanding itself as a religious way-station on our journey toward heaven, must take seriously its role as the sacrament of God's life-giving Spirit. In so doing, the church as God's agent of liberation and community in the world will become a place where the healing processes of critical reflection, memory, grief, protest (even rage), vision, and renewal can occur.

Soul-ed Power

If soul power means the empowerment of the soul, it also means the ensoulment of power! Power without soul is heartless and mindless. It is little more than raw coercion or manipulation. But insofar as the human being is reconstituted in the image of God, we must also expect a "reconstitution of power" (Herzog: 44). In other words, becoming more fully human in Christ requires that power itself be transformed into something human. Thus, "soul-ed power" is power that is shaped in the image of God—power that is liberating, communal, and creative.

Soul-ed power is not just more of the same only now directed toward allegedly new and liberating ends. It really is a new and creative power—a power with a fundamentally new origin, aim, and character. It is a power that suffers with others and yet stands resolutely against all suffering. It is a power that gives life while refusing to take life. It is a power that knows what it means to be powerless and at the same time stands victorious over the forces of death and dehumanization. It is a power that originates on a cross and is vindicated by an empty tomb.

There are those, of course, who would dispute the very notion of a transformation of power. Power is simply power. We may perhaps talk about different uses of power, so the argument goes; but both Jesus and Herod, for example, used the same power—only for different purposes. Certainly the impressive work of Reinhold Niebuhr can be understood as taking something like this kind of position. Thus, the basic paradox of history is that its creative and destructive possibilities are inextricably intermingled. As Niebuhr says, "the very power which organizes human society and establishes justice, also generates injustice by its preponderance of power" (1943:II:21).

We must ask ourselves, however, whether it is not possible for power to be radically reconstituted when born out of and expressed under the conditions of a humanity being restored in the image of God. So, for example, when the prophet Zechariah is told to proclaim that God's will is accomplished "not by might nor by power, but by [God's] Spirit" (4:6), we are being pointed neither to a rejection of power nor to the use of ordinary power for extraordinary purposes. Rather, we are being directed to an entirely new and creative power—a power which, as the cross makes plain, doesn't even look like power any more, but like powerlessness. Soul-ed power, then, is not simply generic power used as an instrument for good purposes; it is power that has itself been shaped and molded in the image of the soul of the universe—in the image of the One whose power is made perfect in weakness (2 Cor. 12:8).

One of the greatest difficulties in moving toward a transformation of power in our lives is the predominance of a one-sided understanding of power throughout the history of Western thought. For a variety of reasons—some philosophical and some downright sinful (we can't blame everything on the Greeks!)—we tend to imagine supreme power in terms of the power to be in control, to determine the outcome of events, or to resist change and outside influence. A powerful man is a "do-it-himself" type. A powerful nation is one with superior weaponry. A powerful God is the Sovereign Lord who is Master over all and can determine the outcome of every event. In this classical view of power, the more perfect a power is, the more coercive, unilateral, and resistant to change it is.

But if we really believe that in Jesus of Nazareth we have discovered decisively who God is and who we therefore ought to be—if it really is in Jesus that we discover "the image of the invisible God" (Col. 1:15)—can we conclude that our conventional understanding of what constitutes supreme power is finally adequate? The God we discover in Jesus is not one who is resistant to change or outside influence, but one who is vulnerable and, in that vulnerability, shares the hurt and suffering of the entire world. That is power! The God we discover in Jesus is not some unchanging monument with whom no mutual relationship can be experienced, but rather the One whose most dependable qualities are responsiveness, patience, and love. This God is supremely powerful because this God is supremely persuasive. This God does not coerce our obedience and worship, but inspires it. So, as in the case of Jesus, supreme power is not the power to dominate, but the power to serve. It is not the power to be unaffected and unswayed by others, but the power to include others, especially the weak and the suffering. Power, in the person of Jesus, is not the power to destroy, but the power to create and redeem.

What this means for compassionate ministry is that empowerment must never be construed merely quantitatively as accumulation of or increased access to raw power. Power itself must be remolded altogether so as not merely to replicate the fear and compulsiveness of the oppressor, by whom the prevalent models of power have been perpetuated. A new style of power must arise from the soul of the transformed human being—the human who is being liberated in community. This power is soul-ed power because it is human power. It is characterized by freedom rather than coercion, by community rather than selfishness, and by novelty and creativity rather than by the stale or the destructive.

Ministry as the authentic empowerment of other human beings simply cannot be unilateral or coercive. And this is not because the would-be empowerer lacks sufficient strength to pull off such an empowerment. On the contrary, no amount of unilateral, coercive power—not even divine unilateral or coercive power—can empower another free being. This is true not because of power limitations on our part or on God's part, but because of the very nature of freedom and empowerment. The only path to becoming free is to become a "subject" (Freire). But no amount of coercive power from another—even God—can force a person to be a subject. God can part Red Seas all day long, but if we have no reason to follow God—if this God does not inspire our confidence and loyalty—the battle for our liberation is over before it has even begun.

The same is true of our own efforts in empowering others. What is required on our part is a power far different from the power to conquer, invade, manipulate, dictate, and intervene. What is required is relational power: the power to influence persuasively through force of love, example, compassion, and dialogue. Empowerment of this sort is effective and authentic because it is mutual and human. Margaret Hebblethwaite cites the following poem written by an anonymous Aboriginal Australian woman:

> If you have come
> to help me

you are wasting
your time.

But

If you have come
because
your liberation
is bound up
with mine
then let us work
together. (94)

In this poem we see glimpses of the remarkable truth that in the liberation of the oppressed is to be found the liberation of the oppressor—that in the life of the kingdom of God it is the oppressed who are ultimately given the enormous responsibility of freeing the oppressor, rather than the other way around. Here again, what is at stake is our understanding of power. As Freire says,

This, then, is the great humanistic and historical task of the oppressed: to liberate themselves and their oppressors as well. The oppressors, who oppress, exploit, and rape by virtue of their power, cannot find in this power the strength to liberate either the oppressed or themselves. Only power that springs from the weakness of the oppressed will be sufficiently strong to free both. (28)

The ministry of empowerment not only aims at an empowerment of the soul, but a radically new experience of power itself.

Justice

There is a well-worn maxim that goes something like this: "Give a person a fish, and she will eat for a day. Teach a person to fish, and she will eat for a lifetime." The contrast readily transfers to the twin dimensions of charity and empowerment. In many ways, charity is giving a person a fish; empowerment is teaching a person to fish. But it doesn't take long before we recognize that, until our angler has relatively free and full access to the fishing hole, and until her fishing hole is free from pollution upstream, she will probably remain hungry. As Hannah Arendt says, "poverty itself is a political, not a natural phenomenon, the result of violence and violation rather than of scarcity" (56). In other words, the poor are not primarily the less fortunate or the disadvantaged. They are the oppressed, the sinned against. Insuring the poor of their rights, opportunities, and freedom from oppression is the heartbeat of a third dimension to compassionate ministry—the ministry of justice.

As a form of Christian ministry, the struggle for justice is in many respects much more difficult to envision and implement than either charity or empowerment. That is because justice and injustice generally operate on a structural level, buried in complex social systems, economic policies, patterns of trade and commerce, and a variety of other frameworks by which we govern and organize our daily living. It is true, of course, that injustice can often be rather easily detected and fought on a purely personal level. If I pay a contractor to pave my driveway and he never does the job, I will have been dealt an injustice. Justice in such a situation will be my receiving restitution from the contractor. If I have to, I can even go to court to seek justice. In this illustration, both the injustice and the path toward justice are relatively obvious and easy to specify. But what about injustice that is less personal and more complex and structural? And, assuming we can even identify such injustice, how do we fight against it?

Disclosing and Exposing

Throughout the Bible, God is portrayed as a just God. This portrayal, however, is never offered for its own sake merely as a piece of theological trivia. The point is not only that God is a just God, but that God desires justice. The Hebrew prophets were heavily impressed, perhaps more than anyone, by this double-edged truth. As a result, they did not hesitate to bear witness to God's justice by consistently pointing out particular injustices in their society, whether in the form of unjust labor policies (Jer. 22:13), trade practices (Amos 8:5), property arrangements (1 Kings 21), legal administration (Isaiah 1:23), sexual exploitation (2 Samuel 12:1–10), or the pretentiousness of living a lifestyle of comfort and prosperity in the presence of excruciating need (Amos 4:1). What we see in these prophets is a dynamic movement back and forth between disclosing God's justice and exposing human injustice. At every turn, the two seem to overlap and imply one other.

Jesus himself took up these twin tasks of disclosing justice and exposing injustice in his own ministry. He died because of it. Christians have traditionally affirmed that the reason for Jesus' death was to save us from our sins. But however true this post-crucifixion interpretation undoubtedly is, there is no avoiding the historical fact that, before any and all theological interpretation, the direct reason for Jesus' death was a power conflict with the religio-political authorities of his day, fueled by his unmasking of cultural and religious myths that perpetuated dependency and poverty, on the one hand, and privilege and wealth, on the other. Jesus attacked the establishment where it hurt the most—

its power to create and perpetuate myths that gave it control over people's lives. Jesus, for example, consistently dispelled the myth, common in his day, that poverty was the result of the sinfulness of the poor. On the contrary, says Jesus, it is the poor who are the inheritors of the kingdom, and the rich will some day beg the poor to dip the tips of their fingers in water and cool their tongues (Luke 16:24). From Jesus' original witnesses forward, Christians have looked back at the cross and seen in it the source of our salvation. It is. But we must never forget that, in the first place, the cross is the penalty for disclosing justice and exposing injustice.

The ability to expose oppressive myths and powers requires a solidarity with victims that provides a perspective from below. One can hardly gain a sense of the dehumanizing power of a myth apart from standing with those who feel its destructive force on a daily basis. By placing ourselves in a position to hear the voices of the poor, minorities, the abused, the victimized, and the excluded, and by critically reflecting on reality through their eyes, a whole new world opens up before us. This world is virtually unavailable—or, rather, unrecognizable—to those whose only contact with impoverished neighborhoods is driving over them on elevated freeways, or whose vision of the poor is confined either to images on television of starving children in Africa or the sight of homeless men at the end of off-ramps holding signs, "Will Work for Food."

I recently visited Disney's Epcot Center in Orlando, Florida, where I sat through a twenty-minute audio-visual presentation entitled *The American Experience*. The captivating show combined music, visual images, and robotics in an awe-inspiring display designed to make true American patriotism well up within every guest. Mark Twain and Benjamin Franklin, robotic puppets on stage, began the episode by reflecting on the question of America's origins. "Where do we begin?" they asked. The answer is easy, one of them responded— "with the coming of the pilgrims on the Mayflower!" Simple, unintentional, seemingly innocuous—someone had made a decision to begin "the American experience" in Europe rather than in America. And so *The American Experience* rapidly degenerated into the American Myth. Likewise, in grade schools, high schools, and even colleges throughout the United States, the story of America is told from the perspective of the conquistador rather than the conquered, the explorer rather than the explored, the invader rather than the invaded. It is no wonder that American history is typically envisioned as being rooted in the discovery of America rather than the embarrassing but more appropriate description—the European invasion. Reflecting on the so-called discovery of America by Columbus, William Baldridge, a member of the Cherokee nation of Oklahoma, says,

From a Native American's perspective, one way to describe the spiritual significance of 1492 is to realize that for the last half-millennium

Columbus and his spiritual children have usurped the role of God and imposed their definitions of reality onto this continent. People now go through life believing that trees went unidentified until Europeans came to name them, that places could not be distinguished and directions could not be given until Europeans arrived to designate one place New York and another Los Angeles. People in the United States accept as self-evident that this continent could not produce food until row cropping was introduced, that water was not pure before filtration plants were introduced, and that conservation is a concept introduced by the U.S. Forestry Service. It is believed without question that this land was godless until the arrival of Christianity. (24)

Disclosing justice and exposing injustice are not merely activities essential for interpreting the past, however. They are also critical skills in the struggle for justice as we examine the present and envision the future. Racism, for example, is a form of structural violence that is increasingly cast in the contemporary American consciousness as the sin of our parents and grandparents. White America has for some time now adopted the posture of congratulating itself for having recognized and moved beyond this tragic mistake in our past. It becomes impossible, therefore, to understand why minority groups would continue to hammer for civil rights or push for affirmative action. On university campuses today, there is still a significant backlash among students who don't see the point of an African-American history week or special departments devoted to the study of minority culture. To white America, this all looks like reverse discrimination. But this perception is born out of the myth that racism is a thing of the past, having been eradicated with the passing of civil rights legislation in the sixties.

At least one of the tasks involved in justice ministry today is exposing racism, in the words of Jim Wallis, as America's "original sin." The word "original" here does not mean something that happened in the past. It means that racism is our fundamental sin, our basic condition, an integral component of American society as we know it and experience it today.

All white people in the United States have benefitted from the structure of racism, whether or not they have ever committed a racist act, uttered a racist word, or had a racist thought (as unlikely as that is). Just as surely as blacks suffer in a white society because they are black, whites benefit because they are white. And since whites have profited from a racist structure, whites must try to change it.

To benefit from domination is to be responsible for doing something about it. Merely to keep personally free of the taint of racist attitudes is both illusory and inadequate. Just to go along with a racist social structure, to accept the economic order as it is, just to do one's job within impersonal institutions is to participate in racism. (91–92)

As I write, over 45 percent of all black children in the United States live in poverty, and over half of all black children are now born to single mothers (Wallis: 90). Up to 50 percent of their parents and siblings who are old enough to work are unemployed. Infant mortality for African-Americans is 17.7 deaths per 1,000 births, a rate that is higher than many third-world countries and about twice the rate for whites in the U.S. Nearly half of all prisoners in the U.S. are now black males (Wallis: 90). If we refuse to conclude that these and countless other similar statistics are the result of a genetic inferiority of ethnic minority groups, we are forced to conclude that in our society opportunity is not equal, justice is not administered fairly, all do not start off on the same footing. White racism is still very much alive and even resurgent in our society.

In North America, our images of reality are quite often little more than a facade. The task of a justice ministry is to unmask that fact. This means, first, exposing our two-track system of justice as the sin that it is and the myths that perpetuate this system as the accomplices to sin that they are. It means, second, a call to repentance. After all is said and done, there is no cure for sin that does not begin with repentance. But repentance in our day is incredibly difficult because we do not typically count passively benefiting from sinful structures as something for which we need to repent. The task of a justice ministry is to expose the fact that we are more than merely inheritors of the legacy of genocide, racism, sexism, and world exploitation in North America; that it is precisely in doing nothing that we are most effective in keeping this legacy alive. And as we continue to do nothing, we will continue to reap the fruits of injustice: violent crime, racial misunderstanding and tension, poverty that debilitates entire communities, and massive mistrust and fear.

Repentance is the first step in paving a way out of this legacy. But repentance, as John the Baptist knew, is not merely a nod to our corrupt past. It is accompanied by fruits—the fruits of converted behavior, of a changed lifestyle, of placing the needs of the oppressed higher than our own wants. Repentance includes reparations that restore some modicum of opportunity and dignity to those who have been victimized, and so it is more than a private transaction between the individual and God. It is going to our brothers and sisters who have something against us and reconciling ourselves with them. Only then can peace be made with God (Matthew 5:24). A compassionate ministry of justice finds its beginning and end in this call to repentance—a call that is directed inward as much as it is directed outward, a call that is born out of the gap between the annunciation of God's justice community, on the one hand, and the denunciation of our inhuman and oppressive social structures, myths, and policies, on the other.

Righteous Resistance

Though silence is betrayal, justice is always more than talk. It is action and resistance. To resist is to assert one's full humanity in the midst of widespread and overwhelming dehumanization. It is a way of being in the world but not of the world. By resisting injustice, we are in fact disclosing God's justice and issuing a call to repentance. Resistance within a compassionate ministry can occur on a number of levels, a few examples of which are protest, advocacy, and community organizing.

Protest, whether through boycott, strike, demonstration, or any number of methods, is a means of visibly expressing our identification with God's resistance against inhumanity and injustice throughout history. We could therefore call protest a sacrament of justice in that it contains the same ambiguity as is present in other Christian sacraments such as the Lord's Supper, Christian baptism, or even the sacrament of marriage. On the one hand, a sacrament points to a reality beyond itself and does not claim to be that reality; it is a symbol or a pointing device. On the other hand, by giving visible form and representation to our deepest experiences, a sacrament makes them public, conscious, and communal, thereby bestowing upon them a new and extraordinary power in our lives. It is not, after all, the written marriage certificate or the wedding ring that is the substance of a marriage, any more than it is the wedding ritual that unites a couple. Yet, there is something critical about publicly proclaiming, sealing, and binding the convictions of our hearts and minds. When we express our faith in Christ through the sacrament of public baptism, for example, we bear witness to our faith before the community and, in effect, lay claim to the accountability of the church and the world. In a similar way, protest is a sacrament of justice. We bear witness to God's commitment to justice and thereby awaken our own commitment from its stubborn dormancy.

As psychotherapy has increasingly helped us discover, silence has great power in our lives. Protest helps us break that silence. Regardless of the extent to which it directly changes the world around us, protest first of all changes us. In protesting against death, poverty, and oppression, we live out our Easter faith. For what is Easter if not a protest against death in all its forms? Of course, the actual results of protest are often mixed, if they can be detected at all. This discourages many people from protesting, and so they ask, "What good will it do?" But we can never know the full impact of keeping pressure on political, economic, or religious structures that distort and corrupt the image of God in human life. And if it is true that transformation does not come overnight, it is also true that freedom is never a gift to be passively received. It must be pursued. It must be won.

Protest is often the only form of expression that the poor and oppressed have for standing higher than the oppression that mires them. And though the direct benefits of protest are not immediately apparent, humanity is discovered in the fight, in creative defiance in the face of domination. Thus, protest as a form of resistance is an indispensable tool, not only for the transformation of society, but for one's own spiritual integrity. The impulse to conform to the passivity and apathy of the world is so strong that the refusal to go along is itself an act of virtue and righteousness. A. J. Muste was undoubtedly one of the most consistent, long-time nonviolent civil resisters our world has ever seen. As one who protested against nuclear proliferation, against the maltreatment of industrial workers, against the lack of rights for black Americans, and against virtually every war in which the United States was involved, Muste, an ordained minister, was a fixture at picket lines, demonstrations, and acts of civil disobedience. Once asked by a reporter at a nuclear demonstration what good his act of protest did at such an obscure site, Muste answered, "I don't do this to change the world, I do it to keep the world from changing me" (Collum: 3). Christian resistance is righteous resistance, not only because it imitates God's resistance and seeks to bring about a more just society, but because it springs from and aims toward a recreated humanity in our own lives.

A second path of resistance in justice ministry is advocacy—standing with victims, pleading their case, and making their cause our own. Advocacy may mean working in the media, on the phone, from the pulpit, or through legislation to effect change. It may mean going to court with a victim of abuse, calling the landlord for a tenant, or securing legal representation for an individual who has been discriminated against. In advocating for another, we reflect God's compassionate activity of incarnation, liberation, and resurrection—of entering into the suffering of others, taking sides on their behalf, and carving out new and creative ways of bringing hope and healing to their need.

Advocacy is a unique mixture of resourcing and confrontation. On the one hand, it is simply trying to dig up resources to set things straight. On a personal level, this might mean working with an elderly woman to insure that her social security benefits are in place, or helping a laid-off worker through the maze of bureaucracy required to register for unemployment compensation until he can locate a new job. In a broader way, it might mean lobbying as a church for more low-income housing, of which we are woefully short in America. On the other hand, if advocacy includes resourcing, it almost inevitably means confronting those in power. It is one thing to advocate for others by holding their hands through labyrinths of paper work, agency appointments, and interviews. It is quite another thing to advocate for someone by calling a landlord to insist that he respond to his tenant's repeated pleas to repair the plumbing or fix a roof leak.

In reality, resourcing and confrontation work together. Former U.S. President Ronald Reagan insisted that there were plenty of resources for the poor in America; the only problem was finding ways for the poor to find out about and access those resources. The war on poverty could basically be won by a combination of cutting out unnecessary social expenditures and disseminating more information about remaining programs. But advocacy for the poor is always more than gaining access to social resources, as important as that undoubtedly is. It is challenging political and economic systems that work against the poor by confronting and calling to accountability those who are the legislators, policy makers, and brokers of those systems. Of course, resourcing, as difficult as it is, is more pleasant and rosy than confrontation. The one who is accessing resources for others will typically receive accolades, while the one who is confronting the brokers of resources will typically receive dirty looks. As Dom Helder Camara, archbishop of Recife, Brazil, once said, "When I give people food, they call me a saint. When I ask why there is no food, they call me a communist" (Brown, 1988: 86). But both dimensions—resourcing and confrontation—are essential to the justice ministry of advocacy.

Because it is typically done by some on behalf of others, advocacy can never constitute the totality of righteous resistance in a justice ministry. The poor and disenfranchised must themselves come together to struggle for justice. And so a third path of resistance is community organizing on a grassroots level. As a local community organizes itself to dismantle an unjust social order and transform it into something more just and human, a concrete face is given to justice. Government officials are forced to look at something other than statistics and to hear someone other than desk-bound clerks, accountants, and staffers. City planners are forced to look into the eyes of the family who is being forgotten by their elaborate blueprints and designs. Utility companies are forced to hear the voices of those who will have to pay disproportionately more of their meager incomes to sustain unfair rate hikes. While the church as a liberation community must always work on a macro level to encourage policy changes and legislation that benefit the dispossessed, there is finally no substitute for justice organizing at a local level.

When a grassroots community organizes itself for justice, it is attempting to change things from the bottom upward rather than from the top downward. It is attempting to subvert the way things are (literally, "to turn from below"). One should not be surprised, then, if a justice ministry that finds its starting point from below is perceived as subversive activity. In fact, it is precisely in this sense of the word that Jesus himself was subversive. In his simple acts of defiance against the establishment—healing on the sabbath, purging the temple courts of greedy religious profiteers, interrupting and overturning legal proceedings being taken against an adulterous woman—all were invited to join, and yet he organized his own liberation community from below. He took a rabble of fishermen, tax-collectors, prostitutes, lepers, and social outcasts and transformed them into his model of the kingdom.

Community organizing is virtually an artform today. There are expert groups, agencies, and resources that can facilitate a local community's attempts to organize itself for justice. The best of these insist on maintaining a careful tension between the absolute priority of leadership from within the community and, at the same time, strong linkages with resources from outside the community. The church itself is not just a tool for a local neighborhood or community to accomplish its quest for justice; the church can, nonetheless, be a natural agent in community organizing. In fact, to the extent that the church abandons a fortress mentality that insulates it from the community, and instead adopts a parish model that sees the whole community as its people, regardless of whether or not they attend its worship services on Sunday, not only does the community stand a greater chance of achieving justice, but the internal structures of the church stand a greater chance of reflecting that justice themselves.

A Justice Community

If justice ministry includes the more negative dimensions of exposing, resisting, and protesting against injustice, it also includes the more positive dimensions of forging a new human community that models compassion and is a constructive agent for justice. Injustice, we know, is a structural and systemic force in our lives and communities. It is difficult to put our hands on. But perhaps what is needed is a counter-structure, a counter-institution, to fight against such evil and provide an alternative to it. Perhaps the best way to fight structural evil is with structural good. Perhaps the best way to fight against institutions of injustice is to construct institutions of justice. The church as a liberation community is called to be just such an institution—a justice community.

The first step in the building of a justice community is to recognize that the church is not the exclusive bearer of justice. On the contrary, the church is a sacrament of justice—a model and agent of the kind of loving, free, and creative humanity that is the image of God. Restoration in the image of God can and must occur wherever and whenever human beings find themselves engaged in the art of daily living. Thus, the church, if it is to be true to its calling, must form "holy alliances" (Batestone, 3) with governments, businesses, educational institutions, the sciences, and the arts, while at the same time maintaining a critical distance from them. In other words, wherever power is molded and managed in our world, the church is obliged to lift its voice and mobilize its resources not only to link up with these power agents, but to challenge and transform them. At the same time, the church must destroy its unholy alliances—its easy identification with cultural, political, and economic structures that oppress and exclude.

If the church as a liberation community is serious about linking charity, empowerment, and justice—whether in the form of food and clothing, job training, adult education, homeownership, or even in the form of soul power, advocacy, and community organizing—it must network and collaborate with a broad range of partners in society, including everyone from federal bureaucrats to neighborhood community groups. The kind of power and power relations that oppressed people require in our context today include not only the ability to put food on the table, but also the ability to hope and to dream. They include not only economic buying power, but also the political clout that can reform schools, pave streets, and close down neighborhood crack houses. Virtually any and all resources in society come to bear on the struggle for empowerment and justice, and so virtually any and all sectors of society become potential allies of compassionate, humanizing ministry.

In constructing a justice community, the church has the ability to do what perhaps no other institution created for the purpose of effecting social change is able to do. The church is able to combine a people's cultural expressions (songs, dance, poetry, art) with intense justice activity in ways that make the struggle for justice something that springs from the soul of the human—something free, creative, and communal. That the church has too often failed to do this in the past is only a mark of its uselessness both to God and to the world. The church that is guided by a compassionate spirituality of justice is able to integrate worship and politics, meditation and legislation, prayer and protest, in ways that a political party, club, agency, or legislative body (as important as these are) never can. The church as a justice community makes sacred space for the world and its needs. And as it does, we discover that the world in all of its need makes space for the church.

Creative Justice: Fighting Fire with Water

As in the case of power, the question arises as to whether or not justice itself can be configured as the restoration of the image of God. Is justice simply justice regardless of who struggles for it or from what starting point it is pursued? Or is there something like a uniquely Christian justice which compassionate ministry seeks to implement?

Historically, reflections on the nature of justice have tended to range somewhere between more utilitarian or pragmatic perspectives, on the one hand, and more retributive or absolutist perspectives, on the other hand. The pragmatic perspective views justice as whatever works in bringing about the greatest amount of happiness or good in human life. In this view, the end justifies the means. The retributive or absolutist perspective, however, holds that persons should get what they deserve regardless of how happy we all feel about it and even if, on balance, it does not seem to benefit the greatest amount of people. In this view, a course of action is either just or unjust, right or wrong, regardless of whether it seems to work. A classic retributive text therefore is the ancient principle of justice found in many cultures and religions: "an eye for an eye, a tooth for a tooth, a life for a life."

What must first be said is that there is nothing distinctively Christian about either of these two views of justice. Each one of them has been advanced on a variety of philosophical grounds and promoted on the basis of a number of religious and even nonreligious outlooks. There may be points at which both positions complement or contribute to a distinctively Christian view of justice, but neither position fully coincides with the kind of meaning that Jesus' original witnesses understood him to have for their lives. In the New Testament, Jesus is presented as one who, on the one hand, was not preoccupied with the costs and benefits of a particular course of action, as viewed from a pragmatic perspective. His actions originate in his resolute determination to do the will of the Father. On the other hand, Jesus explicitly rejected absolutist codes of justice enshrined in such laws as "an eye for an eye."

To the apostles' minds, Jesus offered a new and creative vision of justice that served as a radical alternative to the common wisdom of the day. In the first place, creative justice, like utilitarian justice, is never oblivious to consequences—to costs and benefits. If a course of action is not likely to be redemptive, regardless of how obligated we may feel legally or morally, the Christian is called to reconsider. The heavy burden of being human is the burden of freedom—the freedom to figure out what is or is not the appropriate course of action in any situation. Consequences do matter. We believe that God has a future for us and that our actions either contribute or detract from that future. Thus, the Christian must always be a realist about what works and what doesn't work in participating in God's kingdom.

The vision of justice proclaimed from the prophets to Jesus is not a utopian dream that refuses to take into account the limitations with which we must work and the hard realities we face daily. But what is unique about the Christian vision is that what works is not necessarily what looks like it would work on the surface of things. The cross does not look like it would work. The manger does not look like it would work. Simon Peter would not be our first candidate for the rock upon which the church should be built.

The brand of justice discovered in the life and ministry of Jesus can be called creative because it does not merely react to or base itself on what is, but actually creates new conditions in which justice can flourish. In every hypothetical "what would you do if . . ." with which the Christian is confronted, creative justice is never content with the built-in parameters of the story. The reality of grace means the possibility of something new and creative. And, so, it is not by taking life but by giving life that the sanctity of life is preserved. It is by siding with the weak and the powerless that all are made healthy and whole. This, of course, flies in the face of many classical views of justice.

Another difference between creative justice and utilitarian justice is that while both certainly value the greatest good of the greatest number, creative justice measures this good against our treatment of "the least of these." To common sense, seeking the greatest good of the many sounds perfectly legitimate. For creative justice, however, there is nothing especially noble about a democracy if the wants of the many trample the needs of the few. Instead, Christianity measures a society's justice by its treatment of the powerless and marginalized.

Perhaps the most glaring difference between creative justice and more common views is its blatant rejection of retribution as a means of achieving lasting justice. Without denying the depth of depravity to which human existence falls, creative justice affirms the universality of God's grace which ever precedes, sustains, and restores. It is grace, not sin, that has the first and last word in a Christian view of justice. Thus, it is not the violence that one individual has done to another that is the basis for determining our response to that individual ("an eye for an eye"); rather, it is our universal creation in the image of God that serves as the ground of the new creation—even for that one who has violated the image of God in another.

In other words, the common-sense view expressed in the phrase "fighting fire with fire" is, to creative justice, absolutely ridiculous. Fire doesn't put out fire; water does! It is not by retribution but by creative forgiveness and a commitment to redemptive transformation of criminals (even the most despicable criminals) that true justice is achieved. The possibility of redemption is finally the optimism of the Christian. But this optimism is not utopian. It is an optimism based on what is most real in our world—namely, God's transforming grace. Creative justice does not turn a blind eye to injury and mischief. It is, however, fundamentally proactive rather than reactionary. It seeks to transform and redeem. It persists in doing good as the most powerful and realistic method of overcoming evil.

In sum, it is God's own way of treating us that, for the Christian, defines justice. In God's activity in Christ, justice is not a matter of getting what we deserve; it is a matter of getting what we don't deserve: "while we were yet sinners, Christ died for us" (Rom. 5:8). According to Paul, the penalty of sin is death. But thankfully God does not give us our own brand of justice. Rather, God redefines justice as the extension of forgiveness, redemption, and hope. So too in compassionate ministry, justice is never ultimately about what this or that person or group deserves. It is fundamentally about how God acts. It is making as our own the praxis of God's justice.

The Experience and Ministry of Community

If compassion is entering into community with and liberating involvement on behalf of those who suffer, then there can be no liberation without community and no community without liberation. The two rise and fall together. Where community is missing, liberation breeds new oppression. Where liberation is missing, community becomes something ingrown and cliquish. We can make a theological distinction between liberation and community for the purpose of analysis, but in the practice of ministry there can be no separation of the two. In attempting to imagine a model of the church and its ministry, we must now ask about the experience and ministry of community. What is community? How does it interface with liberation?

Christian Community Is Not a Christian Crowd

Crowds are little more than aggregates of individuals. They hardly constitute a community. Regardless of the satisfaction enjoyed by preachers who, when looking out over their congregations, cheerfully summon forth the veiled self-adulation, "What a great crowd we have this morning," the church must never settle for being merely a crowd. We can best understand the difference between a crowd and a community by understanding the difference between external relationship and internal relationship.

In a crowd, the relationship of the individual to the whole is almost entirely external. The crowd does not in any strict sense need the individual in order to remain itself. Take away one person, add another, it's all the same. In essence, just about the only thing holding together a crowd is its shared physical space. Encounters are often random and anonymous, and one is able to leave those encounters unchanged. Thus, even though some individuals in a crowd may genuinely make a difference to other individuals, the crowd itself is relatively unaffected and unchanged by the joy or suffering, absence or presence, of any one member. Though one of a crowd's chief characteristics is that it is made up of a conglomeration of individuals, it is precisely the individual who counts for so little. This is the most ironic feature of a crowd. In a crowd, the individual fades into facelessness and anonymity.

In authentic Christian community, on the other hand, the individual is not dissolved into a mass humanity. Here the relationship of the individual to the community as a whole is internal—in other words, the whole requires each of its constituents and is not the same without any one of them. In a community, each individual matters to every individual, and where one suffers, so also does the entire body; where one rejoices, the whole body is made glad.

Christian Community Is Not Uniformity, but Unity in Diversity

The basis of cultural Christianity is uniformity. The basis of Christian community is liberating mission in Christ. Just as it is true that liberation is imaginary without community, so the very foundation upon which Christian community is built is the liberation which we both experience and to which we are called in Christ.

Cultural Christianity attempts to construct community on the basis of purely external factors such as language, ethnicity, or socio-economic status, and it undoubtedly succeeds in producing a high level of comfort or increased numerical growth by doing so. In North America, however, as Christians are less and less able to count on cultural Christianity to provide an external cohesive force, the church must either awaken to a unity discovered within diversity as the foundation for Christian community, or it will continue its slide into its ethnic and economic ghettoization.

Authentic Christian community preserves diversity and seeks neither to spiritualize it away nor to segregate it conveniently into homogeneous units. As on the day of Pentecost, Christian community is created not by ignoring, blurring, or overriding cultural factors, but by including diverse groups, each of which hears the gospel in its own language (Acts 2:6). Christian unity, then, is neither superficial nor superimposed from outside; it arises from its inclusive, liberating mission discovered in Jesus Christ.

All this is just another way of saying that in genuinely Christian community, it is mission that creates unity. This is true because faith is not primarily mental but practical. Faith is not only a confidence in the God of Jesus, but also a loyalty to that God. Thus, the unity of Christian faith is always to be measured much more broadly than mere adherence to a common set of beliefs, doctrines, or rituals. The unity of faith is a common loyalty to God incarnated in community through the practice of liberation.

Christian Community Is Spiritual and Therefore Holistic and Inclusive

There are at least two ways of construing the meaning of "spiritual unity" when it comes to our understanding of Christian community. The first way is to treat the word "spiritual" as referring to a nonphysical, nonhistorical plane of human existence that transcends culture, politics, economics, gender, and race. In this view, the Christian conviction that there is "one Lord, one faith, one baptism, one God and Father of all who is over all and through all and in all" (Eph. 4:5–6) means that we must look past the many divisive aspects of our humanity. We must instead keep our focus squarely on the singular faith that binds us together. After all, as Paul says, "there is neither Jew nor Greek, there is neither slave nor [free], there is neither male nor female; for you are all one in Christ Jesus" (Gal. 3:28).

The problem with spiritual unity understood this way, however, is that in the real world there are in fact males and females. There are in fact cultural differences. There is in fact oppression and slavery. By ignoring those difference and looking past them, we make Christian unity abstract and meaningless by making it transcendent of concrete human existence. This brand of spiritual unity thereby forgets and avoids human differences and in so doing perpetuates injustices based on gender, race, or income.

There is, however, another model of spiritual unity that understands the word "spiritual" to refer to the whole of our lives—who we truly are taken in totality. This model, like the previous one, appeals to our unity in Christ. Rather than claim that the basis for this unity is to be found above and beyond our concrete differences, however, this models demands that the church build its sense of community on a deliberate and self-conscious inclusiveness. In other words, the spiritual unity of Christian community is not a transcendent unity but an inclusive unity. The difference is significant.

A transcendent unity is never able to deal with racial, cultural, or gender differences or the concrete oppressions that feed on those differences. It solves the problem of division by shifting our focus away from diversity and difference and toward common features of human existence that transcend our differences. Unity thus conceived does not include and reconcile, it distracts and diverts. It never gets around to the task of learning to live with one another and so inevitably degenerates into a live-and-let-live mentality that reinforces customary social divisions. An inclusive unity, on the other hand, finds the basis of its unity in a reconciliation that is premised on justice. There is no easy unity or harmony for this kind of unity. There can be no peace where there is no justice. A unity built on inclusiveness consciously embraces our differences by recognizing them for what they are. It believes that blind justice is finally unjust.

I recently attended a church meeting where the subject of women's rights was being discussed. Some in the group wanted the church to affirm strongly the rights of women, both in society and in the ministry of the church—to make sure they were included. One individual stood up in the group and was very concerned that the church not single out women for any special treatment or affirmation because, in her words, "We are all one in Christ." Spiritual unity, she argued, demands that we look past worldly differences that divide us and that we focus instead on our faith in Christ which binds us together. What was happening was that a transcendent unity was being advocated as a substitute for an inclusive unity. The phrase, "We are all one in Christ," was used to elevate Christian unity above and beyond the concrete plane of gender or race relationships and injustices. The appeal to spiritual unity thereby became a mechanism that masked injustice and inequality and distorted our obligations to one another in Christian community by spiritualizing them. In a society where individuals are systematically excluded on the basis of gender and race, we dilute our faith by grounding it upon a lofty unity that transcends any and all appearance of partiality.

In the New Testament it is quite clear that the original Christian communities did not understand their spiritual unity to transcend diversity, but rather to include it. Their spirituality was earthy and materialistic. Christian community for these early Christians was undoubtedly based on their common experience of the messiahship of Jesus, but this meant not only a sharing of worship, beliefs, smiles, and friendship, but also a very tangible sharing of, for example, economic resources:

> And all those who had believed were together, and had all things in common; and they began selling their property and possessions, and were sharing them with all, as anyone might have need. (Acts 2:44–45)

Spiritual unity for these believers meant not only that they were "of one heart and soul" but that "not one of them claimed that anything belonging to him was his own" and "all things were common property to them" (Acts 4:32). Christian spirituality is holistic and material; it is the kind of spirituality that we can literally put our hands on.

Christians today must be especially wary of cries for unity in the church. Where there is no liberating mission, no justice, no equality, there can finally be no authentic community. Christian community does not start with unity and then work toward justice and equality. Unity in the body of Christ is an impossibility without justice and equality. The church must tell the truth, even if it hurts and divides. It must struggle for justice, even if that means alienating those within its own fold who prosper from injustice. The church has, for too long, wanted to rush by differences and smooth over diversity in its head-long blitz for unity. The unity achieved in most instances is merely a thin veneer covering our prejudices and divisions. In the long run, unresolved differences always comes back to haunt the church. This is especially true in many evangelical denominations where the creation of inner-city ministries has become a popular endeavor in recent years. Predominantly white, middle-class churches are happy to have token brown and black converts paraded in front of them and are even more than willing to take up an offering to encourage the "great work you're doing down there." But when too many of these ministry by-products begin to show up at their summer camps, begin to ask out their white daughters, or hold hands with their white sons, a strange thing begins to happen. Suddenly, "Wouldn't it be a great idea to create a special camp that could cater to the 'special' needs of these urban youth?" Compassionate ministry is fine as long as it remains at the level of charity. And Christian community is fine, as long as it means never crossing into a genuine justice community with the other, who I really have never gotten around to knowing and loving.

Emilie M. Townes, an African-American womanist theologian, warns the church that wants to bypass justice in favor of a kind of easy unity:

> a unity forged on imperfection, romance, poor vision, limited knowledge, and fissured reconciliation will always benefit those who have the power and leisure to enforce and ignore differences. Unity as a teleological goal can be dangerous and life defeating, for it can overwhelm and neglect equality. Unity is only vigorous in an atmosphere that is unafraid of difference and diversity, an atmosphere that does not view difference as a barrier, but like the proverbial stew makes the aroma richer and provides greater sustenance for the work of justice. (133)

Christian community is indeed born of a spiritual unity. There is one Lord, one faith, and one baptism. But these marks of unity do not distance us from oppression nor do they make us colorblind. They make us color-inclusive! In a society where people are excluded and dehumanized on the basis of their poverty, gender, age, or skin color, the unity of faith must always be a unity of compassion, justice, equality, and inclusion.

Christian Community Is a Celebrating Community

It would be a tragic mistake to overlook the dimension of celebration as a central feature of Christian community. Where people feel united and included, where their life together has mission and purpose, where they are filled with a strong sense of gratitude to, dependence on, and expectation toward God, there we discover celebration. The focal point for this celebration has traditionally been understood by the Christian community to be its public worship. Yet it would be safe to admit that for most North Americans the words "worship" and "church" are not closely associated with the word "celebration." This may even be as true for those who attend church regularly as for those who don't! Church is a place of sheer drudgery, wearisome sermons, stale music, and endless pleas for money. Worst of all, it is an interruption to beautiful weekends, campouts, picnics, and much-needed rest. Those who go twice on Sunday must be gluttons for punishment, and those rare souls who include a Wednesday evening prayer service must be utter masochists. From the perspective of many non–church attenders, public worship is little more than a massive attempt by generally dull people to get a life.

It is somewhat understandable that the experience of worship comes off as overly solemn and even boring in many churches. After all, the Christian life is serious business. But we would do well to ask ourselves, how much of Christian worship is authentic celebration, and how much is stuffy formality and dreary ritual, designed to give what has become largely irrelevant an aura of holiness and significance. Too often, what the church lacks in vitality and pertinence, it makes up for by creating a gloomy atmosphere of sacredness and authority. But the seriousness and sacredness of Christian living need not preclude celebration, nor should worship fail to incorporate the joys and happiness of our daily existence. After all, Jesus himself was a party-goer and one who, when he arrived, did not offer tiresome sermons but his own new wine!

Again the notion of sacrament is helpful. Public worship is not the exclusive moment of celebration for Christians, it is the re-presentative moment. Worship is, or at least ought to be, a sacrament of the joyous life of the believer—a moment of intentional and conscious celebration representing the Christian's daily celebration of life over death, justice over injustice, and love over hate. This duality between the moment of celebration and the life of celebration is just one of the many tensions in the experience of authentic Christian community.

A second tension has to do with the rationale for Christian worship and celebration. On the one hand, worship serves absolutely no purpose. We can fill pages describing the benefits of worship—the way it builds social cohesiveness, strengthens our personal faith, or motivates us to renewed Christian living—but ultimately the act of worship is premised on nothing other than the worthiness of God. Worship is not a "so that ..." kind of activity; it is a "because of ..." kind of activity. Thus, any benefits to worship are purely ancillary to its status as a response to who God is and what God is doing. On the other hand, however, we have to ask ourselves whether we do not in fact need to worship in order to be fully human. Even if our worship is fundamentally oriented toward God and performed entirely as a devoted response to God's character and activity, is it not also true that worship arises out of a human need to respond? If this tension is real, then worship will always involve a duality between orienting *ourselves* to God and orienting ourselves *to God*. It will always include the conscious bringing of all of our life, struggles, culture, hopes, dreams, and needs to the worship experience, and yet it will also always be the alignment and focus of that package toward God.

A third tension in Christian celebration is the tension between hope and suffering. In a sense, it is seems cavalier and insensitive to celebrate the victory of life over death, when so many in our world continue to have death thrust upon them on a daily basis. It seems rather haughty to celebrate Easter when inner-city communities in our nation are still trapped in graveyards. And yet, ironically, it is precisely in the midst of suffering communities that Christian celebration is so vivid and prominent! One thinks, for example, of the vitality of base communities in Latin America where, in the midst of abject poverty and overwhelming oppression, Christian celebration is as passionate, if not more passionate, than in any Christian community throughout the world. So too it is not coincidental that on any given Sunday morning in America for the last two centuries, the place to go to experience the festival and jubilee atmosphere of Christian community has been the churches of oppressed and suffering African-Americans. We should not romanticize worship in such communities, yet the exultation, "Gonna lay down my burdens, down by the riverside," has extraordinary significance for those who carry an extraordinarily large share of society's burdens. Emilie Townes offers the following reflection on the relationship between celebration and the task of building a Christian community from the perspective of a suffering community:

We sing while we build this house. We sing with passion, for passion is what distinguishes us as Christians. We sing when the times of life are failing. Sing when folks tell us we have no gift for singing. Sing when someone has taken the sheet music. Sing in the midst of joy and laughter. We sing using heart and soul. Sing using mind and intellect. Sing using witness and faith. As African-American womanists, we sing because there is a song inside which must be let go. As the song of justice is sung, a house is being built. . . . We are building a house of justice, a liberation community. (143)

A fourth tension in Christian celebration is the tension between worship and justice. The Bible is packed with warnings about worship that is separated from attention to the needs of the poor and the struggle for justice in the world. Such worship is not merely irrelevant, it is downright sinful. Isaiah, for example, instructs the people to cease their endless sacrifices, incense, festivals, feasts, and prayers. They have become a burden to God, and God is weary of bearing that burden. Instead, the people are instructed:

Wash yourselves, make yourselves clean;
Remove the evil of your deeds from My sight.
Cease to do evil, learn to do good;

Seek justice, reprove the ruthless;
Defend the orphan, plead for the widow. (1:16–17)

So also, the prophet Amos chastises those who can hardly wait for church to get over so they can get back to ripping off the poor:

Hear this, you who trample the needy, to do away with the humble of the land, saying, "When will the new moon be over, So that we may sell grain, and the sabbath, that we may open the wheat market, To make the bushel smaller and the shekel bigger, and to cheat with dishonest scales, So as to buy the helpless for money and the needy for a pair of sandals, and that we may sell the refuse of the wheat?" The Lord has sworn by the pride of Jacob, "Indeed, I will never forget any of their deeds." (8:4–7)

For Amos, what God desires first and foremost is not festivals, solemn assemblies, offerings, and music, but rather virtuous character and a just social order:

Take away from Me the noise of your songs; I will not even listen to the sound of your harps. But let justice roll down like waters and righteousness like an ever-flowing stream. (5:23–24)

The notion of integrating worship with justice and righteousness is further reinforced in the New Testament. Jesus continues the tradition of the prophets by forging a more holistic understanding of worship, "I desire compassion, and not sacrifice" (Matthew 9:13, cf. Hosea 6:6). Jesus repeatedly goes so far as to subordinate the whole notion of a sacred day of worship, the Sabbath, to the full range of daily human needs. Paul picks up on this theme and urges followers of Christ to see themselves as a "living and holy sacrifice, acceptable to God, which is your spiritual service of worship" (Rom. 12:1). Worship, then, is not fundamentally ritualistic behavior or song and dance unto God. It is the committed life of Christians themselves.

Celebration is at the heart of the Christian community and is born out of the daily struggles and projects of that community in the real world. Celebration is not a once-a-week activity but is a lifestyle expressed at work and at play, in art and in politics, in love for one's family and in service to those who suffer. As a sacrament of that daily celebration, public worship is all the more important. It especially allows us to integrate into our celebration the essential ingredient of communal activity. Who likes to celebrate alone? Celebration is every bit as much a mark of the true church as any of the classical marks such as unity, holiness, universality, or fidelity to the teaching of the apostles. A Christian community is a celebrating community.

The Compassionate Church as "a Poor Church"?

The church has not always been a friend to poor people. Concerned more often with defending its message theologically to an elite minority of intellectual critics, the church has rarely allowed those without a voice, without power, and without position to make significant claims on its life and ministry. Even when the church has stretched itself toward including the marginalized, it has rarely rethought its nature and mission in view of their predicament. While desiring to play a part in the life of the poor, the church has not always invited poor people to play an integral part in its life. There are, of course, obvious exceptions; one thinks, for example, of St. Francis and the various mendicant orders who, throughout the twelfth and thirteenth centuries, reshaped the entire ecclesiastical landscape because of their commitment to poor people—a commitment that stemmed from their attachment to the image of a poor, naked, and suffering Christ who had neither property nor possession.

In North America today, however, the prevailing structure and organizational patterns of the church are gigantic obstacles to the full and creative participation of poor people in its life, theology, and ministry. Nonetheless, it is possible to transform the church into the community of liberation that God intended it to be. Such a transformation requires a thorough rethinking and restructuring of the church in the light of the massive experience of poverty and oppression on our planet. Indeed, there can be no authentic participation of the poor in the life and ministry of the church where a materially comfortable church of the elite simply invites poor people to join them. A complete reversal of the church's relationship to the poor must take place. In a world that is predominantly poor, the church must first become a church of the poor, or as Gustavo Gutiérrez advocates, "a poor church" (1973: 117).

But what does it mean to be a poor church? Does it mean that there is no place in the church for those who have wealth? Certainly not. It does mean, however, that the church and its ministry must be shaped by the suffering and poverty of the world. When this happens, the church can truly become a compassionate church. The church that allows not only its sense of mission and experience of worship but also its institutional life and internal organization to be shaped by the needs of those who suffer will be revolutionized from outside itself. And this is the irony of the matter. The church is called to change the world. But the world must first be allowed to change the church. As Gustavo Gutiérrez puts it, "The Church must allow itself to be inhabited and evangelized by the world" (1973: 261).

In our world, however, whether we like it or not, the world that stands ready to evangelize the church is overwhelmingly poor. A church that fails to be shaped by that poverty and need, as Jon Sobrino says, is neither human nor Christian. In the first place, a wealthy church is *inhuman* because

> in a world predominantly poor, wealth intrinsically causes the church to distance itself from the real world, to disembody itself from it, and to feign not to understand it. A rich church is, first of all, a church that has failed to become flesh in a world predominantly poor and is, therefore, a "fairy tale" church; in that sense, it is unreal. (84)

In the second place, a wealthy church is not a Christian church "since it does not follow the poor and humble Jesus" (84).

The church that is wealthy, therefore, is actually worthless both to God and to human beings. It does not serve the former, and it has no relevance to the latter. Instead, the wealthy church is a church that deceives itself and others as to the obscene violation of the image of God that poverty and suffering are in our world today. The point is not that wealth is intrinsically evil nor that poverty is intrinsically holy, of course. The point is that in our world it is improper and even deceitful to consider wealth or poverty in the abstract, apart from the motivations and practices that lead to each, and apart from the consequences and paths to which each leads. And nowhere is this more true than in the church.

A poor church, as Sobrino argues, is able to be "rich in compassion," not because it has great quantities of material goods to bestow on the poor, but because it has something even more valuable to offer: solidarity, vulnerability, empowerment, and justice. These are the essential ingredients of compassion rather than an alien or neutral charity trickling down in the form of pity. A poor church, therefore, can be not only human, but also Christian. A poor church follows the example of Jesus in taking sides with the marginalized and outcast of society. When it is following Jesus in the practice of compassion, the church thereby reflects the character of God and serves God. The poor church is evangelical in the sense that its inner life and mission are rooted in the gospel—a gospel that brings liberation and community to those who are oppressed and excluded. The poor church has nothing to conceal. It is free to be a sacrament of life and truth to the world. It is free to be compassionate.

Compassion, then, is both the mark of the true human being as well as the defining characteristic of the true church of Jesus Christ.

> Compassion, as a response [to the suffering of others], is the fundamental action of the complete human person. So conceived, it is not one thing among many other human realities but that which clearly defines the human person. On the one hand, it is not enough to characterize human

beings so, because a human is also a being who knows, hopes, and celebrates. On the other hand, it is absolutely necessary, for in the eyes of Jesus, to be a human person is to respond with compassion. If one does not do so, that person has, at root, perverted the very essence of what it means to be human, as happened in the case of the priest and the Levite who went around the man lying in the road. (Sobrino: 89)

Compassionate ministry is humanizing ministry—it is an expression of and a recovery of the image of God. To be compassionate is not only to be human but to restore the humanity of others. Compassion is more than one ministry among others, and it is not simply a spiritual gift or particular calling that only a few Christians have. If we can talk about the essential character of God, Christ, or even ourselves in terms of compassion, then it certainly must be a constitutive element in the life and mission of the church.

Throughout the world, new communities of liberation are springing up which reflect the compassionate and humanizing mission of the church in the world. At the same time, the church's inner life and structure is being re-imagined and re-invented by that mission. The ministries and experience of liberation and community in this chapter point in the direction of some of the concrete ways that a poor church that is rich in compassion can flesh out this mission. There are undoubtedly other ways this mission can be incarnated in the church's leadership structures, its organizational patterns, and its institutional life. Some of those ways include full utilization of bivocational clergy, prioritizing the meeting of human need in the allocation of church resources, a reversal of traditional decision-making processes so as to give privilege to the voiceless, and an incorporation of training in empowerment and justice ministries along with traditional religious education. It might even be more appropriate for churches to hire ministers of empowerment or ministers of justice rather than simply relying on the standard fare of traditional church staffing menus (youth pastors, ministers of music). Above all, the church's standards of success and growth will require the most profound reformation. If the church is indeed the body of Christ, its less honorable members are to be given the greatest honor, and its most embarrassing and unattractive members are its greatest treasures.

6

Compassionate Evangelism

Let me put it bluntly—Christian evangelism, as it is commonly understood and practiced in North America today, neither lends itself to compassionate ministry nor, if it is consistent with itself, even coexists with compassionate ministry. On the contrary, it excludes and even undermines compassionate ministry. In this chapter, I will attempt to suggest why this is so, survey the options before us, and offer an alternate vision of evangelism that attempts to reflect the breadth and diversity of the biblical understanding of salvation.

The Popular Consensus

Unless I am mistaken, there is something like a popular consensus among Christians as to what evangelism is and is not. This consensus is relatively wide-spread and, though largely the creation of Protestant evangelicals, it has had a tremendous impact not only on the way non-Christians understand Christians but on the way Christians understand themselves. Not all Christians would concur with the features of the consensus described below, but its influence can hardly be ignored, especially by those who are engaged in ministry. If the church is to take up the ministries of liberation and community whole-heartedly, the question inevitably arises as to where evangelism fits, if at all. Is compassionate ministry to be considered evangelism in the truest sense of that word or is it perhaps something contradictory to, the consequence of, along-side of, or preparatory to real Christian evangelism? To answer this complicated question, we need to clarify the fundamental features of the prevailing evangelism consensus.

(1) The pedestal upon which the predominant evangelism consensus stands is a fundamental dualism between an immortal soul and a perishable body that houses this soul during its relatively short journey on earth. Corresponding to this body-soul dualism are two distinct planes of existence in which human

143

beings live and move—the spiritual and the physical. The former is eternal (and therefore most valuable), while the latter is transitory and finite (and therefore of little or no value).

While this dualistic starting point has held tremendous sway in the history of Christian thought over the last twenty centuries, there is nothing especially biblical about it. Its origins lie in classical Greek philosophy and in a religious system known as "gnosticism" that grew out of it and thrived during the first centuries of Christianity. The fact that the Western Christian tradition has clung to this dualism for so long only shows how powerful and pervasive the Greek intellectual tradition has been on Western civilization.

It is hardly surprising that the Greco-Roman world was so ruffled by the flagrant materialism of Judaism and Christianity. For Greek thought, the world is an inferior and imperfect shadow of something more real, unchanging, and perfect. For the Jew, however, the physical world is the creation of God and essentially good. While Greek thought envisioned salvation in terms of the soul's escape from its earthly prison, Hebrew thought operated from a view of salvation with roots in its doctrine of creation, its historical experience of exodus from Egypt, and its vision of a holy people and a holy nation. Whereas for Greek thought, history is cyclical, for Judaism, history is going somewhere, and it is God who is guiding it. What we do, therefore, matters because it either contributes to or detracts from God's purpose for the world. Even when elements of salvation, understood as a postmortem existence, began to enter relatively late in Judaism, this salvation was understood not in terms of an immortality of the soul but a resurrection of the body. To the Greek mind, why the body would be of such importance was anybody's guess.

With the advent of Christianity and its claim that God became incarnate in Jesus Christ, the conflict between Hebrew and Greek modes of thought became even further intensified. Here was the ultimate insult to a philosophical world-view that firmly believed the divine and the physical do not mix and that salvation consists of escape from this world rather than its redemption. Early Christian apologists, however—seeking to make Christianity more respectable and accepted in the Greek world, especially in the face of gnostic challenges—inevitably adopted Greek systems of thought, especially the body-soul dualism and the accompanying compartmentalization of reality into a spiritual realm and a physical realm. The legacy of this transmutation of holistic Jewish and Christian forms of thought into dualistic Greek forms of thought is our inheritance today. This legacy is one of the fundamental building blocks of the contemporary evangelism consensus.

The natural by-product of this dualism is an understanding of the kingdom of God as essentially private, other-worldly and ahistorical. After all, if the soul is eternal and the body is temporal, and if we really catch the full significance of this difference, what possible value could our world, our history, and our bodies have, apart from being merely a testing ground or a ticket station for what is truly important, eternal, and valuable? In other words, if we believe in the human soul in the same way as the predominant consensus does, then we must join in with the chorus:

> This world is not my home, I'm just a-passing through.
> My treasures are laid up somewhere beyond the blue.
> The angels beckon me from heavens open door.
> And I can't feel at home in this world any more.

The implications for evangelism are obvious. Save souls.

(2) The second point of consensus in evangelism today is its clear preference for personal salvation over corporate salvation. Communities don't get saved; only individuals do—at least in the only sense of the word "saved" that finally matters. This view is, in many ways, a natural result of dualism, but it is also the by-product of an entrenched individualism that saturates North American culture. Salvation, in this view, is strictly a matter between the individual and God. At best, this exclusively private and personal salvation may have implications for our corporate life together. And so, within the predominant consensus today, the emphasis is placed on what has come to be called "personal evangelism"—the effort to lead individuals to a personal relationship with Jesus.

(3) A third feature of the prevailing consensus of evangelism is its view of human existence as a test rather than a constructive project. This feature builds on the prior two characteristics: dualism and individualism. What else could human existence mean if our world, our history, and our bodies are passing away and if it is only the salvation of our eternal souls that matters? Evangelism, in this view, is envisioned and carried out as an effort to get people to pass the test, enter the lifeboat, get their ticket, or the like. Really, it could not possibly be otherwise. If the soul of a person is all that finally matters, any form of evangelism that spends even the slightest bit of energy on anything not directly related to the ripening and harvesting of souls for eternity is doing nothing more than putting a new coat of paint on the Hindenberg. Given this third point of consensus, compassionate ministry along the lines of charity, empowerment, justice, and community is nothing more than a sentimental distraction or, at best, a tool for real evangelism. Indeed, compassionate ministry is not evangelism at all in the proper sense; it can be no more than a means to a greater end.

(4) The fourth point of consensus of contemporary evangelism is its predominantly (if not exclusively) other-worldly or next-worldly understanding of salvation. It should be obvious how this feature fits in with the

others already mentioned. Salvation is the guarantee of one's future; it is the determination here and now of where one's soul will spend eternity. Salvation is the avoidance of hell and the insurance of heaven. Again, this life is but a test to see where one will end up. Admittedly, the confidence that Jesus is our personal savior and that we will spend eternity with God in heaven makes life more abundant here and now, but it is consistently from the "there" and "then" that any meaning for the "here" and "now" must be drawn.

(5) A fifth feature of the contemporary evangelism consensus hinges on the first four points and is an emphasis on the quantitative rather than the qualitative in our salvation. If what matters most about human existence is the eternal salvation of our individual souls, then mass evangelism—or at least personal evangelism on a mass scale—will have to be our greatest priority. Here again, changing the *quality* of physical, social, and political life is of relatively little importance in comparison to the greater task of filling the lifeboats as quickly and as completely as we can.

(6) Finally, a sixth feature of this predominant consensus is its measurement of the normative Christian experience of salvation in terms of an instantaneous conversion experience referred to by phrases such as "accepting Jesus as your personal Savior," "allowing Jesus into your heart," or "being born again." Such phrases are, of course, of relatively recent origin among Christians. Even the phrase "born again," though scriptural, has taken on an unprecedented life of its own in the past few decades. What this popular jargon actually means, then, is difficult to determine—not only for those on the outside looking in, but also for those who actually use the lingo. What, for example, does the whole notion of "accepting Jesus" mean? And just what is implied by the phrase "personal Savior"?

Like any other religious phenomenon, there are wide ranges in the use of language to describe it. For some, a phrase such as "accepting Jesus" may mean little more than a mental acknowledgment of the divinity or Messiahship of Jesus. For others, it may mean a more intimate and mystical relationship with the resurrected Jesus. Thus, Jesus becomes one's personal Savior. But even here, the phrase sounds more like something borrowed from our modern, fast-paced, narcissistic world where individuals have their own personal trainer, personal lawyer, personal secretary, or personal masseuse. But even more to the point is the fact that a personal relationship with Jesus can be anyone's possession in a matter of minutes or even seconds.

What we have here is more than just jargon. In the prevailing evangelism consensus, the entire experience of salvation has been reduced to a single momentary decision and experience. The phrases used to describe it are what we would expect when describing a salvation that is basically dualistic, individualistic, private, and other-worldly. The question is no longer about the content of Jesus' message, the particular life that Jesus leads and calls for as the authentic response to a compassionate God. Nor is the most important question any longer about the particular allegiances which participation in the kingdom demands, the political and human preferences which correspond to God's own compassionate taking sides with those who suffer. Rather, all these fall by the wayside in favor of getting saved. Anything that would discriminate or divide, anything that would set up an obstacle to an individual becoming a Christian, is either bracketed or diluted. Instead, what finally and eternally matters is what anyone can do in a matter of seconds: namely, accepting Jesus as personal Savior.

Theological Suspicion

Perhaps one of the most important contributions of contemporary liberation theologies is their call for the application of a thoroughgoing suspicion to all forms of thinking, especially theology. This suspicion proceeds on the assumption that because of the concrete life commitments and social location out of which our beliefs arise, some data have not been taken into full account while other perhaps less important data have been given a primary role. I recently attended a meeting where all pastors were to give their annual reports to a body of delegates. The pastor of one of the largest and most affluent churches in the group began his report with great flair and authority by quoting the words of Jesus recorded in Luke 4. He spoke each word with passion, eloquence, and precision: "The Spirit of the Lord is upon me because he has anointed me to preach the gospel!" He then went on to give his report.

I doubt if anyone noticed his omission of the last three tiny words of Jesus' sentence—"to the poor." But the preacher's revealing deletion (whether conscious or unconscious) was a concrete example of the way the allegiances and commitments of all of us form a kind of lens through which we read the Bible and which daily flesh themselves out in all kinds of beliefs and actions.

When we look closely at the theology represented in the predominant consensus about evangelism today, we must first ask about the relationship between that theology and how it functions in certain social contexts. So, for example, we must ask whether the personal, other-worldly, test-oriented, and quantitative evangelism of today (what I will henceforth refer to as "soul evangelism") is not uniquely suited for reinforcing the status quo in society. I think that we will find it is. On the one hand, soul evangelism allows white middle and upper classes to retain their social privileges and comfort and still consider themselves Christian. After all salvation is private, internal, a matter of the soul, and has primarily to do with where we end up when we die. On the other hand, soul evangelism allows minorities and the poor in our society to adjust psychologically to their exclusion and dehumanization, to put up with it. Soul evangelism assures them that someday there will be a place where every tear is wiped away and where everyone will own a mansion. But for now, the simple assurance that their souls are saved and their mansions reserved should be satisfaction enough.

Now perhaps it is merely a coincidence that the consensus theology of evangelism fits in so well with the maintenance of patterns of domination and subordination, racism and segregation, sexism and oppression in our society, not to mention the destruction of our planet's natural biosphere. But given the ever-present tendency of the church to mirror the world rather than challenge it, and given the way purveyors of the evangelism consensus have traditionally neglected social reform and compassionate ministry, the suitability of evangelism for maintaining the status quo seems hardly a coincidence.

Of course, it might be objected that my portrayal of soul evangelism is merely a reactionary caricature. Soul evangelism need not be so antithetical to compassionate, humanizing ministry. Let's don't throw out the baby with the bathwater! If evangelism is carried out correctly, people who authentically accept Jesus as their personal savior will, as a matter of course, begin to transform society and work to overcome poverty and injustice.

But why should they? Why tinker around trying to fix features of our existence that finally don't even matter at all? "Just 'cuz" is a good argument, I suppose, but it doesn't go very far with most adults. As crazy as it may seem, we human beings like to think that what we do with our lives has purpose, that it contributes to something we can understand and draw meaning from. Thus, while this objection sounds sensible at first glance, the actual practice of those who operate by the consensus theology speaks volumes against the possibility of its reform. The problem here is that we're looking at more than just a paradox, but rather a contradiction. And the cognitive dissonance between holding to a dualistic, privatized, and other-worldly evangelism, on the one hand, and a commitment to social redemption, humanization, equality and justice, on the other hand, is just too difficult to sustain.

Theology really does make a difference in how we go about the practice of ministry. If what ultimately matters is the spiritual, then anything can be done to the physical—to our bodies, to animals, to the planet, to history. One cannot say in one breath that what finally matters is the final destiny of one's soul, determined by a private and instantaneous decision in this life, and then in the next breath say that making this world a decent place to live has any ultimate purpose. If what really matters is the eternal destiny of our immortal souls, and if this world and this history are purely a testing ground, then we should not be surprised that any activity that does not lead to the salvation of immortal souls is considered a distraction. We should also not be surprised that contemporary

Christians are so little concerned with the plight of inner cities or with global poverty and ecological destruction. In such a view, the only reason to struggle against hunger and disease would be to give people more time to accept Jesus. No wonder a Christianity that operates on the popular evangelism consensus seldom moves beyond charity toward empowerment, justice, and community building. In the rush to save the soul, we have forgotten the human being.

The Options Open to Us

If the consensus with regard to evangelism today is anything close to what I have described, can there be any kind of positive or even complementary relationship between evangelism and the kind of compassionate, humanizing ministry described in this book? Can the two work together? Will one need to be subordinate to the other? Will one simply have to disappear? I propose that we understand at least the following three options as open to us:

(1) The first option is to assign compassionate ministry something like a "sweatshop" role in Christian evangelism. This option attempts to implement compassionate ministry from within the prevailing consensus of soul evangelism. Compassionate ministry, in this model, is merely a slave to real evangelism and, at best, provides an open door to bigger, better, and more eternal things like people's souls. Compassionate ministry, in this view, has no intrinsic value. Social problems such as unemployment, illiteracy, lack of affordable housing, or discrimination receive only soup today and heaven tomorrow. But, of course, why do more? Remember, given the evangelism consensus, our fundamental nature and destiny as human beings are thoroughly individualistic and private. People are not essentially social; rather, it is their individual and personal destinies that matter. All else is secondary and peripheral. This option has the merit of at least being consistent with itself.

(2) A second option wants to have it both ways. It can be called the "Italian dressing" option. It attempts an oil-and-vinegar mix of soul evangelism, on the one hand, and compassionate ministry, on the other. Here Christ's redemption is understood to have a social dimension that complements traditional evangelism. Stirred up enough, it looks like the oil and vinegar have mixed. But stop the cheering and the mixture settles back down to a simple duality of two elements that have little or nothing to do with one another. In most instances, this option either avoids the question of the contradiction between soul salvation and social change or is willing simply to live with the contradiction. Perhaps we cannot intellectually reconcile what God wants us to do, and so our job is simply to do it without asking questions. But while it is possible to silence reason over the short run and to proclaim that ignorance is bliss, the inevitable product of living with this contradiction is that spirituality and social ministry

go their separate ways. Spirituality becomes ingrown, narcissistic, and irrelevant, while social ministry becomes manipulative, interventionist, and hollow.

(3) A third option can be termed compassionate evangelism, though it is nothing other than cooperating with God's own compassionate activity of restoring human beings into His image as free, communal, and creative. In this view, Christian evangelism is any and all activity that leads to our becoming human. Nothing more. Nothing less. To be a compassionate evangelist is to be a model, witness, and agent of the true humanity discovered decisively in Jesus and made real in our lives, in our communities, and in our world by the work of the Holy Spirit. If evangelism is that broad and inclusive, it is only because salvation is just as broad and inclusive. In compassionate evangelism, we are creative participants in Jesus' outrageous vision of the coming of the kingdom of God—a liberation community—on earth as it is in heaven. And in this historical and earthly project, we are not so presumptuous as to believe that our own efforts simply are the kingdom of God nor even that this world is all there is, but neither are we inclined to give up on the possibility of a truly human community in favor of an other-worldly community way beyond the blue.

In every respect, compassionate evangelism stands opposed to the prevailing evangelism consensus. It is holistic rather than dualistic. What needs saving is not a soul, but a human being. And this human being does not merely have a body, a spirit, or a mind, but is a body, spirit, and mind. The human being that needs redemption does not merely have relationships, but in the truest sense is those relationships. Any talk about either a ministry to the body or a ministry to the soul is downright misleading and the by-product of thought forms that are foreign to a biblical anthropology. Compassionate evangelism rejects from the start any such dualism. There is only one plane of existence in which our lives are led and in which our salvation is accomplished. That plane is neither physical nor spiritual, but human. Either-or as well as both-and models of evangelism are bound to fail because they refuse to cast off this dualism. The either-or model argues that either the spiritual plane or the physical plane is more important than the other and is the proper field for evangelism. The both-and model simply slaps the two together and says both are important. The infinite difference between the two makes any genuine unity impossible, however. Inevitably, the two spin off in their own separate directions.

There are other differences between compassionate evangelism and the predominant evangelism consensus. Compassionate evangelism is corporate as well as personal. It aims not only at the transformation of the individual, but also of that individual's community and world. Compassionate evangelism understands human existence as a creative project rather than a life-long test. It is radically this-worldly though it is never willing to equate any human enterprise, regardless of how humanizing and compassionate, with the kingdom of

God itself. It emphasizes the qualitative over the quantitative in salvation. It calls for repentance and conversion to a particular set of values, commitments, and allegiances re-presented in Jesus of Nazareth, rather than some private and personal salvation experience that requires no change in loyalties and can be obtained in a matter of seconds or minutes. If what it means to be human includes every aspect of our existence—our work, play, politics, sexuality, art, business, and religion—it also includes the whole of our life from birth till death. Human existence is just as lengthy as it is broad. So also is an evangelism that genuinely cares about the entirety of human existence.

Worldly Salvation

In my church, I grew up hearing a lot about world evangelism but not very much about worldly evangelism. It is only by doing great damage to the biblical witness, however, that we miss the earthy and materialistic dimensions of salvation and of the evangelism that attempts to be a model, witness, and agent of that salvation. Once we are confronted with the rich historical strands that weave together to form the biblical tapestry of salvation, the reduction of salvation to a private assurance of one's postmortem existence in heaven seems like a tofu substitute when we were expecting steak.

In attempting to come to grips with the sumptuous vision of salvation served up in the Bible, the Jewish understanding is the place to start, at least for those Christians who consider the Old Testament any kind of significant authority for their lives. Jesus, as we shall see, does not radically overturn his own native Jewish faith, but only intensifies and radicalizes it. In the Old Testament, there are hundreds of experiences, prophetic utterances, songs, stories, and narrative accounts that interlock to form a magnificent structure of witness to God's salvation in their lives. It is difficult to single out one or two bricks in this edifice and proclaim, here is the Hebrew understanding of salvation. Perhaps we can, nonetheless, identify a few fundamental pillars, or overarching themes, of that witness which, taken together, give some indication of the lavish diversity of the Old Testament witness as a whole.

A first pillar is the Hebrew understanding of creation as essentially good. Modern Christians, under the heavy influence of individualism and dualism, often try to be more spiritual than God. We are quick to reject the physical as something less than perfect, simply because it is material, temporal, and changing. From a Hebrew perspective, the worldliness of the world—its sheer physicality and temporality—are hardly the problem. The problem is what we human beings do with the good world we have been granted. For Jewish faith, creation and salvation are inextricably linked. That God is the creator of the planet, of nature, and of our bodies is hardly a trivial theological artifact. Unless we are willing to say that God somehow goofed in creating the world (for the gnostic it was actually a lesser deity's goof), we must agree that the creation of the world has a purpose and a meaning. We must agree with God's pronouncement on creation, "It is good!" The world is what God desires, and, regardless of what we do to it, it is redeemable. It is no wonder that salvation, throughout the Old Testament, is something earthy and concrete. Even animals get in on the act. They not only suffer the devastation of sin, but are included in the salvation that God intends for the entire planet. Even the original rainbow covenant between God and Noah explicitly included the animals of the earth (Gen. 9:8–15). In the same way, our physical bodies are hardly outward shells to the Hebrew mind. Our bodies *are* us and are animated through and through by the breath of God. Because of this, sexuality is intrinsic to the true human being and hardly something that one wears on the outside like a jacket. There simply is no room for a body-soul dualism in Hebrew faith.

A second pillar in the Old Testament witness to salvation is its understanding of history as the history of God's saving activity. History is not some repetitious cycle, endless spiral, or dead end. It is meaningful and important, because it is going somewhere. History is holy. This characteristically Hebrew view of history is rooted, of course, in God's act of deliverance from the hand of oppression in Egypt. As the Red Sea is parted, Moses says to the people, "Stand by and see the salvation of the Lord which He will accomplish for you today" (Ex. 14:13). Salvation here has nothing at all to do with one's personal survival after death. It has to do with a survival that is much more immediate, critical, and this-worldly. In this decisive display of salvation, Moses is understood as a "savior" sent by God to "defend" and "deliver" the people (2 Kings 13:5, Isa. 19:20). Salvation is historical and worldly. The long—and to many modern readers, boring—historical narratives of the Old Testament are hardly included in what we take to be an inspired Bible simply to fill space. They reflect the premium placed by the Hebrew people on their history, not so they could brag to one another of their great historical achievements; on the contrary, the historical accounts are sober and often critical self-assessments that serve to point to God and to God's saving activity throughout time and history.

A third pillar is the Hebrew understanding of salvation in terms of the building of a holy nation and a holy people. Rarely in the Old Testament do we find God saving one Israelite at a time. The people are saved as a people. It is not simply individuals, but nations that can be born again. The covenants between God and Noah, Abraham, Moses, and David are covenants between God and the community. God's deliverance of Israel out of Egypt is for the purpose of creating a covenant community: a community that lives in dependence upon God. This community models, proclaims, and is an agent of God's peace and justice in the world. Thus, the experience of God's salvation within the Jewish faith can well be summarized as shalom, the well-being of the community that derives from its corporate sense of peace and harmony as well as the reality of just social relations in its midst. Here again, there is nothing especially other-worldly about salvation as covenant and shalom. And there is certainly nothing private or individualistic about it. It is a state of affairs here and now. The creation of this world and of human beings is not a temporary measure until we can be scuttled off to something more real and important. We are created for community with each other and with God. In whatever way life after death may be said to continue that community, it is certainly not the essence of salvation.

Finally, a fourth pillar is the Hebrew understanding of atonement as central to what it means to experience God's salvation. There are a number of features that could be cited by way of describing this major theme. Unfortunately, Christians, looking back on it after the death of Christ, have tended to interpret it almost exclusively in ritualistic terms, so as to play Christ's once-and-for-all sacrifice off the endlessly repetitive sacrifices and offerings of the Jewish temple system. But first and foremost, the path to forgiveness of sins in Hebrew faith through sacrifice and offerings is a grand witness to their corporate confidence that salvation is something solid and tangible in daily life. Salvation is experienced as atonement for sin in the present tense. Furthermore, atonement is not only a guarantee of one's right standing before God, it is also a symbol of one's right standing in the community. The highest holy day in the Hebrew calendar, the day of Atonement, is a day of corporate forgiveness of sins. The very idea that people are saved together may be foreign to our theological imagination, but for Israel, not only is the experience of forgiveness a this-worldly experience, it is an intensely social experience.

If these four pillars can be said to constitute even a portion of the central witness of Jewish faith to salvation, we already have a gloriously worldly salvation on our hands. And it is not just the presence of this worldly witness that is so striking. What is perhaps even more remarkable is that the Hebrew people can sing and praise God for salvation in the context of a virtual absence of any other-worldly hopes. The ancient Hebrews, up until two or three centuries before Christ, did not even believe in a life after death, except for the shadowy continuation of sheer existence in Sheol, a place (if it can be called that) where nothing happens or is known: "For there is no mention of Thee in death; In Sheol who will give Thee thanks?" (Psalm 6:5)

That Jewish faith could maintain such a vibrant testimony to God's salvation despite the lack of any eternal compensation after death seems almost incredible, especially given our contemporary tendency to identify salvation exclusively with a guarantee of heaven. Never in the Old Testament is heaven even held out as a place where saved people go (with the possible exception of Elijah who was said to have been caught up in a whirlwind into heaven). All of this need not force us to discard belief in life after death in order to give this world and this history the kind of salvific meaning and significance that the Bible gives it. But it should help us to put other-worldly hopes into proper perspective. Jewish hope was in no way focused on one's alleged soul and what happens to it after death. It was focused on God and what God was up to in the world. Thus, the Psalmist can declare that "the Lord is my light and my salvation," and the faith that arises from this conviction is the confident reply, "Whom shall I fear?" (27:1) Justo Gonzalez makes the following observation:

> Indeed, if the central message of the Bible is that our souls can be saved and live eternally, then the Hebrew Scriptures are at best prolegomena to the real message, and at worst a misunderstanding of the message itself. In the "books of Moses," God's "salvation" is the deliverance from Egypt. In Judges, "salvation" is a successful uprising against oppressors. In Isaiah and several of the prophets, it is freedom and return from exile. In the Psalms, it is the destruction of one's enemies. If all this has nothing to do with "real salvation," then it is difficult to see why these books are considered sacred and inspired scripture. (90)

When we turn to the New Testament, we must of course bear in mind that Jesus himself was not a Christian! Jesus was a Jew and remained a Jew. The writers of the New Testament were Jews. There are a number of important theological implications of this fact, not the least of which is that the historical, holistic, and worldly understanding of salvation to which the Hebrew faith bears witness does not suddenly disappear with Jesus or the first Christians. In many respects, it is even further intensified. The kingdom of God preached by Jesus is a concrete state of affairs where liberation and community characterize the human project here and now and where the conversion demanded is a conversion to one's neighbor in need rather than the flimsy adoption of an abstract creed, the mechanical observance of a starched legal code, or the instant procurement of a private mystical experience. While the corporate nature of salvation is retained in the teaching of Christ and the apostles, however, there is certainly a heightened attention to the personal decision required for our own creative participation in the kingdom. But even here, the decision required is a decision to live in a new covenant community; it is a decision to join in a common struggle for humanization in the world. Nowhere in the New Testament is the name of Jesus waved around like a talisman that guarantees one's individual passport into eternal bliss. Conversion to Jesus is a conversion to the way of the cross. It is a conversion to compassion as a life commitment.

All this is not to imply that there are no other-worldly or futuristic overtones hovering around the understanding of salvation that makes its way into the pages of the New Testament. The point is that salvation cannot be reduced to these overtones. Throughout the Bible salvation is referred to in past, present, and future tenses. So, for example, Paul can say that it is "in this hope we were saved" (Rom. 8:24) or that God has already "saved us and called us" (1 Tim. 1:9). At other times Paul can talk about "those who are being saved" (1 Cor. 1:18, 2 Cor. 1:15) or he can instruct the Philippians to "work out" their own salvation (2:12). At still other times, Paul can say that "our salvation is nearer now than when we first believed" (Rom. 13:11). But just as the temporal dimensions of salvation vary throughout the New Testament, so also does its basic meaning. While Paul generally refers to salvation as deliverance from sin and judgment, he can also use the word to describe rescue from imprisonment. At other times, Paul goes so far as to envision salvation on an explicitly cosmic scale where even creation itself is promised liberation (Rom. 8:21). Elsewhere in the New Testament salvation can have religious meaning as well as physical meaning. The word "salvation," for instance, is used to describe the physical healing of Jairus's daughter, the woman with a hemorrhage, and the blind Bartimaeus. In fact, often it is only the context that gives us any clue as to whether the word "salvation" or "healing" should be used.

For compassionate evangelism, salvation is both personal and corporate, public and private. Salvation is a past confidence, a present project, and a future hope. Compassionate evangelism urges individuals to make a decision to live by faith, and at the same time it lobbies politicians to pass legislation that more closely approximates the reign of God on earth as it is in heaven. In compassionate evangelism, the word "soul" is but a metaphorical way of talking about who we fundamentally are, not apart from our bodily actions or social relationships, but precisely in and through those actions and relationships. If I am saved, I am saved as a human, not as a soul. But to be a human is to be interconnected with other human beings. To be a human is to be interconnected with a biosphere of plants and animals on which I depend for my existence and which (to a much lesser degree) depend on me for their existence. Thus, while salvation most definitely entails the enjoyment of an intimate relationship with God, there is another sense in which there is no salvation apart from "the indivisible salvation of the whole world" (Soelle, 1971: 60).

For Christians to have any relevance to the world today, the old paradigms of liberal versus conservative, spiritual versus physical, personal piety versus social action simply have to be discarded. They no longer work. Did they ever? There can be no personal salvation where there is no genuine social redemption, just as there can be no meaningful social change apart from personal transformation. So, for example, it is nonsense to talk about my being saved from sins like greed or covetousness, when our entire society is built on the premise of a deadly consumerism. It is nonsense to talk about my being saved from sins like selfishness and manipulation, when our entire national politics and economic fabric are premised on exploitation and colonialism. If there is any sense in which we can talk about the salvation of the individual, or the recovery of the image of God in that person, it is to the extent that he or she is a full and creative participant in the humanizing process of, for example, transforming an economic system that prizes competition over cooperation and rewards greed while penalizing selflessness. That is not to say that salvation is merely economic rather than spiritual. It is to say that the dualism between the two is obsolete. What compassionate evangelism requires, as John Cobb says, is a "deprivatisation of our understanding of human existence and of salvation." We must bring every aspect of our worldly existence to the table of salvation and we must take back from that table something for every corner of our world.

We have been created in God's image as free, creative, and social beings. Sin is the violation and corruption of that image and an attack on our true humanity. For that reason, the Philippian jailer's question, "What must I do to be saved?" is today none other than the question "What must I do to be human?" Christian evangelism answers that question by pointing us to the truly human one, Jesus of Nazareth. But as we rush toward him in our mad dash to save our souls and get our ticket to heaven, we should not be surprised to find him standing squarely in the world and inviting us back to be with him in the world. It is there that salvation takes place. It is there that he offers us the possibility of being human. And though we are more interested in the mysteries of what occurs beyond the grave, Jesus would rather talk to us about collard greens, sheetrock, mayoral elections, the price of milk, bus tokens, and crack houses. Evangelism is never turning away from the world to find God somewhere else. It is always plunging ourselves into a thoroughly worldly world—a world that needs our words, deeds, and presence. And when we plunge into that world, we will discover that we are not alone. Christ is already there.

Conclusion

The Hope of Compassion

Is it possible for the world to be transformed into the liberation community that God intends it to be? Would we be too naively optimistic to live our lives or navigate our ministry on the basis of such a hope? Such questions are hardly rhetorical when set against the backdrop of the kinds of suffering and injustice that span our globe and reach into the depths of human history. It is not difficult to understand why for many, including a number of Christians, there is not much for which we can hope—at least in this world and in this history. Hope is essentially a way out, a diversion, a distraction. In the previous chapter I tried to show how one of the effects of such a hope is the reduction of evangelism to an exercise in preparing people to die rather than to live. The hope of compassion, on the other hand, is a positive and quite earthy hope that in and through the experience of compassionate community with victims, liberation is possible —here and now, in our time and in our place.

Living with such a hope—indeed, sharing this hope with others—is no easy task in Christian ministry. We know today that no amount of news, radio, television, graphic pictures of starving people, or letters from relief organizations will make us more compassionate or hopeful. In fact, many of us suffer from what can only be called compassion fatigue. The more we see and hear, the less we are moved to compassion. The more we know about the problems of the world and the more we become aware of the need for liberation, the more paralyzed we feel and the more inadequate we consider ourselves. As individuals, the problems of the world and the transformation required to solve those problems is overwhelming. Our brain circuits becomes overloaded and our hearts shut down. The result is all too often the precise opposite of compassion and hope: despair, apathy, and even anger.

The thesis of this book is that the experience of Christian community can provide a creative and liberating channel between the suffering of the world, on the one hand, and our helpless and hopeless individual responses to that suffering, on the other. In authentic Christian community, we hear the cries of hunger and abuse; we see the destruction left by disease, poverty, and neglect. But we neither turn our heads nor cover our eyes. In Christian community, the sights and sounds of suffering do not dissipate behind cold stained glass nor do they translate into resignation, paralysis, or panic as so often happens in the case of each of us as individuals. In Christian community, we find strength for compassion. We discover that through the bond of the Spirit, we can do far more together than any of us or all of us can do individually. In Christian community, we discover hope.

That is why a Christian community that intends to be a liberation community can never be a mere aggregate of human beings who have banded together to step out of the world, even for a moment. We are, instead, a community of hope. We are neither driven together out of shared fear, desperation, or anger, nor are we attracted to one another as an escape from the world. Into this community we are drawn into and united by a deep shared calling to be visible bearers of the very compassion of God in our world. In Christian community we discover a new way of being together: a new way of living together, working together, and playing together. And, thus, our special gifts and talents, our individual attitudes, and our personality traits do not divide but unite. For compassion is never the special calling or talent of this or that individual, nor is it a spiritual gift bestowed on only some in the church. Compassion is first and foremost a way of living together in the world and for the world—a way of being together to which all Christians are called and gifted by the Spirit. It is in this place of compassion that we discover the Christ who is the compassion of God and that we find the strength to share that compassion with others.

As ministers, then, our calling is not only to liberation but to community. Indeed, it is at the intersection of the two that compassion ceases to be a mere notion and becomes, instead, a practice. I think it is true that our hopes and dreams for the world don't generally die because they are not compelling or sound. Nor do they perish because we fail once we attempt to put them into practice. They die because we do not know how to put them into practice— because, as individuals, we have nowhere to put them into practice. Christian community is that place where hope becomes real and is structured into creative patterns of response and imaginative habits and practices.

A few years ago, my wife and I lost our three-month-old daughter, Karla, to a genetic disease. Experiencing Karla's death was, of course, excruciatingly painful. While living with her for three months was incredibly joyful, the simple and constant awareness that her time was short also brought a certain degree of sorrow. But perhaps none of the suffering we experienced could compare to the first time we were told by doctors just a day after her birth that

Karla had a fatal disease and would die within months. It is impossible to describe the emptiness and hurt of that moment. I was an urban pastor at the time, and the Christian community—both lay parishioners and fellow clergy—made it a point to come visit us.

Many of the clergy who visited us tried to help us make sense of the tragedy. Some insisted that God's ways are not our ways; they instructed us to trust in God's inscrutable plan. Some tried to assure us that the joy of Karla's eternal destiny in heaven far outweighed our present sufferings. One pastor's wife chided us for even accepting the doctors' forecast and urged us to have faith for a miracle of healing.

In striking contrast to these responses, however, was a memorable visit from three of our parishioners, all three impoverished single mothers, all three with an incredible number of worries and problems of their own. They had no intelligent answers to offer, no neat theological explanations to serve up. They could only wrap their arms around us, cry with us, and whisper "It'll be all right." It seemed as if their suffering was every bit as great as ours, and perhaps more. But it was in those moments that we experienced true compassion and, strangely enough, felt most at peace and most hopeful about the days to come.

Authentic Christian hope can never be merely lobbed over at others like a brick over a fence. It is born in compassionate community with those who suffer—in identification with their wounds and in a courage that brings healing and liberation in creative and even unexpected ways. And while never triumphalistic, Christian hope is nonetheless unyieldingly confident in the ultimate triumph of compassion over all forms of tyranny, alienation, bondage, and suffering. By using the word ultimate here, I do not mean that compassion is triumphant only someday or in the end. To believe in the ultimate victory of compassion means that regardless of appearances, compassion is the most authentic and real way of living and ministering here and now, today, in our world. To have Christian hope today means to have a confidence that radiates from Christ's resurrection—a confidence that expects the triumph of life over death, love over self-interest, freedom over slavery, and creativity over despair —not merely someday, but today.

John records that before raising Lazarus from the dead Jesus dialogues with Martha, the sister of Lazarus. Lazarus has been dead and buried for four days, and Martha, upon hearing that Jesus has gotten to town, goes out to meet him. She sees him just approaching the gate of the city, runs out to him, and says courteously,

Lord, if you had been here, my brother would not have died. Even now, I know that whatever you ask of God, God will give you. (John 11:21–22)

It's clear that Martha is here being simply polite. She really believes that Jesus could have saved her brother. Mary and Martha have probably repeated the thought in their minds a hundred times since Lazarus died, "If only Jesus had been here. . . ." But now it's over. The mourners and embalmers have already come. The body has been wrapped. The tomb has been sealed.

Jesus says to Martha, "Your brother shall rise again." And to this Martha rejoins, "I know that he will rise again in the resurrection on the last day." Notice Martha's final words, "on the last day." Martha had done what we so often do. She had misunderstood the true nature of hope and resurrection. She could recite the creed, and she knew her doctrine. But she had substituted a dry orthodoxy for a present and liberating hope. She believed in the resurrection. But she didn't understand resurrection hope! Jesus counters Martha's declaration by proclaiming, "*I am* the resurrection and the life!"

Christian hope is not ultimately about what happens to us someday or in the end. It is not, in the first place, about where we as individuals end up. In fact, it is not primarily about us at all. Christian hope is about God and God's power to resurrect the deadest of the dead, whether that be dead people or dead neighborhoods. It is in that hope that Christian compassion is born, nourished, and lived. And such a hope is hardly a naive or overly optimistic dream. The hope of compassion is eminently realistic because it is rooted and grounded in the reality of a compassionate God.

Bibliography

Alvez, Rubem
   1984   *I Believe in the Resurrection of the Body*. Translated from the Portuguese.
          Philadelphia: Fortress Press.

Arendt, Hannah
   1967   *On Revolution*. New York: Viking Press.

Baldridge, William
   1993   "Reclaiming Our Histories." In *New Visions for the Americas: Religious
          Engagement and Social Transformation*. Edited and translated by David
          Batstone, 23–32. Minneapolis: Fortress Press.

Banks, Robert
   1993   *Redeeming the Routines*. Wheaton: Victor Books.

Batestone, David (ed.)
   1993   *New Visions for the Americas: Religious Engagement and Social Trans-
          formation*. Minneapolis: Fortress Press.

Brown, Robert McAfee
   1978   *Theology in a New Key: Responding to Liberation Themes*. Philadelphia:
          Westminster Press.
   1984   *Unexpected News: Reading the Bible with Third World Eyes*. Philadelphia:
          Westminster Press.
   1988   *Spirituality and Liberation*. Louisville: Westminster Press.

Bultmann, Rudolf
   1952   *Theology of the New Testament*. Two volumes. London: S.C.M. Press.

Cobb, John B., Jr.
   1982   *Process Theology as Political Theology*. Philadelphia: Westminster Press.

Collum, Danny
   1984   "Clues to the Future." *Sojourners* 13:11, 22.

Cone, James H.
   1969   *Black Theology and Black Power*. Twentieth Anniversary Edition (1989).
          San Francisco: Harper and Row.
   1972   *The Spirituals and the Blues*. New York: Seabury Press.

Creighton, Louise
   1904   *Life and Letters of Mandell Creighton*. Two volumes. London.

Crichton, Michael
   1990   *Jurassic Park*. New York: Random House.

Dayton, Donald W.
   1976   *Discovering an Evangelical Heritage*. New York: Harper and Row.

Freire, Paulo
   1983   *Pedagogy of the Oppressed.* New York: Crossroad.
González, Justo L.
   1992   *Out of Every Tribe and Nation: Christian Theology at the Ethnic Round-*
             table. Nashville: Abingdon.
Grant, Jacquelyn
   1992   "Poverty, Womanist Theology, and the Ministry of the Church." In
             Standing with the Poor. Edited by Paul Plenge Parker, 47–59. Cleveland:
             Pilgrim Press.
Gutiérrez, Gustavo
   1973   *A Theology of Liberation.* Translated and edited by Sister Caridad Inda
             and John Eagleson. Maryknoll: Orbis.
   1978   "Two Theological Perspectives: Liberation Theology and Progressivist
             Theology." In *The Emergent Gospel.* Edited by Sergio Torres and Virginia
             Fabella, 227–255. Maryknoll: Orbis.
Hall, Edward T.
   1959   *The Silent Language.* New York: Doubleday.
Hebblethwaite, Margaret
   1994   *Base Communities: An Introduction.* Mahwah, NJ: Paulist Press.
Herzog, Frederick
   1980   *Justice Church.* Maryknoll: Orbis.
Isasi-Díaz, Ada María and Yolanda Tarango
   1992   *Hispanic Women: Prophetic Voice in the Church.* Minneapolis: Augsburg
             Fortress Press.
King, Martin Luther
   1986a   "The Drum Major Instinct" (originally delivered on 4 February 1968). In
             A Testament of Hope: The Essential Writings of Martin Luther King, Jr.
             Edited by James M. Washington, San Francisco: Harper and Row, 1986.
             259–267.
   1986b   "Remaining Awake Through a Great Revolution" (originally delivered on
             31 March 1968). In *A Testament of Hope: The Essential Writings of Martin*
             Luther King, Jr. Edited by James M. Washington, San Francisco: Harper
             and Row, 1986. 268–278.
Kozol, Jonathan
   1992   "Education with Savage Intent: An Interview with Jonathan Kozol" by
             Niki Amarantides. *The Other Side* (May–June).
Longenecker, Richard N.
   1964   *Paul, Apostle of Liberty.* Reprint (1976). Grand Rapids: Baker Book
             House.
Marxsen, Willi
   1976   "Christology in the New Testament." In *The Interpreter's Dictionary of the*
             Bible: Supplementary Volume. Edited by Keith Crim, 146–156. Nashville:
             Abingdon.
McNeill, Donald P., Douglas A. Morrison, and Henri J. M. Nouwen
   1982   *Compassion: A Reflection on the Christian Life.* Garden City: Doubleday.

Mesters, Carlos
1981 "The Use of the Bible in Christian Communities of the Common People." In *The Challenge of Basic Christian Communities.* Edited by Sergio Torres and John Eagleson, 197–216. Maryknoll: Orbis.

Moltmann, Jürgen
1983 *The Power of the Powerless: The Word of Liberation for Today.* Translated by Margaret Kohl. San Francisco: Harper and Row.

Niebuhr, Reinhold
1932 *Moral Man and Immoral Society.* New York: Charles Scribner's Sons.
1941– *The Nature and Destiny of Man.* Two volumes. New York: Charles
1943 Scribner's Sons.

Nouwen, Henri J. M.
1972 *The Wounded Healer.* Garden City: Doubleday.

Ogden, Schubert M.
1982 *The Point of Christology.* San Francisco: Harper and Row.
1986 *On Theology.* San Francisco: Harper and Row.
1988 "The Agency of God: Twenty-One Theses." An unpublished contribution to a convocation with William J. Abraham, Perkins School of Theology.

Patton, John
1990 *From Ministry to Theology: Pastoral Action and Reflection.* Nashville: Abingdon.

Perrin, Norman
1976 *Rediscovering the Teaching of Jesus.* New York: Harper and Row.

Ruether, Rosemary Radford
1983 *To Change the World: Christology and Cultural Criticism.* New York: Crossroad.

Schumacher, E. F.
1979 *Good Work.* New York: Harper and Row.

Segundo, Juan Luis
1976 *The Liberation of Theology.* Translated by John Drury. Maryknoll: Orbis.
1984 *Faith and Ideologies.* Volume One of *Jesus of Nazareth Yesterday and Today.* Translated by John Drury. Maryknoll: Orbis.
1985 *The Historical Jesus of the Synoptics.* Volume Two of *Jesus of Nazareth Yesterday and Today.* Translated by John Drury. Maryknoll: Orbis.
1986 *The Humanist Christology of Paul.* Volume Three of *Jesus of Nazareth Yesterday and Today.* Translated by John Drury. Maryknoll: Orbis.
1987 *The Christ of the Ignatian Exercises.* Volume Four of *Jesus of Nazareth Yesterday and Today.* Translated by John Drury. Maryknoll: Orbis.
1990 "Two Theologies of Liberation." In *Liberation Theology: A Documentary History.* Edited by Alfred T. Henelly, 353–366. Maryknoll: Orbis.

Sobrino, Jon
1993 "The Economics of Ecclesia: A Poor Church Is a Church Rich in Compassion." In *New Visions for the Americas: Religious Engagement and Social Transformation.* Edited and translated by David Batstone, 83–100. Minneapolis: Fortress Press.

Soelle, Dorothee
  1971   *Political Theology.* Translated by John Shelley. Philadelphia: Fortress Press.
  1984   *To Work and to Love: A Theology of Creation.* Written with Shirley A. Cloyes. Philadelphia: Fortress Press.

Taylor, Mark Lewis
  1993   "Transnational Corporations and Institutionalized Violence: A Challenge to Christian Movements in the United States." In *New Visions for the Americas: Religious Engagement and Social Transformation.* Edited and translated by David Batstone, 101–126. Minneapolis: Fortress Press.

Tillich, Paul
  1951   *Systematic Theology.* Three Volumes. Chicago: University of Chicago Press.
  1954   *Love, Power, and Justice.* London: Oxford University Press.

Townes, Emilie B.
  1993   "Keeping a Clean House Will Not Keep a Man at Home: An Unctuous Womanist Rhetoric of Justice." In *New Visions for the Americas: Religious Engagement and Social Transformation.* Edited and translated by David Batstone, 127–144. Minneapolis: Fortress Press.

Vincent, Marvin R.
  1979   *A Critical and Exegetical Commentary on the Epistles to the Philippians and to Philemon* (*International Critical Commentary*). Edinburgh: T. & T. Clark

Wallis, Jim
  1994   *The Soul of Politics.* Maryknoll: Orbis Books.

Welch, Sharon
  1993   "'Dreams of the Good': From the Analytics of Oppression to the Politics of Transformation." In *New Visions for the Americas: Religious Engagement and Social Transformation.* Edited and translated by David Batstone, 172–193. Minneapolis: Fortress Press.

Wesley, John
  1979   "On Working Out Our Own Salvation." In *The Works of John Wesley*, Volume VI, 3rd Edition. Kansas City: Beacon Hill Press.

Index

abortion, 38
"Action-Reflection-Action," 1, 12
Acton, Lord, 108
advocacy, 126–127
Alves, Rubem, 54
Arendt, Hannah, 120
atheism, 48
atonement, 153

Baldridge, William, 122–123
Banks, Robert, 101
Batestone, David, 128
Bible, the, 14–15
blues, the, 10
Bresee, Phineas F., 16, 115
Bresee Institute, xv
Brown, Robert McAfee, 1, 46
Bultmann, Rudolf, 95
Bush, George, 41, 102

Câmara, Dom Helder, 127
capitalism, 36, 62
CELAM, 16
celebration, 136–139
chaos, 65
charity, 103–108: creative, 106–107;
    resident, 104; taking sides and,
    105–106
Christology, 69–71
church, the: models and metaphors of,
    97–101; as a poor church, 140–142
Church of the Nazarene, 16, 115
circle, between theology and ministry,
    1–17
Cobb, John B., Jr., 156
Columbus, 122–123

commitment: practical consequence of,
    15–17; priority of, 10–17; theoret-
    ical consequence of, 13–15
community: created for, 27–29; creativity
    and, 32–34; freedom and, 29–32;
    "in Christ," 94–96; the kingdom of
    God and, 78; liberation and, xii,
    132; the ministry of, 132–139
community organizing, 127–128
compassion, xi–xii, 44, 141–142: conver-
    sion to, 52; knowing God and,
    51–53; liberation and, 59–60;
    misplaced, x; pity and, xii
compassionate evangelism, 150–156
compassionate ministry, xi–xii, 44, 63:
    evangelism and, 149–156; as
    humanizing ministry, 84–85; salva-
    tion and, 51; theology of, xii;
Cone, James, 9 10, 81, 105 106
consciousness-raising (conscientization),
    112–113
context: and theology, 4–5, 11
conversion, 146–147: the kingdom of
    God and, 75, 79–81
creation: "new creation," 92–94; partici-
    pation in, 39–40; salvation and,
    151–152; story of, 19–20
creative justice, 130–131
creativity: community and, 40–41;
    created for, 34–39; freedom and,
    39–40; the kingdom of God and,
    73–75; sexuality and, 37–39; work
    and, 35–37
cultural Christianity, 133

Dayton, Donald, 115

development, 109–110
dualism: of body and soul, 111, 143–144,
    151–152; the kingdom of God and,
    77–78; ministry and, 107; spiritu-
    ality and, 6

East, Mark, 20
Einstein, Albert, 2
empowerment, 108–120: consciousness-
    raising and, 112–113; development
    and, 109–110; of the soul, 110–120
evangelism: compassionate ministry and,
    149–156; humanization and, 81;
    oppressive, x; and the poor, 80–81;
    popular consensus regarding,
    143–147
exodus, the, 57–59

faith: and decision, 52; liberation from
    sin and, 88–92; a "new creation"
    and, 92; and works, 51–52
fasting, 8
Francis of Assisi, 15, 140
freedom: community and, 26–27, 62–63;
    created for, 23–25; creativity and,
    25–26
Freire, Paulo, 102, 106, 111–114, 119, 120

gender: and community, 31–32
global perspective, xiii
God: activity of, 42; compassion and, 14,
    55–56, 62–64, 65–67; creativity
    and, 64–67; freedom and, 62–64;
    images of, 44–45; justice and, 121;
    liberation and, 59–60; love and, 57;
    as social, 55–56; solidarity with
    victims, 55–57; as taking sides,
    58–64
González, Justo, 154
governing authorities, and the Christian,
    93–94
grace, 41–43
Grant, Jacquelyn, 31
Greek philosophy: dualism and, 144;
    God's nature and, 56
Guatemala, 33–34

Gulf War, 41
Gutiérrez, Gustavo, 12, 103, 140

Hall, Edward T., 37
Hartshorne, Charles, 27, 56–57
Hebblethwaite, Margaret, 114,
    119–120
Herzog, Frederick, 117
holiness tradition, the, 16, 114–117
Holy Spirit, the, 114–117
hope, 157–160

ideology: the kingdom of God and, 77;
    theology reduced to, 5–6
image of God, 19: community and,
    27–34; creativity and, 34–41;
    freedom and, 23–27; to be
    recreated in, 84–85; theology of
    compassionate ministry and, 20
imagination, 1–3
"in Christ," 86
Isasi-Díaz, Ada María, 82

Jesus of Nazareth: as the answer to the
    question of who God is, 54; central
    proclamation of, 75; as the
    compassion of God, 68, 71; the
    humanity of, 69–71; the Kingdom
    of God and, 73–81; poverty and,
    14; surprise and, 66–67; as taking
    sides with the oppressed, 61, 70;
    witnesses to, 72
Jonah, ix–xi
Jurassic Park, 64
justice, 120–132: creative justice and,
    129–132; exposing injustice,
    121–124; knowing God and,
    48–50; worship and, 138–139
justice community, a; 128–129
justification by faith, 51–52

Kierkegaard, Søren, 10
King, Martin Luther, Jr., 26–27, 29–30,
    82–83
kingdom of God: creative participation
    in, 73–84; evangelism and,

144–145; as a liberation community, 82–83; proximity of, 76–78
knowing God, 45–53
Kozol, Jonathan, 41

liberation, 101–102: community and, xii,
62–63, 132; the kingdom of God
and, 77–78, the ministry of,
103–32
liberation community, xvi: the kingdom
of God and, 82–83; as a model of
the church, 17, 101
liberation theology, 16, 147
Longenecker, Richard N., 86, 94

Magnificat, 59–60
Marx, Karl, 5, 81, 105
Marxsen, Willi, 72
Mary, 59–60
Mesters, Carlos, 116
ministry: apathy and, 74; humanizing,
84–85; grace and, 42–43; self-
reliance and, 75; theology and, xiv
Moltmann, Jürgen, 116
Muste, A. J., 126

Negro spirituals, 9
new creation, 92–94
Niebuhr, Reinhold, 90–91, 108, 118
North American context, xiii
Nouwen, Henri, 70, 99

Ogden, Schubert M., 19, 42
oppression, 102–103: internalized, 111

Patton, John, 4
Paul: on Christian community, 95–96; on
faith and works, 51; on freedom in
Christ, 86–92; on God's anonymous activity, 54; on "new
creation" in Christ, 92–94; on the
significance of Jesus, 85–96; on sin,
87–91
Paul VI, Pope, 116
Perrin, Norman, 73
play, and work, 37

poverty: the destruction of creativity and,
32–34; the destruction of relationships and, 27–28, 30–31; as a form
of slavery, 24, 26; and the kingdom
of God, 80–81
power, 108–109: ensoulment of, 117–120
practical theology, xiv
practice, and theory, 1–10, 52
praxis, 113
preferential option for the poor, 15–17
prevenient grace, 42
protest, 125: and the blues, 10

racism, 31, 115–116, 123–124
Reagan, Ronald, 34, 127
religion, and economics, 5–6
repentance, 124
resistance, 125–128
resurrection, 159–160
retributive justice, 130–131
rich, the: and the kingdom of God, 80–81
Ruether, Rosemary Radford, 80

salvation: conversion experience and,
146–147; corporate, 145, 152, 155;
history and, 152; liberation and,
87–91; other-worldly, 145;
personal, 144, 155; the poor and,
80–81; worldly, 151–156
Schumacher, E. F., 36
Segundo, Juan Luis: on the kingdom of
God, 73–75, 79–81; on mass relationships, 32; on Paul's theology,
88, 94; on priority of commitment
to the oppressed, 11–12, 13
sexuality, 37–39
sin, 87–92: community and, 26; freedom
from, 91–92; grace and, 42; racism
and, 89; structural, 89–92; unemployment and, 35
Sobrino, Jon: on the church, 141–142; on
compassion, xii; on Jesus, 68
socialism, 36, 62
sodomy, 91
Soelle, Dorothy: on creation, 40; on sexuality, 37–38

168 Index

"soul power," 110–117
spirituality, 6–7: holistic, 7–8; as the path from ministry to theology, 3–10
suffering, xiii: privileged perspective and, 13–15

Tarango, Yolanda, 82
Taylor, Mark Lewis, 33–34
theology, xiv: of compassionate ministry, xii; of evangelism, 148–149; ideological use of, 13; imagination and, 1–3; ministry and, xiv, 1–3; of ministry, xiii, 17; suspicion and, 147–149
theory, and practice, 1–10, 52
third-world theologies, 10–11
Tillich, Paul, 20, 108

Townes, Emilie B., 136
transnational corporations, 33–34
Tutu, Desmond, 60

underemployment, 35–36
unemployment, 35
unity, 133–136
utilitarian justice, 130–131

view from below, 13–15, 18

Wallis, Jim,
Welch, Sharon, 111
Wesley, John, 42, 73–74
work, 35–37
works-righteousness, 50–52
worship, 136–139